Cultura

Kevin Landis and Suzanne MacAulay

Cultural Performance

Ethnographic Approaches to Performance Studies

First published 2017 by
RED GLOBE PRESS

Red Globe Press in the UK is an imprint of Springer Nature Limited, registered in England, company number 785998, of 4 Crinan Street, London, N1 9XW.

Red Globe Press® is a registered trademark in the United States, the United Kingdom, Europe and other countries.

ISBN 978–1–137–60424–8 hardback
ISBN 978–1–137–60423–1 paperback

A catalogue record for this book is available from the British Library.

A catalog record for this book is available from the Library of Congress.

Contents

Acknowledgments

There are so many people to thank and influences that have formed our views on the topics in this book. The artists and scholars who have written case studies both contributed content *and* inspired us to challenge our own viewpoints and assumptions. We wish to acknowledge our colleagues in the Department of Visual and Performing Arts at the University of Colorado, Colorado Springs, for their dedication to interdisciplinary education and for their advice and expertise. To our friends and the many people in the scholarly community who helped us gather our information and recommend writers: Christina McMahon, Monica White Ndounou, Paige McGinley, Una Chaudhuri, Tomie Hahn, Pannill Camp, Mark Gordon and Kristin Valentine. To Kevin's colleagues at the Public Theater in New York for their support and brainstorming sessions: Oskar Eustis, Ciara Murphy, Laura Caton, Drew Broussard, Andrew Kircher, Michael Friedman, and Shariffa Ali. To Suzanne's loyal group of folklorists, who listened to various versions of different case studies, and supported the idea of this book from the very beginning. Above all, we acknowledge our editors at Palgrave, Nicola Cattini and Clarissa Sutherland, for their gentle guidance and impressive patience.

List of Images

Notes on Contributors

David Afriyie Donkor earned his PhD in Performance Studies and doctoral certificate in African Studies from Northwestern University, where he was a Gwendolyn Carter Doctoral Fellow. He received his MFA in Directing and MS in Multidisciplinary Studies (Ethnic Studies, Speech Communication, Educational Foundations) from Minnesota State University, and a Diploma in Theatre from the University of Ghana. Dr. Donkor engages theatre/performance as forms of public address in African cultures. His ethnographies of Ghanaian stand-up comedy, popular theatre, and storytelling explain the interplay of a trickster ethos (based on folk figure Ananse) with performance, political liberalization, and economic (neo) liberalization in Ghana.

Sean F. Edgecomb is Assistant Professor of Theatre at the College of Staten Island/CUNY and teaches at The Graduate Center. His work focuses on the intersection of queer performance and theory and he has published in numerous edited collections and journals. His book, *Charles Ludlam Lives!: Charles Busch, Bradford Louryk, Taylor Mac and the Queer Legacy of the Ridiculous Theatrical Company* (2017) is the latest contribution to The Triangulations Series at University of Michigan Press. His new book project considers how animals and anthropomorphism have been used as symbols of queerness in rituals and performance throughout human history.

Tomie Hahn is an artist and ethnomusicologist. She is a performer of *shakuhachi* (Japanese bamboo flute), *nihon buyo* (Japanese traditional dance), and experimental performance. Tomie's research spans a wide range of area studies and topics, including: Japanese traditional performing arts, Monster Truck rallies, issues of display, the senses and transmission, gesture, and relationships of technology and culture. Her book, *Sensational Knowledge: Embodying Culture through Japanese Dance* was awarded the Alan P. Merriam prize (Society for Ethnomusicology).

She is a Professor in the Arts Department at Rensselaer Polytechnic Institute, where she is also the Director of the Center for Deep Listening.

Shawn Hall is an interdisciplinary artist, painter, and educator who views her practice as an act of participation in the biological world. She is currently represented by Cole Pratt Gallery in New Orleans and Red Arrow Gallery in Nashville.

Kevin Landis is an actor, director, and theatre historian. He is Associate Professor and the director of the Theatre and Dance Program at the University of Colorado, Colorado Springs, founder and producer of the *Prologue Lecture Series* and a Scholar in Residence at the Public Theater in New York. Dr. Landis' scholarly interests include culinary intersections with performance, the historical avant-garde, Eastern European actor training methods and Nordic theatrical landscapes.

Suzanne MacAulay is an art historian and folklorist. She is Professor and Chair of the Visual and Performing Arts Department, University of Colorado, Colorado Springs (UCCS). Before UCCS, she developed a culturally oriented art history program for New Zealand's Whanganui Polytechnic Institute and became Head of the Fine Arts School. Research interests include South Pacific and Spanish Colonial textiles, ethnoaesthetics, performance theory and personal narratives, memory, diaspora, globalization and social class, as well as the scholarship of teaching and learning.

Callie Oppedisano received her M.Phil in Irish Theatre and Film from Trinity College, Dublin, and earned a PhD in Drama at Tufts University. She is now an Independent Theatre Scholar based in Salt Lake City, Utah, where she continues to review, research, and write about Contemporary Mormon Theatre. Her reviews and articles have appeared in *Theatre Survey, Theatre Journal, Ecumenica,* and *BYU Studies.* In addition, she writes about local theatre for Utah Theatre Bloggers.

Pearl D'amour is the interdisciplinary theater company of Katie Pearl and Lisa D'Amour. Launched in 1996 with a 14-hour performance on the side of a busy street in Austin, TX, PearlDamour creates experimental, often interactive, work that ranges from intimate (*Bird Eye Blue Print*, a performance tour in a small suite of offices) to epic (*Lost in the Meadow*, a work created specifically for a 40-acre meadow). PearlDamour's touring work includes their OBIE-award-winning *Nita & Zita*, the 8-hour performance installation *How to Build a Forest*, and *MILTON*, a spoken and sung performance with video created for five towns named Milton throughout the USA. www.pearldamour.com

Sean Williams teaches ethnomusicology as well as Irish Studies and Asian Studies at the Evergreen State College in Washington State. She plays more than thirty instruments and sings in several languages. Ireland, Indonesia, and Brazil are her primary areas of focus, but she is particularly interested in liminality, social justice, and ecomusicology.

Introduction

Image 1 *Cambodian Shadow Puppets* © Kevin Landis

"What should we call this book?" The question is one we have been grappling with for months and the story of the struggle is instructive as you approach your learning in this field. But what is the field? What do we aim to study in a book now titled *Cultural Performance: Ethnographic Approaches to Performance Studies*? In a sense, that *is* the question.

The answers are ongoing and, we hope, will be debated in your class and in various institutions. For us, the increasing interest in interdisciplinary practice in universities around the world reflects a pedagogical understanding that in an era of globalization and of digital media, it is critical for students to make connections, to see overlap and similarities in their artistic practices and intellectual inquiries. In turn, it needs to be understood that our myriad artistic impulses are based in the mores and methods of the cultures and communities that have influenced us.

It is equally important to acknowledge at the outset of this study that the scholarly connection of ethnography, folklore, and performance traditions is certainly not new, in fact it has been around for a long time. Richard Schechner, whom you will read more about in coming pages, pioneered the discipline of performance studies, and, with the anthropologist Victor Turner, encouraged scholars and students to assess performance—to look at human behavior through the lens of performance. Similarly, folklorists like Roger Abrahams, Richard Bauman, Dan Ben Amos, and Barbara Kirshenblatt-Gimblett emphasized the importance of context to performance and many other anthropologists found it necessary to understand communities and cultures based on their physical movements, sensory awareness, storytelling, and tradition making.

As with any anthropologically aligned field, there is always danger when researching peoples and tying their traditions to varied modes of thought. As you will see, great care, respect, and ethics need to go into studying cultures and their traditions. In addition, performance studies scholars have been assiduous in understanding and delineating the difference between "performance as art" and "performance as cultural expression." This is a critical understanding and one that should not be ignored. The categorization is rather simple and perhaps is best seen with a couple of basic examples. A creation of an avant-garde dance to be "performed" in a town square can likely be seen in a different light than the celebration of the Eucharist at a Catholic Church. The dance may appropriately be seen as an event that focuses on artistic value and entertainment, while the taking of the host, though celebratory in nature, speaks to cultural and religious significance of a different kind. The way one approaches the study and discussion of these two examples necessarily must be different and nuanced. And yet there are many similarities that exist between the two performances. In this book, we intend to offer many examples of the ways in which performance art and entertainment utilize cultural methods to deepen and enrich the practice.

We know that approaching a topic that deals broadly with performance studies, a field populated by exemplary scholars and myriad detailed studies, is fraught with challenges. But this is also precisely the reason we want to tackle these subjects. With a renewed interest in interdisciplinary education, we are acutely aware of the swirling complexity of our field. In fact, we cannot even limit our topic to one field! The often-cited challenge with performance studies as a discipline is its ineffability. It is somehow too big, too broad to be described. There are too many experts from varying disciplines with competing viewpoints. From the outset, Schechner wisely acknowledged this. He writes, "Theoretically, performance studies is wide open" (Schechner, 2006: 1). But he is careful to note that the field is not valueless; rather it is an embracing discipline that requires contextualization and acknowledgment of personal experience, bias, loves, interests, and desires. There will be differences of opinion. The anthropologist might blanch at the lens that a theatre artist uses to understand the dance of a shaman. The musician might balk at the description of the sonic environment provided by an art historian. A sociologist might titter at an oversimplification of a community gathering by a dance scholar. But at the same time, we are continuously reminded of our similar approaches and our need to recognize overlap and fluidity.

A couple of years ago, we both attended a workshop on Deep Listening, a practice founded by musician and composer Pauline Oliveros, that encourages participants to focus on the intricacies of the sounds in the space in which a group is gathered. As we experienced several of Oliveros' exercises, we both individually (we learned later) thought about how many similarities there were with our own practice as artists and teachers of the arts. Oliveros may have been trained in music, but her work resonated strongly with our own experience. And this is how it often is in an interdisciplinary artistic world. We find these blendings in so much of what we do and, thus, think it is critical to revisit some of the concepts that find resonance in a discipline that we might call ethnography, performance studies, folklore, anthropology, sociology, theatre, music, dance, and so on. Simply put, we hope to explore with you, a new scholar and artist, the ways in which culture and art blend so that we can use the knowledge to be more astute observers of performance.

This requires a certain amount of daring and humility for us. And it will for you as well. Suzanne MacAulay is a folklorist and art historian. Kevin Landis is an actor and theatre historian. We have learned from each other over the years and have long wanted to collaborate on a study like this, a study that mixes our fields and helps the budding student see our perspectives *while* creating her own conclusions. But how to do that? We have already established that the field is impossibly broad, overlapping with so many disciplines and methodologies. So, rather than run from that reality, we want to embrace it and we hope that you will too. We asked several scholars and artists to join us and contribute case studies for this book in an effort to see the various ways that cultural performance can be accessed and assessed.

Of the many goals of this book, perhaps the most important is to develop our understanding of cultural performance in context so that we can better understand the broad range of human attitudes, behavior, expressiveness, and creative ingenuity embedded in performance. Each chapter begins with a mini-case study, which helps frame the topics that the chapter attempts to illuminate. By the end of the book, you will have dozens of examples of cultural performance to add to your own experiences of the world. We also provide questions and exercises at the end of each chapter that will encourage you to bring your own cultural and performance backgrounds into rich discussions and projects, which will help you make sense of these exciting areas of study. This is a central point and one that will be reiterated throughout the book. One cannot approach ethnographic study and performance studies without continuously remembering the centrality of individual experience. As we describe performance and culture, we do so with the humility that we cannot know all details of performance reception because it is unique to the viewer in the moment of viewing and experiencing. To that end, you must also bring your individual experiences to bear. In fact, you will see that our look at performance ends with considerations of the specific human body and its place in nature and the world.

Books and courses require structure and, finally, it would be inaccurate to imply that we are here only giving a collection of artistic examples, without an overarching methodology. To the contrary, over the years, we have looked at our disciplines and the ways that we teach and noticed patterns in our observations of culture and performance. We see an approach that looks at cultural performance from three standpoints: aesthetics of experience, place and space, and the sensory body. Each section begins with a chapter that broadly considers the topic from a performance-centered standpoint and uses several mini-case studies to illuminate the concepts (Landis). It is followed by a chapter that applies these concepts to a more detailed analysis of ethnographic study through singular case studies (MacAulay). Each chapter is accompanied by a contribution from a different scholar, which addresses a similar theme. In this way, we augment our own areas of expertise with the viewpoints of scholars who may approach cultural performance in new ways and, certainly, with different life experiences.

Aesthetics of Experience approaches some of the broader concepts of performance and cultural overlap by looking at tradition and community and the reasons for performance creation. Inspired by the field of anthropology of experience, the aesthetics of experience adds a consideration of the creative elements accompanying human action and interaction. This notion of creativity and improvisation extends to the natural world of nature and nonhuman engagement in the final chapter. Concepts that broadly demonstrate human needs exercised through cultural performance will be introduced in the first section and applied throughout the book. In "Performing Traditions," you will learn, through specific cultural examples, the basic parameters and goals of performance and various ways to define performance. In "Experiencing Community," those performance building blocks will be added to a discussion of communities and societies and the ways that they approach performance within their social and belief structures. This chapter thus incorporates the ethnographic lens to performance.

Place and Space situates performance in *physical* location and asks how geography, nature and architecture affect and direct performance events. "The Architecture of Performance Space" focuses on the way buildings, human constructed structures, and deeply considered spaces guide and are guided by cultural performance. "The Topography of Performance" dives deeply into a consideration of New Zealand Maori culture and the cultural politics of performance in the creation of place. The second part of the chapter uses a pictorial representation of a revived cultural performance to raise questions about a socio-religious campaign of place-making to revitalize spirituality in a specific locale.

The Sensory Body focuses on the corporeal in the context of performance. "The Somatic Experience" uses several theatrical traditions as examples of performance that centers on the way a body responds to stimuli and the way that performers address body in the time and space of creation. We will look at the consumption of food and the internalization of sounds as, themselves, moments of performance. How is individual body response essential in the reception of cultural performance? "Bodies in Nature" situates the human and nonhuman animal body in the context of the world, how the body then becomes implicated in the performance in collaboration with nature. In this chapter, we also investigate themes at the intersection of performance studies, environmental studies, and animal studies. Interspecies collaboration is a useful concept when applied to the interdependency of various human and nonhuman participants in performance.

At the end of this book, you will have many tools that you may use to better understand the place of performance in the world, and, likewise, the way you and your community perform deliberately and, perhaps, without knowing. The specificity of our disciplines (theatre and folklore) certainly colors our understanding of cultural performance and you will see that in our descriptions. What we choose to focus on may not be the same things that you want to address, and that is the beauty of the field. As long as you are looking at cultures and performance with a rigorous, thoughtful, empathetically acute mind you are well on your way. Our questions throughout and at the ends of the chapters will help you personalize the topics of this study.

Our contributors include theatre historians, ethnomusicologists, folklorists, musicians, and dance scholars. They write about traditions from several cultures and through their own unique analytic lens. It is important to remember that any book of this sort is, necessarily, always far from comprehensive. As scholars, we must do our best to recognize our own tendencies, cultural biases, and influences, and since we are both American citizens our writing may, indeed, have a western slant. We attempt to flag that within the text and encourage you, as well, to understand your background and its influence on your thinking. The critical anthropological work of uncovering and describing comes with the myriad responses that you bring to the classroom and your lives. Let's begin!

Part I

Aesthetics of Experience

1

Performing Traditions

Image 2 *Harar Hyena Feeding* © Kevin Landis

There is a town in Ethiopia that is famous for its hyena man. Legend has it that if the hyenas in the desert are not appeased, they will penetrate the gates of the ancient walled city of Harar, steal the children as they sleep, and enjoy a delicious feast. The villagers, obviously, chose to avoid the disastrous possibility and put their trust in hyena men who traditionally feed the wild beasts a buttery porridge. The practice has grown and now, almost every evening, Yusuf, a local celebrity, sets up camp just outside the gates of the town. He arrives with sticks and plastic buckets filled with raw meat.

Hyena viewers arrive, too, sometimes with meat to donate to the cause. In this part of Africa, the hyenas carry enormous cultural signifi-cance and are met with respect by Hararis. Just after sundown, jeeps pull up through the dust and sand, their headlights flooding the ritual space. Tourists and locals alike come to watch the unusual event; they sit in their cars, Yusuf in front of them with his sticks and buckets. Slowly, through the darkness of the vast desert, the twinkling reflections of several sets of eyes emerge: far in the distance at first and then eerily closer. Soon they come into view, the squat, muscular beasts, at once ferocious and mesmerizing. A single hyena could kill Yusuf but he does not appear afraid as he baits a stick with meat and puts the end in his mouth. The boldest hyena approaches him and gingerly gnaws the meat off the stick. Then others follow as the hyena man baits other rods and facilitates a canine feast.

Soon, the tourists are invited out of their jeeps to get a closer look at the spectacle, and even to participate in the ritual feeding. Eventually, the hyenas are being fed by a dozen locals and tourists, all under the watchful gaze of the hyena man. He acts as a sacred moderator, a shaman of sorts, facilitating this act of ritual and performance.

After some time of feeding, the hyenas, fully satiated, retreat into the darkness.

The story related above quickly introduces us to many important terms and ideas related to cultural performance and should give us several questions to grapple with. There is a lot to uncover here. What is meant by *performance, culture, ritual,* and *tradition*? Couldn't we look at this story and, in a different light, call it a *play*? What if we were to say that Yusef was an *actor* and that the hyenas were fully trained circus animals?

What if the tourists were simply called *audience* and the jeep's headlamps were *theatrical lighting*? The hyena man's sticks and buckets are his *props* and the events of the night happen precisely the same way every evening, as if it were a *script*. When put in those terms, you might suddenly think the entire event was a fraud, not worth study or consideration. But if you think on it longer and consider your own traditions and rituals, you will see that they too can be folded into the larger category of *performance*. Perhaps you are Buddhist. Temple ceremonies can be assessed through the language of performance: theatre, actors, props, scripts, costumes, lighting. So, too, can the Catholic mass or a Jewish Bar Mitzvah. For some, these are difficult and even uncomfortable juxtapositions.

In this chapter, we will take a look at these juxtapositions so that we can get a better idea of the myriad ways that cultures perform their identity. We will introduce you to many terms and ideas that are foundational for studying performance and its relationship to culture. We will see that societies use performance not only as a way to symbolically identify themselves, but also as a central facet of their cultural being. The cultural performance of the hyena man is now perhaps the most famous aspect of Harar. Tourists who visit Harar may not know anything about the people of the village but they do know something about the mysterious nightly performance.

What Is Performance?

The hyena man with his evening feeding ritual neatly fits under that category of cultural performance. But what exactly is meant by cultural performance? This is a tricky question, and we can look to some writers and performers who have attempted to identify the nature of the term and what it means to them. As with any complex idea, it is best that we break it down into its component parts, and to do that we have to have a working idea of the basic term, **performance**.

You might be surprised to know that there are many books dedicated to the topic of identifying performance and there are many different ways of defining the term. It is probably safe to say that we all have a sense of what we each understand as a performance. Consider things that you believe to be examples. You might think of a play, a concert, a musical comedy, or a speech. But what about a report that you give in front of your class? Is that a performance? How about the presentational style of a waiter at a restaurant? Or even the way you dress or use your voice? These examples underline an important aspect of this course of study that we have to become comfortable addressing. What are the elements of some events that make them stand apart as formalized performances as opposed to examples of everyday life in action? Three basic tenets immediately come to mind, though we will refine throughout the study:

- *Location*: We accept that for a performance to take place we need a place to perform. This may seem obvious at first, but as later chapters will explore, the actual place of the event is a critical component to understanding of performance. For now, let us accept that we must first have a location if we are to have a performance.
- *Audience/performer*: For a performance to exist, we generally understand that there is a relationship between a *work of performance* and a *viewer of performance*. Can a performance be viable if there is no one there to see it? Alternatively, if an audience gathers and no one shows up to be watched, is there a performance? The simple answer seems to be no, but as this book will demonstrate, this may be more complex than first thought. At the very least, this relationship has to be considered in performance analysis.
- *Skills/product*: If we agree that there is a necessary relationship between viewer and creator, it follows that we assume that the creator of the work has something to show. As in every question in performance, this too becomes tricky and gives rise to many other questions. Is something less of a performance if the quality of the skill or product is inferior? What constitutes a skill or product? We will investigate this throughout this chapter and book. For now, let us say that when we speak of skills or products, we are referring to the *thing* that is being presented, shown, experienced, or heard.

In *The Empty Space*, one of the great studies on theatre, the British director Peter Brook wrote, "I can take any empty space and call it a bare stage. A man walks across this empty space whilst someone else is watching him, and this is all we need for an act of theatre to be engaged" (Brook, 1968: 9). This description quite well identifies the general nature of performance that we have been highlighting and the definition holds up fairly well. For a performance to happen we need these three basic elements: an empty space, an audience/performer relationship, and something to be shown. But Brook introduces another concept in his famous description above that needs some consideration: **theatre**. "Theatre" as a term can represent many different things. Simply, we often understand it to be a structured performance event with conventions accepted by the culture that creates it. We generally expect that there is a story that is being told in the theatre, perhaps with a considered emotional outcome for the audience. Alternatively, "theatre" can be an idea that represents a feeling that something is performance-like, or based in spectacle: "Oh, you are so theatrical!" some might say. "Theatre" can also simply refer to a building where a performance takes place, and indeed, in this book, we will look at those examples as well. We will be careful to remember that theatre and performance cannot be assumed to be one and the same. Or can they? This is a central question that we encourage you to continue to unpack in the course of this study.

Perhaps already, you can see that our limited idea of performance and theatre as concepts may not go far enough and certainly are more complex than a simple definition can offer. As many theatre and performance anthropologists have outlined in the past, there are myriad ways that the audience/performer relationship can be highly complicated. Take the following example as a jumping off point in our inquiry: The great Polish theatre practitioner Jerzy Grotowski spent much of his professional career creating performance that actively questioned what an audience really was. Could an audience actively participate in a performance and, when that happens, what becomes of the all-critical audience/performer interplay? He eventually came to believe that an audience was not necessary. He developed what he called *paratheatre* or a theatre without any audience, where everyone in attendance in the space of performance created the theatrical event.[1] Paratheatre focused not on

---

[1] www.grotowski.net/en/encyclopedia/paratheatre

the final product but on the experience of discovering performance, its influences, and the community connections that it fostered. That might mean that the spectators stood up and danced, joined the performers in the playing space and, thus, helped create the skill or product. Alternatively, it could mean that the performers themselves might run and play in the woods for hours and then return home. In fact, this was one of the actor training methods employed by his acolyte and paratheatre practitioner Wlodzimierz Staniewski at his center for performance in Gardzienice, Poland. "The night run is led by precise rhythms sustained through the stamping feet on the ground. The group bunches in behind the leader, affirming the initial rhythm through those who run behind or in front, sometimes in complete darkness" (Hodge, 2006: 236).

These "night runs" based in music, beats, rhythm, physical exhaustion, and sensory challenges may seem, on first exposure, to be preposterous and unrelated to our conventional views of theatre. But the techniques that Grotowski gave rise to were picked up by others and continue to be debated and questioned to this day. Rena Mirecka, Grotowski's lead actress, furthered his ideas of performance and paratheatre and has described the relationship that she sees with the spectator of the event:

> For me, I couldn't have an observer and even people as witness is impossible. The people who are outside, they are in a total different state of consciousness, they observe and they judge. They observe and think "this is good, this I don't like." The mind has vibration, the energy of the mind and especially when it's negative, it makes it difficult for people who participate in the research of the group. People who are sitting in the comfortable chair, they eat the energy of actors and they think "I paid for a ticket, I have to receive something." They don't help. Paratheater is the doer, it's not actor.[2]

As we will see, there are numerous examples of theatre, performance, and ritual that exist beyond the borders of easy definition. Already, we have examples of people who actively question some of the basic tenets

---

[2] Rena Mirecka, interview with the author, Sardinia, Italy, 19 June, 2008.

of performance. But you will notice that Mirecka identifies the loose concept of audience as "people who are outside" and this is a critical distinction for our understanding. In Mirecka's ideal performance, the audience is not really eliminated but rather the performer becomes the audience just as the audience becomes the performer. In this paratheatrical example, people begin to take on different roles. Performance relationships thus can be analyzed based on being outside versus inside of a performance. And with this understanding, we are starting to dip our toes into the pool of cultural performance.

What Is Cultural Performance?

It is obvious perhaps that cultural performance must address the needs of a culture, but we probably should not assume that **culture** is an easily definable term. Indeed, there is much nuance here, too. Generally speaking, culture is an amalgam of the beliefs, practices, arts, and mores of a certain group of people. They can be material or nonmaterial, meaning, for example, that culture can be represented in the way we decorate our houses (material) to the laws we pass and the religious rites we practice (non-material). Sociologists remind us that cultures evolve over time to reflect the needs of the people who make up their fabric, that their facets are understood and shared by the members of the society, and are reinforced through the socialization process (Landis, 1992: 72). In other words, we are taught what is acceptable in our given societies.

To further clarify performance, let us borrow from Richard Schechner, one of the great scholars on the subject and the creator of a line of inquiry called performance studies. Schechner elucidates the role of performance by identifying what he calls overlapping spheres or functions of performance. He contends that performance aims (1) to entertain, (2) to make something beautiful, (3) to mark or change identity, (4) to foster community, (5) to heal, (6) to teach, persuade, or convince, and (7) to deal with the sacred and demonic (Schechner, 2006: 46). If we accept our three basic components of performance (place, audience, skill) and add to them these seven goals of performance, we now have many exciting points of analysis for performance that allow us to peel back the layers and explore the nuances. If we ask "what is the goal of a performance?" we can begin to see its cultural necessity.

Certainly, we have a sense of several of Schechner's tenets. Entertainment may seem like the most obvious of the goals; we perform to entertain ourselves and our group of observers. Beauty and its definitions are perhaps more complex and we will deal with that when we discuss aesthetics. However, in several of Schechner's criteria (identity change, foster community, teach, deal with the sacred and demonic), the need of an audience and community is clearly implied. In fact, he notes that audience has a critical role in the equation because it necessarily identifies performance as separate from other behavior (Schechner, 2006: 12). In paratheatre, the need for experience is necessary, even if the performer and the audience roles are one and the same.

You may have noted that Schechner indicates in his outcomes that performance often has as its goal the fostering of relationships between people. People coming together to view or perform a skill (or both!) conjures up the idea of **community**, or a group of like-minded individuals sharing a space and/or ideals and culture. If we go back to Yusef, the hyena man, and start to alter our view of the tourists who watch him in the Ethiopian desert, we immediately see that performance can have a very powerful influence on the development of a society. The tourists now are engaging in a tradition that has helped define Harar. All of the participants are, in their own way, fostering community engagement and identity. Is Yusef's role a component of the cultural make-up of Harar? Is the tourist feeding the hyenas becoming part of the fabric of the community of Harar? The answer to both of these questions is yes. In Chapter 2, we will look deeper at the definitions of communities and the way they gather.

You will notice that the term **performative** is also used quite often in performance analysis and it is critical to see the difference between it and performance generally. To put it simply, elements of performance may be performative. Evolving out of JL Styan's speech act theory, for something to be performative, the communication taking place, is, in itself, an action. For example, when a marriage officiant pronounces "you are now man and wife," the words are performative since their utterance completes an act. The American presidential oath of office, likewise, is performative in that the speech itself, in context, makes that person the leader of the country. You will see throughout this book examples of the performative in cultural performance, times in which an action or speech fundamentally changes a person or community.

The power of performance and the performative are now coming into view and we are honing in on an understanding of cultural performance, the key term that we are attempting to better understand in this book. So, what is it exactly? The anthropologist, Milton Singer, coined the phrase in the 1950s because he began to recognize patterns of behavior in Indian culture that highlighted specific events that defined who they were as people. Much like the hyena feeding in Ethiopia, Singer noticed events like weddings, temple festivals, plays, musical events, and others that, in line with our definitions, contained skills, location, and a performer/spectator relationship and also were specific in content and had a considered duration. These events, he argued, defined the culture. "Indians, and perhaps all peoples, think of their culture as encapsulated in such discreet performances, which they can exhibit to outsiders as well as to themselves" (Singer, 1959: xiii). This is a fairly remarkable observation, as Singer here notes that performance is the defining mechanism of a culture, a way of showing cultural identity to the outside and reaffirming it for the members of the society.[3] In the years following his writing, cultural performance became a term that acquired much attention, to the point where most *anything* could be considered a performance. Indeed, the field of performance studies is an offshoot of this idea and is a field of inquiry that actively assessed the performance elements in the everyday.

At this point, we may say that cultural performances are those events that create, highlight, or perpetuate a certain culture. We have already looked deeply enough to be able to say that elements of performance are

---

[3] The deep problems that can exist when anthropologists or scholars generalize about a particular culture, especially when they are not members of that culture, should not go unnoticed. My "reading" of the hyena feeding may not accurately reflect Harari intentions, especially since I viewed the event as a tourist. Perhaps Singer's assessment of Indian culture may be too broad for such a sweeping statement. This challenge will not be ignored. In the next chapter, we will consider the ethnographer's ethical responsibilities to the cultures studied. For an in-depth, ethnographic analysis of the Harari feedings, see Marcus Baynes-Rock (2015).

everywhere, from the way we speak, to the way we dress and the events that we attend. But what are the events, specifically, that fall under the umbrella of cultural performance? This is a tough question and one that is contested in many circles. If we think that everything is a performance, then the word starts to lose its meaning. In order to further refine cultural performance, let us go back to the hyena man and look at a couple of qualities that might be quite obvious but are necessary to unpack if we are to find a solid way to hold on to the idea of cultural performance.

For the sake of argument, we should reassess the case study that began the chapter with a caveat that may disqualify it from our assessment as performance. What if we told you that the feeding of the hyenas happened only once—it was never repeated—and the audience of tourists just happened to have seen it as they were making their way to dinner? All of a sudden, this does not seem nearly as important as before. The hyena feeding has cultural significance only when we know that it takes place every evening, it always includes audience and, indeed, that anthropologists have written about it. What makes this then more important is that the performance now is invested with the need for repetition. The society has deemed it critical enough to happen over and over again. In this way, the element of tradition enters our understanding of cultural performance.

What Are Traditions and Rituals?

Perhaps your family does the same thing every year on Christmas Eve. You have a special dinner, hang your stockings on the mantel, and leave cookies at the hearth for Santa Claus. Maybe you gather around the Christmas tree and sing carols or exchange gifts. Even if you do not do this precisely, or celebrate other holidays, you can probably think of many things that you or your family does every year in the same way. Likewise, you might consider the things that your country does habitually. Inaugurations of presidents, speeches to parliament, and national anthems sung before sporting events might qualify as traditional occurrences. In fact, the repetition of the hyena feeding in Harar could be assessed in this way.

With just these general and generic examples, it is easy to see that a **tradition** is something that is done by a group or a community over and over again. But there is something more to the term. We must ask why? Why do your parents teach you traditional Christmas carols? Why do they prepare the same dinner year after year on the same evening? Why does your government perform the same ceremony every four or six years to initiate new politicians? The answer lies in the importance of cultural performance more generally. Cultural performance often fits in the repetitive nature of tradition because the very act of repeating a thing or action invests that thing with temporal power. That is, if we know that our family has eaten the same dinner every year for generations and will, presumably, continue to do so into the distant future, we are drawn to the importance and connectivity of our family unit. It gives us a sense of place in the world, permanence, and a feeling of comfort in its pre-dictability. Likewise, national traditions do the same thing for countries and societies. They serve the purpose of connecting the communities under the national banner such that we have a sense of being, place, and strength. There is comfort in knowing that the King's or Queen's address to parliament will have the same traditional elements in place year after year. When seen in this way, traditions are very important. Nations and communities have realized that traditions are so central to their existence that many create traditions that actually have no basis in history. In his seminal study on tradition, Eric Hobsbawm details that a tradition seeks "… to inculcate certain values and norms of behavior by reputation, which automatically implies continuity with the past" (Hobsbawm, 1983: 1). The word "implies" is noteworthy in this context since it indicates that the tradition may not actually be linked to the past as deeply as the community believes. By creating repetitive behavior, even if it is made up, a society can add weight and importance to its existence. This is an important addition to your understanding of tradition. We often think that tradition is fixed and rooted in the distant past. Resist this notion. Just as your traditions are mutable and changing based on circumstances, so too are many of the performance-based traditions that are discussed in this book. While tradition, as Hobsbawm notes, is often rooted in an implied connectedness to the past, remember that all tradition is change and evolution.

We have to take a quick step back and recognize that another term is often mentioned that is central to our developing understanding of cultural performance. What exactly is a **ritual** as opposed to tradition? If we are to accept a tradition as being some act or series of acts that tie a community or group of individuals together, rituals are more codified actions, enacted in the same precise way and repeated. In a sense, we may look at many traditional events as being made up of rituals. For example, a World Cup match begins with the ritual of the coin toss. The toss of the coin contains the critical elements of a ritual in that there is an outcome that fundamentally changes the trajectory of the game. Rituals are often associated with the sacred and contain a series of actions, done in exactly the same way to perpetuate tradition and cultural unity. The Catholic mass, especially the holy Eucharist, is a prime example of a ritual. Going to church on Sunday, then, is a tradition.

Traditional acts and rituals can bind our communities together by creating common goal posts as we progress through life. The anthropologists Arnold van Gennep and Victor Turner identified these "rites of passage" in their respective studies of tradition and ritual. We can all identify rites of passage in our own life: naming ceremonies, baptism, confirmation, bar mitzvahs, marriage, graduation ceremonies, funerals, etc.. These are rituals that allow a person or people to pass through a threshold, to become someone or something that they were not before. We can easily identify this as a "growing up" process or as an initiation into a community or even as a passage through to a different realm of existence. In this way, these rites of passage confirm the participant within the community through a traditional practice. Turner, in his *The Ritual Process*, refers to the **liminal** as that time when a person or people are in the midst of a rite of passage, when they have shed their past characteristics but have not yet fully entered the next phase of being. In those moments, they are "betwixt and between," neither here nor there. This is an important cultural place because the liminal allows for, as Turner notes, a "recognition of a generalized social bond" that has changed and is transforming into other social structures (Turner, 1997: 95–96). These are the moments when many cultural traditions are most richly performative. Throughout this book, you may ask yourself what cultural performances bear this stamp of the liminal, performances that mark some sort of community or individual transition.

You should be asking yourself if every repeated action thus must be considered a tradition or a ritual. Is going to the dentist every year for a cleaning a tradition? Perhaps you take your car through the car wash every second Friday. Tradition? As we have grown accustomed by now, this enters us into a sticky area of debate. Hobsbawm classifies these sorts of things as routines, in that they "have no significant ritual or symbolic function" (Hobsbawm, 1983: 3). Certainly, we could say that these things become tradition for some people. But there seems to be a lack of gravity, of ideological importance to sufficiently qualify as a tradition. In that way, we can assume now that a tradition must do something that symbolically affirms and reaffirms the identity of a group of people. The hyena feeding, again, is an excellent example. Begun as a way to appease and respect the hyenas and keep the residents of Harar safe, the repetition of the invented ritual, now a tradition, has become a way to identify as Harari. It is an act that reaffirms the culture, perpetuates identity, and defines the community. It is a cultural performance predicated on tradition.

By now you can clearly see that ritual and tradition make up many aspects of our lives and they can range in value and importance. When placed in the context of cultural performance we intend to look at how these rituals and traditions are expressed by communities and why they are important in defining the community. We can see then that rituals and traditions can be either religious in nature or secular but that they have a purpose and we must do our anthropological due diligence in trying to understand why the cultural performances have developed in the ways that they have.

Aesthetics, Experience, and Presence

It should be reiterated at this point that we are broadly introducing you to terms that are closely tied to the idea of cultural performance, a subject that is highly complex and filled with nuance and opinion. Nowhere is this complexity more evident than when we start discussing beauty and aesthetics. Indeed, there are entire books written on the subject. As we saw before, Richard Schechner identifies "beauty" as one goal of performance, but he is quick to affirm that it is notoriously difficult to define. He writes: "Beauty is not equivalent to being 'pretty.' The ghastly, terrifying events of kabuki, Greek tragedy, Elizabethan theatre, and some performance art are not pretty… but the skilled enactment of horrors can be beautiful and yield aesthetic pleasure" (Schechner, 2006: 48). To use those examples that Schechner mentions we may conjure up images of bloody deaths and maiming, humiliation of kings and queens and even the terrifying facial expressions of the Maori war dances. We may not like what we see in these sorts of performances but we must be able to acknowledge their aesthetic value.

Aesthetics are the principals that underlie the relative beauty of a work of art. Aesthetics add a particular color to experience and deepen it in terms of sensory awareness, affect (feeling, emotion), style, and meaning. Aesthetics may refer to a society's taste and traditional style. Aesthetics analysis may not convince you that a piece of cultural performance is pretty, to use Schechner's word, but may, with careful practice, allow you to look deeper at the component elements of the work of art. When you are asked to learn, describe, and critically engage with the aesthetics of a performance, you are required to assess many things. How does the work affect you as an observer? What does the history of the community tell you about the choices that the artist has made? How does the artist employ **craft**, the skills that went into the creation of the work of art? We must continue to focus and refocus on aesthetics as we shape our awareness of what we are seeing and feeling. We might discover that the aesthetics of a performance may be horrifying and ugly. In fact, in the eighteenth century, the philosopher Edmund Burke referred to a concept called the **sublime**, in which greatness and beauty are not necessarily pleasurable. Some art is powerful when it both attracts and repels us at the same time. Some art, therefore, is aesthetically complex because it terrifies us.

At this point we have a dizzying mix of elements that must be brought to the analysis of cultural performance. The combination of tradition, ritual, spatial intentionality, beauty, terror, and general aesthetic analysis fuse to a point of cultural **experience**. Experience can be individual or communal, and in this book, we will explore both of those aspects as they relate to cultural performance. The geographer Yi-Fu Tuan writes that experience is a process of learning, influenced and made fuller by thoughts and feelings—human emotions (Tuan, 1977: 9–10). Imagine an experience that you may have had. Inevitably, there is a sense of duration, growth, and greater understanding that comes from the process of experiencing something. In the realm of performance, Schechner writes that a performance takes off when a "presence" is manifest (Schechner and Appel, 1990: 10). That presence may be a connection that you have with the other people engaged with the performance, generally in shared time and place.[4] Thus, we might say that a performance experience occurs when, through our senses and emotions, we are engaged. Often, through a feeling of presence with audience and performers, we learn and grow as a community or as individuals. In the next chapter we will look at how presence and experience are related and how an understanding of the concepts is fundamental in our evaluation of cultural performance.

We end with the hopefully exciting prospect that many of the characteristics of performance, theatre, and cultural studies require deep thought and personal reflection. As you study, you should consider your own traditions and rituals and see how they fit into the discussion. This can often become a difficult inquiry, as we seem to instinctively worry that the more traditions look like performance, the less authentic the experiences they create. People often do not want their religious ceremonies to be classified as performance for precisely this reason. Let us go back to our original example. The hyena feeding that began the chapter evoked feelings of community tradition, spiritual connection, and even, something sacred. The anthropologist Marcus Baynes-Rock has devoted an entire book to the chronicling of the relationship between the hyenas and the people of Harar. But, in a concerned note early in the book, he describes the rise of multiple hyena feedings around the town and the

---

[4] Presence and experience are complex words when discussing many contemporary art forms, especially related to digital content. It is worth asking yourself how you differently define an experience or presence if you are viewing a performance on YouTube.

worry that some now are geared toward the watchful gaze of an audience of tourist outsiders. The baiting of the hyenas with meat and sticks suddenly feels problematic. He writes: "And so begins the slide down a slippery slope towards a world of spotlights and bleachers, handlers reeling off scripted commentary into headsets, and family tickets with set start and finish times for the performances" (Baynes-Rock, 2015: 45). Now, our seemingly exciting story of an Ethiopian ritual seems tainted by the framing of performance and the need for authentic experience. We may choose to look at it this way, and indeed, there is truth in that concern. Continue to assess warily, as performers and anthropologists, the line between **authenticity** and the cultural mirage. Even as you conclude that some cultural performances perhaps lack the stamp of the authentic that we admire, the very nature of its inauthenticity is ripe for discussion about how that too speaks volumes about the specific cultures of creation. Why does a culture create a false performance? Is there such as thing as false performance or is every performative act a moment of authenticity? Perhaps then, what we should concern ourselves with are the motivations behind the performance and how they illuminate the nature of the communities that create them.

Finally, if you now have more questions than when you started, you are in a good place to begin your journey of learning about cultural performance. In the case study that follows, David Donkor describes a traditional performance in Ghana and furthers our understanding of performance as a site of community discourse (discussion or conversation). You will see how a specific African community uses performance, storytelling, and tradition to continue a feeling and definition of community. In addition, pay close attention to the way the people use storytelling for their performances, and places where they rely on audience interpretation of narrative to guide the spectacle. Donkor will introduce the concept of "parody" as it applies to the Akan performance traditions. The study will give you an excellent example of the power of community engagement and critique, as well as demonstrate how a scholar observes and analyses a performance. You will see that ritual, tradition making, and cultural performance are not trapped in history. Rather, through audience involvement, they continue to change and, as the author states, are integral components of the actual identity of the communities that create and perform them.

Terms and Ideas for Study

- Performance
- Theatre
- Culture
- Community
- Performative
- Cultural performance
- Tradition

- Ritual
- Liminal
- Aesthetics
- Craft
- Sublime
- Experience
- Authenticity

Questions for Discussions

- In your estimation, what are the differences between theatre and performance?
- What sorts of performance traditions define your community? What are your communities?
- What makes up your sense of aesthetics? What are the things that make up your idea of what is beautiful in art?

Creative Project

- In groups, create an idea of an imaginary community. Define some of its cultural traditions, rituals, and practices. What sort of performance might develop to express the society? Present to the class a detailed description of the performance that you imagine for this community (or, even, perform it!)

Case Study

Trickster's Double-ness: The Cultural Performance of Akan Storytelling

by David Afriyie Donkor

I first heard about the storytelling village of Ekumfi-Atwia, an *Akan* (Ghanaian ethnic group) community in the Central Region of Ghana, during a class when I was an undergraduate theatre student at the

University of Ghana. I learned that unlike the storytelling sessions that my own family held whenever there was nothing good on television or we were hit with an electric power outage, storytelling at Ekumfi-Atwia included elaborately staged public events that involved the entire community and that with the passing of time such elaborate performances had grown very infrequent in the village (Akyea, 1968: 83; Arkhurst, 2007: 169). I heard again about storytelling at Ekumfi-Atwia nearly a decade later when, while studying in the United States, I returned to Ghana to conduct fieldwork for my doctoral dissertation. Professor Esi Sutherland-Addy of the University of Ghana kindly informed me that the village was staging a special storytelling event for a visiting group of tourists from the African diaspora. I recognized the rare opportunity the professor had informed me about and set out to the village for the event.

I went to the Ekumfi-Atwia event primarily because I was interested in the importance of *Ananse* to the communities whose stories he often dominates. Ananse is a spider trickster character in the stories of the Akan. Trickster characters are one of the ways in which many cultures speak about themselves in folklore. I wanted to learn more about Ananse and Akan people not simply from the stories, which, as an Akan myself, were already part of my childhood, but, importantly, from the enactments that make up the cultural performance of the stories. After all, cultures tend to use performance as an integral and concrete component of their identity and to symbolically identify themselves. The term *Anansesem*, which bears Ananse's name, refers to both the stories and the storytelling performance itself (Sutherland, 1987: 3). What would the study of Anansesem *performance* tell me about trickster Ananse and, in a larger sense, Akan communities? Basically, the question that I sought to explore was about the relationship between cultural performance and identity. The people of Ekumfi-Atwia are a coastal *Fante* subgroup of the Akan. Indeed, Akan people are diverse, sharing a language but showing variety in dialect and cultural particularities. However, as one of the few Akan communities that retain a distinctively public tradition of storytelling, the event at the village presented a good case study for the relationship between a cultural figure (the trickster), cultural performance, and identity.

Two Stories: "The Origins of Co-Wife Rivalry" and "An Explanation for Tree-Bear's Cry"

I arrived at Ekumfi-Atwia in the afternoon. A crowd of the villagers had gathered by a pile of timber logs on the outskirts of the village. Singing, waving cloths, and moving around in a feet-shuffle dance of welcome, they led the tourists to *Kodizdan* (House of Storytelling) the modest community theatre building in the center of the village where I, also, joined the many villagers gathered to welcome and perform for the tourists. Several florescent lights illuminated the stepped-down central arena of the Kodzidan, where two performers from the village served as Ekumfi-Atwia's principal storytellers for the evening.

The first of the two storytellers to perform was a middle-aged woman, probably in her 50s. The story that she told went as follows:

> Once upon a time there lived a couple, married for thirty years without children. One day the husband, a hunter, brought home an antelope that he had killed in his hunt. He saved one thigh and hung it on the kitchen wall where it stayed days after the couple had eaten the rest of the meat. About the same time, the couple realized that an unidentified helper was doing the household chores. The husband decided on a vigil to find out the identity of this benefactor and discovered that the antelope-thigh had turned into a beautiful woman that did their chores. Struck by her beauty, he begged her to stay human and be his junior wife. She agreed but only upon his promise of secrecy about her animal origin. However, when the displeased senior wife demanded to know the origin, he broke his promise and disclosed it to her. One day, in a dispute between the co-wives the senior one insulted the junior one by calling her "a mere antelope thigh." When the junior realized the husband's betrayal, she transformed back into an antelope's thigh. Disappointed, the husband scolded his senior wife thus: "You women and your marital rivalry, you will never be rid of it." From then on, co-wife rivalry became an enduring thing in the world!

The story by the second storyteller, a younger man probably in his early 30s, went as follows:

> All the animals of the forest gathered together and made an agreement to publicly disclose their secret *mmrane* (identity poem or personal accolade

extended into poetry). But, Tree Bear refused to make the disclosure—not even to his own wife. She begged and coaxed him, until Tree Bear finally promised the disclosure to her alone. Unbeknownst to Tree Bear, his wife asked Hare, the sharp-eared messenger drummer for all the animals, to eavesdrop upon the disclosure. At the next meeting of animals, when Tree Bear still refused to disclose his mmrane, Hare asked for a drum and then recited the secret poem for all to hear in drum language. A very upset Tree Bear thus decided to hide away on a huge tree nearby. As he climbed up he met Osebo, the leopard, who tried to grab him but merely detached his tail. Placing the source of all his woes in his wife's betrayal he shook his head and cried, "Oh the treachery of woman!" And that is the meaning of the tree-bear's cry.

One can immediately point to a few general things about the Akan people from these stories: for instance, that antelope hunting, polygamy, poetic self-identification, and drum communication were once part of the Akan societies. Further, one can interpret the stories as Akan cautionary tales about the keeping of confidences, the betrayal of trust, and/or the placement of community interests over personal ones in the society. These were all information that one needn't see the performance to deduce. They were accessible simply by an acquaintance with the stories, even as transcribed narratives on a page. However, what I was really interested in were the new and deeper understandings of the relationship between the cultural performance and Akan identity that storytelling *activity* could open up for me.

To Be Believed and Not to Be Believed: Parody and Narrative Turmoil in Anansesem

One of the main insights that I received from experiencing Anansesem in an elaborate cultural performance at Ekumfi Atwia, instead of merely reading or hearing the stories, is that this Akan storytelling practice is in part a *parody*. The thinking that led me to see a particular parody in the Ekumfi-Atwia performance began when I recognized similarity between the story of co-wife rivalry and another about the origins of the Fante *Adwenadze* coastal clan:

Once, a widower met a beautiful maiden on the beach and asked her to be his wife. The woman gladly accepted him. They set up a home.

After some time, she decided to visit her parents alone but the man asked to accompany her. He followed her to the beach and when they dived into the sea and arrived at a beautiful courtyard he realized he had married a fish. She forbade him to reveal to anyone that she is a fish. They returned to land, had children, and the man took a second wife. One day, in a quarrel between the wives, the second taunted the first for being a fish. At that moment the fish woman realized the man had betrayed her confidence and so left the house and returned to the sea. However, the children they bore became the founders of the clan and *adwen* (a type of large catfish) their symbol.

Commonly folktales, novels, historical accounts, and other narrative genres are seen to discuss or present a world of the imagination (fiction) or a real world (fact/non-fiction) based on agreed-upon criteria for what is real or factual. I recognized that except for a shift from fish and fishing to antelope and hunting, and other minor elements, the above story and that of the Ekumfi-Atwia story are practically the same. Yet, Akan do not regard them as equally factual. Whereas Akan regard the co-wife story and other Anansesem as fiction, some Ghanaian scholars describe the stories as born of the creative imagination or "a figment of imaginative delight" (Ayeh, 1978: 3; Yankah, 1997: 146–147). They regard the Adwenadze clan story as *tetesem* (from the Akan word *tete* or past), as history, as true accounts of actual events in the past. In short, tetesem purport to be factual accounts of the origins of Akan people and their important cultural institutions. (Van Dyck, 1966: 23)

How did I arrive at parody from the above? Parody implies similarity because, by definition, it is "a form of *imitation*" (Hutcheon, 1985: 32). However, "imitation" is not merely a similarity, it suggests an action— an act of copying or replication. The question that the similarities in the stories raised for me was the following: is there an action of imitation beyond just the similarity? Every imitation has a *target* (the imitated thing) and if imitation was present, it is likely that the fictional Anansesm story was imitating the "factual" tetesem Adwenadze story. No imitation completely replicates its target: there is always a difference or "distance" between them. In parody, this is a *critical* distance. In other words, parody arises when an imitation comments on a target by cueing us to its alikeness to and difference from that target (Rose, 1996: 32). I shall call this the *parodic relationship*. It is from such cues and commentary in the Anansesem performance that I concluded it had a parodic relationship with tetesem.

How did the Anansesem performance manifest the contours of parody that I have described above? It did so in part by its juxtaposition—placing side-by-side—of *fictional* and *etiological* frames. What do I mean by this? Although there is a consensus of sorts in Akan tradition about the status of Anansesem stories as fiction, that status does not remain a tacitly agreed upon thing in storytelling—it is the convention for the storyteller to verbally establish it as fiction before proceeding to tell the story. This declaration is an elaborate, sometimes over the top act and, at Ekumfi-Atwia, involved the following exchange between each storyteller and the audience:

STORYTELLER: Anansesem is not to be believed
AUDIENCE: It is for keeping.

An etiological frame, on the other hand, is different from the fictional frame. Etiological narratives (from the Greek *aitia*) purport to explain origin, something fact based. In Anansesem performance, it is conventional for the storytellers to announce what the story is about and if it purports to explain origins—it establishes an etiological (factual) frame (Pelton, 1989: 68-69). During the performance at Ekumfi-Atwia, each storyteller proceeded immediately from establishing the fictional frame to establishing an etiological frame: The first storyteller announced, "I'll tell you how co-wife rivalry came into the world," and the second declared, "I'll tell you how the tree bear's cry came about." Clearly, they were setting up stories and, as noted, they said already that the stories are *not* to be believed.

But, consider what happened next. It is important to note that villagers at Ekumfi-Atwia were not mere bystander audiences but rather participants of sorts in the performance. We can already see this in the fact that the declaration by which the storytellers established fictional frames involved the audiences' verbal participation. In the course of each storytelling act there was more of this participation. Villagers in the audience interjected questions that, in jest, asked each storyteller for some kind of indication about the factualness of the story. "Were you present (when all this happened)?" asked one participant during the first story. To this, the storyteller insisted with a mock defensiveness, "I was there!" Another participant asked during the second story: "what was the name of Tree-Bear's wife?" The storyteller replied with affected seriousness, "Aba," as if he personally knew her.

So, how is this parody? Because both storytellers established the fictional frame at the start of the performance, it had overriding force. Thus the subsequent factual frame ended up as an imitation of the latter. In other words, the factual frames, juxtaposed against the larger fictional frame, indicated that part of the pleasure to be derived from the performance would come from this pretend play, this delightful teasing. Villagers' jocular demands that the storytellers verify the factualness of the stories through eye-witnessing and name-dropping were part of this collaborative pretend play.

As I indicated earlier, parody is more than mere imitation. Parodic relationships must cue us to the alikeness *and* difference in a "critical" way—i.e., by making a comment on the target. The parodic relationship is not necessarily belittling but can be "playful" and "critically constructive" (Hutcheon, 1985: 32). True to this characteristic of parody, there was something more profound in the Anansesem at Ekumfi-Atwia than mere imitation. The storytellers' fictional *and* non-fictional framings of their stories, combined with the playful audience interjections, yielded what I call *narrative turmoil*—a collaboratively staged and productive confusion/uncertainty about the "truth" of the stories. By declaiming, "This is not to be believed" yet paradoxically insisting "I witnessed it all" in front of the participants who kept asking "were you there?" the storytellers and participants collaboratively connoted that whatever they tagged "not to be believed" may well be something potentially "to-be-believed" and, more importantly, whatever is assumed to be factual may be worthy of contest (Donkor, 2016: 76–79). One of the collaborative features of Anansesem, called *mboguo* (literally means, "knock down") helps to intensify the narrative turmoil. The term describes participants' permit to periodically break a storyteller's narration and supplant it with their own lively contributions of music, dance, mimed action and/or comic skits. By displacing anyone's sole authorship of and sole authority over narration, *mboguo* allows the larger storytelling community to be more intensely involved in staging a productive confusion/uncertainty about the "truth" of the stories.

How does this sort of parodic cultural performance demonstrate Akan identity in complex ways? Kwesi Yankah has observed that in several cultures of Ghana, criticisms are associated with obliqueness (or indirectness) as part of the aesthetic of communication (Yankah, 2000: 141). A mark of aesthetic sophistication is a capacity to use cryptic language when channels for public challenges and opposition are limited. In Akan tradition, elders and principal officers such as royal linguists are the official custodians and conveyors of factual stories.[5] So, directly raising questions may be considered disrespectful to the custodians and the heritage itself (Van Dyck, 1996: 13, 23). Anansesem performers, by imitating tetesem, critically draw attention to differences. Through the narrative turmoil Ekumfi-Atwia performers opened space for ordinary Akan to confront aspects of their tradition: particularly, the common understanding of tetesem as completely factual and the notion that this shared understanding ought not to be questioned.

Enter, Trickster Spider: Doubleness and the Ananse-likeness of Anansesem

Here, I must return to the significance of the trickster Ananse—the reason why I went to the village of Ekumfi-Atwia in the first place. The storytelling performances at Ekumfi-Atwia show Anansesem as a tradition that is grounded in collaborative fabrication. Akan people name their storytelling Anansesem not only because the stories have Ananse in many of them (though, neither of the two stories at Ekumfi-Atwia had Ananse as a character) but *also* because storytelling is considered crafty, imaginative talk

---

[5] I use the term "tradition" quite a lot throughout this essay and I thought I ought to point out certain caveats about my use of it. I use the term "tradition" not to freeze Akan culture into an ahistoric entity whose identity and values have and always will be a particular way. Not only is that scholarly untenable, it also goes against the trickster spirit itself! However, I use the term in recognition that this kind of expected social circumspection remains present in certain arenas of Akan culture today.

and therefore a practice that is associated with the character of Ananse himself.[6] In the stories, Ananse's capacity for trickery has to do with his ambivalence. Ananse compels the questions: Is he god or not, human or not, wily/creative or actually treacherous/dangerous? To each, the answer is both "yes" *and* "not yes," and "no" *and* "not-no" because it is impossible to limit Ananse to one side or other of these distinctions. This trickster spider, then, is the very embodiment of duplicity—of doubleness. Since there is nothing unequivocal about Ananse, he is wary of any "just-so" claims (claims that discourage questioning) on the suspicion that they might lead to the development of an oppressive ideology.

Because ideologies present a *particular* image (partial truths as whole truths) to win others to a particular way of seeing the world and may work to bind people to a particular order of society that is against their interests, Ananse, whose doubleness resists singular perspectives can be understood as the embodiment of an opposition against ideology. This kind of opposition is one that rejects singularly focused outlooks. It recognizes that much of what we take for granted socially are ideological constructs. Trickster Ananse reminds the Akan people to question such stories—to, in a manner of speaking, ask: "were you there". In the Akan tradition, not only is trickster Ananse the folkloric embodiment (because of his doubleness) of the capacity to generate multiple conversations and ideas, that quality of the trickster is very much embedded in the practice of storytelling itself.

Cultural performances are usually a concrete and integral component of the identity of the people who enact them. The storytelling at Ekumfi-Atwia indicates that in the Akan tradition, cultural creativity can be a challenge to dominant narratives through ambiguity. They suggest, in a performance-centered manner of speaking, that no one has an absolute claim to the direction of the narrative. The ultimate goal of the trickster Ananse, then, is not so much to unequivocally repudiate the existing Akan social order. What we see in the example of Anansesem is not the

---

[6] For a discussion of Anansesem as the likeness of Ananse, see Donkor, *Spiders of the Market,* 2016, 73–76.

use of cultural performance to directly challenge the Akan social order but rather to interrupt its claims, to draw attention to its limits and assumption, and to reposition it as one of the many possible voices in an ongoing dialogue.

References

Akyea, E. Ofori. "The Atwia Ekumfi Kodzidan: An Experimental African Theatre." *Okyeame* 4.1, 1968: 82–84.

Arkhurst, Sandy. "Kodzidan." In *The Legacy of Efua Sutherland: Pan African Cultural Activism*, edited by Anne V. Adams and Esi Sutherland-Addy, 165–74. Banbury, UK: Ayebia Clarke, 2007.

Ayeh, E. O. *Mmrehua*. Accra: Ghana Publishing Corporation, 1978.

Brooker, Peter. *A Concise Glossary of Cultural Theory*. New York, NY: Oxford University Press, 1999.

Donkor, David A. *Spiders of the Market: Ghanaian Trickster Performance* in *a Web of Neolbieralism*, 73–83. Bloomington, IN: Indiana University Press, 2016.

Drewal, Margaret Thompson. "The State of Research on Performance in Africa." *African Studies Review* 34.3, 1991: 1–64.

Hutcheon, Linda. *A Theory of Parody*. New York, NY: Methuen, 1985.

Pelton, Robert. *The Trickster in West Africa: A Study of Mythic Irony and Sacred Delight*. Berkeley, CA: University of California Press, 1989.

Rattray, Robert Sutherland. *Akan-Ashanti Folk-Tales*. Oxford: Clarendon, 1930.

Richards, Sandra. "Writing the Absent Potential: Drama, Performance and the Canon of African American Literature." In *Performance and Performativity*, edited by Andrew Parker and Eve. K. Sedgwick, 65–87. New York, NY: Routledge, 1996.

Rose, Margaret. *Parody: Ancient, Modern, and Postmodern*. Cambridge: Cambridge University Press, 1996.

Storey, John. *Cultural Theory and Popular Culture*. New York, NY: Routledge, 2000.

Sutherland, Efua. *Marriage of Anansewa and Edufa*. Harlow: Longman, 1987.

Van Dyck, Charles. "An Analytical Study of the Folktales of Selected Peoples of West Africa." PhD Dissertation, Oxford University, 1966.

Yankah, Kwesi. *Speaking for the Chief*. Bloomington, IN: Indiana University Press, 1995.

————. "The Question of Ananse in Akan Mythology." In *Perspectives on Mythology*, edited by Esi Sutherland-Addy, 134–47. Accra: Woeli, 1997.

————. "Nana Kwame Ampadu and the Sung-Tale as Metaphor for Protest Discourse." In *Frontomfrom: Contemporary Ghanaian Literature, Theatre and Film*, edited by Kofi Anyidoho and James Gibbs, 135–53. Amsterdam: Rodopi, 2000.

Yeboa-Danqua, Jonas. "Storytelling of the Akan and Guan in Ghana." In *Ghanaian Literatures*, edited by Richard K. Priebe, 29–42. Westport, CT: Greenwood, 1988.

2

Experiencing Community

Image 3   *Penitentes* © Suzanne MacAulay

Good-bye, all those present,
All who accompany me ...
Good-bye all my neighbors,
And do not forget me.
The End – The End – Amen.

Adios todos los presentes
Que me van a acompanar
Adios todos mis proximos
No me vayan a olvidar.
Fin – Fin – Amen.[1]

From within the room next to the small chapel sanctuary where families and friends gather in the dark, a Penitente Brother shouts out "*Ave Maria!*" His prayer is followed by a cacophony of clanking chains, sounds of rattles, feet pounding on the floor, clapping hands, and soulful moaning. For those Catholics sitting in that cramped sanctuary, the clamor and commotion, intensified by the disorienting blackness of the chapel and the lingering scent of extinguished candles, symbolically represents the chaos and shadow that enveloped the earth as Jesus Christ died on Good Friday. At last, the strident noises fade into a recitation of prayers for the souls of the dead, for the Penitente Brothers and their families, and for those of us present. During this litany, I, along with other villagers, become witnesses to the power of memory as the living prayerfully commemorate the dead in the aftermath of the still reverberating echoes of sonic disorder. Sitting in the darkness—separate but together—amidst our palpable physical and emotional uncertainties, we hear our names called out with the rest, firmly binding us all together in a pledge of remembrance not only to the dead but to ourselves as well.

Every year toward the end of Holy Week the time-honored religious ceremony of *Las Tinieblas* (Darkness) is enacted by *Los Penitentes*, a society of devout lay Catholic men known as Brothers (*Hermanos*), performing their role as spiritual guardians and memory-keepers for their **community** (past and present). For this local chapter of the Brotherhood,

---

[1] *Adios al mundo*, transcribed and translated by Alice Corbin Henderson, as cited in William Wroth, *Images of Penance, Images of Mercy* (Norman: University of Oklahoma Press, 1991), 62.

the ceremony always occurs in a remote chapel (*morada*) in the foothills of the Sangre de Cristo Mountains on the eastern perimeter of the San Luis Valley in south central Colorado. However, fraternities of the Brotherhood are active in remote villages throughout southern Colorado and northern New Mexico. With beliefs retaining traces of sixteenth-century Spanish mysticism, the Brotherhood has maintained a modicum of secrecy in order to protect their privacy from years of popular misunderstanding and alienation from mainstream Catholicism as well as public scrutiny.

The Holy Week ceremony of Las Tinieblas is also known as *Tenebrae*, and throughout the Catholic world dramatically recreates the tumult and confusion following Jesus' death, when the dead were believed to rise and walk the earth (hence the pounding on the floor accompanied by choruses of moans and prayers). Penitentes is the popular name for the Brotherhood, *La Hermandad de Nuestro Padre Jesus Nazareno*. Its shortened version refers to penitents, and derives its name from performing penance during Lent such as a dedication to a strict schedule of severe physical deprivation (fasting) and bodily punishment (e.g., flagellation or whipping themselves and walking barefoot over difficult rocky terrain). Through acts such as these, Penitentes identify with Christ's suffering and death.[2] This empathy with Christ's travails is registered as deeply in the body as in the imagination. In the eyes of the *Hermandad*, the great achievement of penance is to try to surmount embodied worldliness by transforming the heart and the spirit.

Every year, weeks before Easter, the Brothers sequester themselves in their moradas (chapels) to fast and pray for the welfare of all Catholics in the area—as if their prayers could uphold the delicate symmetry between the community's spirituality and fate. During the Lenten

---

[2] There are chapters of lay Catholic penitents all over the Spanish-speaking world. A news article dating to the late 1990s describes one harrowing scene in the Philippines, where ten men underwent crucifixions by being nailed to crosses and hung there for several minutes in fulfillment of celestial bargains they made earlier for various reasons such as for the sake of a mother, who was cured of tuberculosis, or a son, who recovered from another incurable disease, etc.. This ritual of extreme self-mortification has continued for more than fifty-five years in San Pedro Cutud village north of Manila. "Filipinos mark Easter with crucifixions." Wanganui, New Zealand, *Wanganui Chronicle*, 3 April 1999, p. 1.

interval, the Penitente assumption of the role of custodians of communal spirituality is consonant with their historical status as yearlong caretakers of village mores, informal arbiters, and helpers for families of the sick or recently deceased. The real meaning of the Brotherhood's commitment lies in upholding an essential balance among the group's corporatism, shared humility, and individual religious vows.

The term "morada" (chapel) also signifies the Brotherhood itself. As both a space and a concept, it allegorically represents the guardianship of community values and beliefs achieved through the Brothers' exemplary yet harsh behavioral codes and socio-religious commitment. In the words of one of the Brothers, Juan Estévan Medina, conjuring up the image of convertible sacred space, he says, "Any place you pray … is *morada*. Any place you pray Rosary or a prayer or … something" (Medina, 1993). Thus, the morada is an actual physical place for communal ritual action and a conceptual space for individual contemplation and prayer. These unassuming structures (basically, one room plus an anteroom) dotting the rural southwestern landscape attest to the continual presence of Penitente chapters extant since the Spanish Colonial era. They are the sites of centuries of penitential religious practices associated with the Catholic religious calendar. As we have learned, Penitentes perform these rites in the belief that in order for their actions and physical suffering to really benefit the greater good of the group and their community, they must honor their pledges and vows in the spirit of Christ's death for the redemption of the world.

Cultural Performance

This chapter focuses on cultural performance and **ethnographic practice** relative to communities and folk groups in terms of perceptions of identity, social values, tradition, evolution, invention, and change. By now, you should be somewhat familiar with the notion of cultural performance as it was introduced in the first chapter. In this chapter, we carefully relate culturally embedded performances to folk groups and community. A few ethnographic methods and their application will also be introduced here to help guide you through the thicket of meaning and interpretation. Recall that Milton Singer is mentioned in Chapter 1. His description of cultural performance acknowledges the significance of cultural conventions or traditions as framing the performance as "repeated and significant actions that are deemed by custom and authority to be appropriate for a particular occasion" (Valentine, 2002: 293). We should note that tradition as construed as "repeated and significant actions" also entails change and transformation according to each cultural circumstance. Tradition is dynamic and evolving, changing within the context and changeable in performance. Singer's explanation, however, does emphasize one of the important consequences of these performances, which results in solidarity among participants, unifying them while strengthening and reinforcing their commitment to certain values and beliefs. Review the description of Penitente Holy Week rites, and try to identify those ceremonial aspects that conform to expectations of cultural performances. Consider Penitentes' social marginalization on the fringes of San Luis Valley society, and their intense physical and spiritual interpretation of Catholic liturgy. In fact, their self-sacrificial practices seem more appropriate to a **folk religion.**

In order to understand more about cultural performance, we need to look at other analyses of performance. Scholars have offered different interpretations of cultural performance ranging from the concept of bounded, repetitive, intensified sacred, and secular rituals to communal opportunities to reflect who we are, and to "*show ourselves to ourselves* in ways that help us recognize our behavior ... as well as our unconscious needs and desires" (Victor Turner as quoted in Madison, 2012: 154). With these thoughts in mind relative to Penitente devotional actions, how do we go about investigating sacred ceremonies as performance while still acknowledging and respecting the religious depths of these rituals? We also need to acknowledge the profound nature of certain ritual's relationship to the spiritual well-being of a community. In the case of the Brotherhood, performance is obviously not entertainment. According to Richard Schechner, performances, among other things, "mark identities, bend time, reshape and adorn the body, and tell stories" (Schechner, 2006: 28). Speaking more generally, Erving Goffman says, "A performance may be defined as all the activity of a given participant on a given occasion which serves to influence in any way any of the participants" (quoted in

Schechner, 2006: 29). Penitente Lenten rites appear to encompass a bit of both descriptions. Toward the end of this chapter we will encounter more examples specifically focusing on cultural performance, and consult criteria derived from analytical models or templates that can aid us in charting our course through the complex interplay linking sacred rites, cultural reenactments, performance, traditions, variations, actors, processes, objectives, scripts, setting, and audience in context.

One aspect of learning about cultural performance is learning how to interpret performances *in situ*, that is, as an audience member or participant in a certain time and place or during **fieldwork** in a specific locale. On the one hand, when we are in the "field" (that is, simply being in a particular situation or context whether near or far away), and viewing public cultural reenactments, we may not even be aware of the significance of certain dramatic and aesthetic contents or how deeply they are entangled in various aspects of performance and cultural representation. It is often during reflection afterward that meanings emerge. On the other hand, we may also underestimate the importance of our own background and experience, which we bring to these situations. We may not realize how strongly our training and sensitivity are implicated in the eventual climactic fusion of performance components and to what extent this affects our ultimate "reading" or interpretation of the cultural event. Thus, acquiring an ease and familiarity with the process of **self-reflection** or **reflexivity** helps us understand the complexities, and also the subtleties, of rituals and ceremonies relative to our positions.

In Kristin Valentine's cultural analysis model, arising from her fieldwork with the Yaqui Indians during their annual Easter ceremonies in Guadalupe, Arizona, she describes the steps leading to a perceptive (and sensory) rendering of what one is witnessing during cultural performances. The overarching theme of Valentine's work with the Yaqui involves the ethical concept of "intense spectatorship." She starts with the notion that as guests in a cultural situation and as fieldworkers, who are there to learn and document the event, we show respect and behave in harmony with the moral principles of our hosts. Valentine's idea of "intense spectatorship" also aligns with the anthropological concept of "deep observation"—paying careful attention to everything happening around us. Thus, her model encompasses stages of self-reflection in order to sort out certain autobiographical traits that determine how we shape our views of a particular cultural performance, prior knowledge of cultural and historical circumstances around the event, and our awareness of the moment of fusion where mind, body, and environment come together during the performance. The idea of fusion, or blending together, represents the merging of all these diverse elements, usually at the climax of the ceremony. This final stage includes the ultimate unification of performance elements, including atmosphere, multiple audiences (more about this later), and culminates with the performers in their roles at the most powerful, revelatory moment of the ceremony—the point when all is consummated. Finally, Valentine's last concept reverts again to the process of self-reflection or reflexivity in order to look back and contemplate the meaning of all that took place vis-à-vis cultural circumstances, individual spectators, and transformative experience. Reflexivity is one of the modalities we use to enact experiential observation. It is a personal feedback mechanism whereby we are deeply aware of how we observe ourselves and others through self-reflection. Reflection and interpretation are at the heart of writing ethnographies. These modes provide the platform upon which we construct our observations and impressions of what occurred.

Let's review Valentine's four steps to help us understand a way to evaluate cultural performance. First, "engage in self-reflection," which focuses on one's own personal history and circumstances as well as influences that may shape one's perspective on the cultural performance. Second, "investigate cultural and historical explanations related to the performance event." Third, try to identify where the intersections and overlaps (the "blurred boundaries") occur among the atmosphere, audience, performers, their roles, and the highlights of "saying and doing" at the heart of the ceremony or performance. Fourth, reflect on the learning experience of the cultural performance (Valentine, 2002: 282).

Ethnography

On our way to understanding how performance and community work together, let us now examine the ethnographic process, which is one of the "tools" we use to acquire knowledge and understanding in cultural contexts. Ethnography is how we actively learn about another culture by being in the situation (i.e., local and specific), and conversing dialogically with the people about whom we are learning and with whom we are collaborating. We become acquainted through dialogue. The key to any cultural analysis is ethnographic practice and a means of getting to know other human beings intimately and well. Therefore, ethnographers closely examine the cultural processes and activities imbedded in the cultural sediment of the field site, whether it is rites enacted in a remote chapel in the Sangre de Cristo foothills or a Fourth of July Rodeo parade on a downtown street in the western United States. In other words, the principal idea of ethnographic practice is to notate everyday life through the descriptive analysis of culture in intense communication with others. By heeding process and dynamics, we recognize the fluid nature of ethnographic practice, its open-endedness, its multiple voices, its sensorium (awareness of engaging all the senses), and its susceptibility to change and evolve as we learn more and more about each other. Folklorist Henry Glassie defines ethnography in the same lively and animated spirit in which we aspire to study the dynamic processes of cultural performance as "interaction and collaboration." Specifically pertaining to ethnographic practice, he cites "the ability to converse intimately [with others]" (Glassie, 1982: 14). Elsewhere, Glassie says that scholars "need imagination to enter between the facts, to feel what it is like to be, to think and act as another person" (Glassie, 1982: 12).

Participant Observation

Empathy also figures in anthropologist Clifford Geertz's notion that ethnography is the discovery of a particular group's perception of "who they think they are; what they think they are doing; and to what end they think they are doing it" (Geertz, 2000: 16). In order to uncover answers or follow their lead, it requires the ethnographer or student who is involved in fieldwork to fully and empathetically participate in a cultural group's activities through intense engagement. This is usually achieved by a methodology of both observing and participating. It is what is understood by the label, **participant observer**, which is a term associated with a more holistic and applied understanding of cultural performance with its various plots and roles. As participant observers, we are part of the cultural experience at the same time as we are observing it. In a more profound sense, we are co-performers in an "intimate involvement and engagement of 'co-activity' or 'co-performance' with historically situated, named, 'unique individuals'" (Johnson, 2013: 9). At times, this experience can be unsettling and can feel like one is operating under a dual perspective or split consciousness: The somewhat distanced analytical ethnographic view of the observer is juxtaposed with the close-up, more intimate view of the individual enacting their role as participant. Another way to grasp this concept is to refer to it in theatre terms describing the state of mind of an actor onstage as a "double agent," that is, being oneself and not being oneself at the same time (Hughes-Freeland, 1998: 6). In other words, by experiencing a different culture as the *outsider within*, the ethnographer is directly focused on cultural practices of the community while at the same moment turning the lens back on herself by reflexively scrutinizing one's own actions and reactions within a given situation.

The very condition of "being within" also raises another series of questions, which complement Geertz's set of inquiries mentioned before. The following sequence characterizes the ethnographer's viewpoint based on the experience of being an outsider deeply involved with the internal workings of a particular cultural group or community. These classic ethnographic queries arise from a position of being both inside and outside a culture or community. "What is it like to be a member of this society?" "How does it feel to live in a culture such as this one?" And the ultimate "outsider" quandary, "Can we ever know how it feels?" (MacAulay, 2000: xiv). The final question resonates with the age-old metaphysical conundrum of wanting to know the minds of others: "How can we ever know?" Imagine situations in which you were both participant (that is, co-performer) and observer. Perhaps this occurred at a Thanksgiving dinner, a wedding or a Jewish Passover celebration. Under what circumstances did you feel confident and at ease to fully participate? Did your background knowledge and experience help prepare you for this event? What factors caused you some discomfort and unease? In what way was your understanding and interpretation of the event affected by your feelings?

In this chapter, we will look beyond basic definitions of the ethnographer's relation to community captured in the spirit of such action verbs as observing, participating, describing, evaluating, writing, etc. to question how we can apprehend the deeper meaning of cultural expressiveness through our attentiveness. Victor Turner was an anthropologist, who made essential and very important observations and discoveries about ceremony and cultural performance stemming from his work with ritual and performance among African societies. We have already encountered his succinct appraisal of performance to "*show ourselves to ourselves.*" A variant on this thought, which is another frequently quoted Turner insight, is especially pertinent to this book; "We will know one another better by entering another's performances and learning their grammars and vocabularies" (cited in Schechner, 2006: 19). In tandem with Turner's idea of a kind of reciprocal performative action is his central notion of humans as performing beings—not merely "knowing" beings, *homo sapiens*, but also *homo performans*, that is, humans as performers and members of a performing species. Turner wrote:

> If man is a sapient animal, a tool making animal, a self-making animal, a symbolizing animal, he is no less, a performing animal, *homo performans*, not in the sense, perhaps that a circus animal may be a performing animal, but in the sense that man is a self-making animal—his performances are, in a way, reflexive; in performance he reveals himself to himself. (quoted in Madison, 2012:166)

Traditional ethnographic practice has moved beyond scholarly textual inscriptions as representations and interpretations of cultural experience primarily confined to words on a page to embrace other ways of knowing such as sensory awareness and actively co-experiencing the impact of cultural expressiveness through participant observation. At the heart of ethnography is the desire to deeply know a culture and to be able to communicate in a broad sense each cultural particularity such as worldview, history, place, specific context, cultural performance repertory, social dynamics, evolving identities, and active, engaged, lived experience in as meaningful and truthful way as possible. Consider the southern Colorado Penitentes as they perform their isolated yet crucial caretaking role once a year to spiritually safeguard their Catholic village communities, and be attentive to how they fulfill this responsibility. What does the brief introductory description at the beginning of the chapter tell us about the belief system of the group participants and their relationship to community? How are these connections enacted and consummated through religious and cultural performance? Is there an audience and who are the constituents? Or, is everyone a participant? Beyond the display of a type of devotional altruism, there are also questions of power and its distribution, and how this is manifest through ceremonial action. In light of this, think about how the Penitentes, an obviously less privileged group of Catholic lay people in light of the majority of San Luis Valley society, acquire power through their ceremonial role of praying for the souls of the rest of the community. This power arises through performance and underscores the penitential mission of spiritual caretaking, which continues to be amplified throughout the year whenever a Brother helps a disadvantaged community member.

Community

We usually begin thinking about **community** by identifying characteristics or traits in common that cohere to make a united entity, in other words, a group. Is location a determinant? Are solidarity of purpose and governance strong factors in group formation? What about communal action? Art historian Nicholas Thomas suggests that community is formed in *opposition* to something else. Community is defined or demarcated by what it is not. He writes, "… the idea of community cannot exist in the absence of some externality or difference, and identities and traditions are often not simply different but constituted in opposition to others" (Thomas, 1992: 213). For example, the Penitentes are a folk subculture of the institutional Catholic Church, but their extreme ritual practices such as flagellation, etc. place them more in opposition to traditional Catholic observances. Thus, they are considered outsiders in terms of official Catholicism, and are defined as such by the established Church. But, internally Penitente communities are composed of "multiple interactive worlds of individuals" making up a whole, which is united in a certain religious attitude and purpose (Noyes, 1995: 458). As Thomas continues to probe the idea of community, he eventually circles back to align his thinking with the customary folkloristic view of community delineated by folklorist Dorothy Noyes as having a shared culture, a common interest, often sharing a common descent or lineage, living in a specific locale, engaging in collective activities, and "*emerging from performance*" (Noyes, 1995: 452 author's italics). Congruent with these basic identifiers, Thomas ultimately expands his initial statement about community formation in opposition to something, to state that difference is not as important a factor in distinguishing community as the "actual histories of accommodation or confrontation that shape particular understandings of others and thus determine what specific practices, manners, or local ethics are rendered explicit and made to carry the burden of local identity" (Thomas, 1992: 213).

Let us look again at Noyes' string of salient characteristics defining group or community. What does she mean by "emerging from performance?" In order to make that statement Noyes proposes "that we distinguish between the empirical [i.e., observable] network of interactions in which culture is created and moves, and the community of the social imaginary that occasionally emerges in performance" (Noyes, 1995: 452). Imaginary is the realm of the imagination. When linked to the notion of "social," it connotes the enactment of a shared vision or utopian ideal—a principle acknowledged and held in common. The community is still recognized as representative of ideals, values, etc. but the notion of community and its identity is effected or brought about through performance. This emergence of identity through performed action is an active, participatory condition of creative and aesthetic dimensions. Performance is generative (brings something into being) not only representational. It creates presence through ambiance, setting, action, props, etc. as well as creatively transforming the actors, the audience, space and time, and all who witness the event or participate in it.

How does community emerge from performance? Again, we can provide an example from rituals of the Penitentes. On Good Friday afternoon, Penitentes gather to reenact Christ's steep climb carrying his cross up the torturous route to Calvary, where he will be crucified. As their stage space for this religious pageant, the Brothers chose a precipitous uneven and slippery slope strewn with jagged rocks behind the morada in the village of El Rito. This ceremony is named *El Calvario* in Spanish for the hill upon which Jesus was crucified, and melds two forces of collective religious action together. One is the ritual procession over rough terrain on foot (some go barefoot), which emulates the physical travails of Christ along the "*via crucis*" (refers to the Catholic Stations of the Cross) on his way to being crucified. The other integral part in the ceremony is the commemoration of the Fourth Station of the Cross—the place where Christ meets his mother as he ascends the path to Calvary. In Spanish, this rite is called *El Encuentro*, the encounter. All those present are also reenacting and meditating upon the sorrowful meeting between mother and son as the group of worshippers clamber over the rock-strewn path to the top of the hill. The ritual begins with everyone inching slowly along while praying and dropping to their knees on sharp rocks every few steps to recite the Rosary (prayers dedicated to Jesus' mother, the Virgin Mary). The El Encuentro ceremony culminates in prayers and more recitations at the summit of the hill with an invitation to all participants to step forward to caress and personally cherish the plaster image of the Virgin. They also kiss the crucifix, which is carried by members of the Brotherhood, who stand and offer both these objects to the procession of penitents and supporters until everyone has filed past. Following the ritual climax, there is a sense of palpable intimacy among the group, which binds everyone to each other in honoring death as much as life.

The powerful feeling of intimacy is not merely a by-product of performance but directly *emerges* from this sequence of performed actions (i.e., walking, praying, touching, honoring, and descending on the path back to the morada). In this way, the shared sense of enacted community binds all celebrants to each other through suffering, sorrow, love, and compassion. The concept of ceremonially co-experiencing the physical and emotional suffering of the divine mother and son thus becomes part of the repertoire of the "social imaginary" (that is, a shared vision) joining this particular community together through common beliefs and the efficacy of devotional action. In the tradition of Victor Turner's notion that "community is a felt reality," this affective community is mutually created by Brothers out of their religious beliefs, and binds them together through sensory experience and deep feelings (see Noyes, 1995: 466). Sensory awareness is crucial to understanding and experiencing the depth of these sacred rites on this very cold day in March. In this instance, the preeminent senses, visual, auditory, and kinesthetic, intensify our perceptions of the affective spiritual presence embodied in ritual through us physically struggling with the extreme cold and blowing snow upon our faces, coping with dizziness from fasting, making our bodies move excruciatingly slowly along the grueling path, and enduring the pain from kneeling abruptly on slippery jagged rocks. All of these sensations are essential to comprehending the core spiritual and physical practices of Penitente cultural performances.

Combining Dorothy Noyes' earlier description of community identity as "the empirical network of interactions in which culture is created and moves," with her view that the constitution or essence of the group or community is fully realized in performance when interactions involved in culture making are in dialogue with the notion of the "social imaginary," we see that Penitente group performances exemplify both the "empirical network" and the "social imaginary." We began this chapter by describing a particular Penitente ritual, Las Tinieblas, which demonstrates the interconnectedness of religious observance and the moral commitment of the Brotherhood. This interplay between belief and action defines the Penitente community and privileges the interactive network of relationship at the core of its spiritual culture. Collectively, belief and performed actions constitute the melding of a network of interaction with the "social imaginary," which on multiple levels signify Penitente ceremonies as cultural performance.

Temporary Communities

Penitente chapters are centuries old, but how do the two descriptions of community—one concrete and observable ("network of interactions") and the other abstract and theoretical ("the social imaginary")—apply to **temporary communities**, for example, a group gathering around a particular finite and bounded performance during an afternoon? Those temporal groups, united in the moment as a community and resembling a community in every way for the short term, possess all the elements of cultural cohesion mentioned throughout this chapter. However, for the most part they do not endure in bonds of affinity and solidarity beyond the moments of one-time enactments. Let's examine one such example,—a community-based poetry and arts project called *Poetry of the Wild*, and see what else we can learn about secular (nonreligious) communal performances and community dynamics. In 2003 Ana Flores, an activist artist who creates work inspired by environmental issues and cultural politics, conceived Poetry of the Wild (POW) as an ongoing artistic and literary project that according to her original idea invites the public "out for a walk" to freshly experience their world through word, sound, and image. Inspired by pro-totypical birdhouse designs, these unique configurations of poetry boxes combining art and poetry were temporarily installed for just a few weeks in communal spaces throughout the United States and England on trails, in parks, on city streets, on the seashore, following migration routes through the Mexican borderlands, along rivers and wetlands as well as "shelved" in bookstores and library stacks, e.g., one box was installed in a library under its Dewey Decimal address: English poetry 811 (MacAulay, 2016: 106).

Each iteration of a different POW community emerges and coalesces around aesthetic expressiveness and performances where the culture in common is re-experienced, recreated, reconstructed, and reshaped according to circumstance. These are community-driven projects lasting up to a month or more where poets and artists collaborate on the design, execution, and siting of the boxes. Since there are no restrictions on participation, Poetry of the Wild is a radical project about aesthetic democracy or the democratization of art and poetry. Through the years and in many places, it has involved poets, poet laureates, students, interested citizen-artists, artist guilds, poetry clubs, actors, filmmakers, teachers, professors, corporate executives, and retired professionals, etc.. Once installed, the search for these boxes is akin to a magical treasure hunt where walkers, hikers, bird watchers, etc. encounter these boxes in unexpected places. Poetry of the Wild is regarded as a series of cultural performances because each iteration created in a different setting embod-ies the aesthetic values of a specific group in a particular context and draws on its shared culture for inspiration and consensus.

Poetry of the Wild not only inspires and elicits individual and com-munal creative expressiveness, but also gives people agency. What does "agency" mean in these circumstances? Community participants are the catalysts for designing boxes, fabricating them, composing or researching poems, and arranging for the performance readings. The denouement of all this activity is a peripatetic community gathering of all involved, including on-site poetry readings and long walks together as a group in search of the next box. Artists, poets, and spectators are the agents that make things happen. This is a fundamental premise of the anthropology of experience—that people are active agents who construct their own world. Anthropologist Barbara Myerhoff expressed this as, "we are the authors of ourselves" (Bruner, 1986: 12). Everything about Poetry of the Wild is predicated on the transitory nature of emergent social connections where creativity, artistic and cultural ties, collaboration, and continuity simultaneously ebb and flow. This project is concretely manifest within a certain timeframe and setting. When all is over, it becomes a fleeting afterimage upon the landscape and in people's memories.

As mentioned, each enactment of Poetry of the Wild has a special celebratory climax where members of the community sponsoring the project, including the artists and poets responsible for the boxes, gather to view all the art and poetry collaborations, and listen to the poets recite their work. Most attendants are either meeting each other for the first time or just getting to know each other, yet there is an instantaneous feeling of mutuality and camaraderie. Feelings such as these resonate with folklorist Deborah Kapchan's thoughts about community formation emerging out of performance, in particular, that the performances "play an essential ... role in the mediation and creation of social communities" (Kapchan, 1995: 479). Her ideas also parallel Noyes and Turner in emphasizing the creation of communality out of the emergent dynamic effects of performing together—in this instance, reading and listening to poetry being read.

The following passage describes one of the Poetry of the Wild culminating events occurring in conjunction with the tenth anniversary in 2013 when I was present. On a hot summer day in late June at a gathering in Mystic, Connecticut, the POW group transformed itself into a temporary community by association, distinct from the hordes of tourists streaming through the streets seeking ice cream or beer. All afternoon, I and the poetry group moved against the flow of tourists and pleasure-seekers as we followed various poets and artists to different urban locations of enchanted poetry boxes. These were placed around the town and along its outskirts. The tangible aspects of poetry boxes are the visual elements, the poetic words, and the boxes' actual materiality. The intangible aspects center on the feelings and experience of the group, enhanced by spontaneity and an instantaneous sense of community revealed in people lauding each other's creative efforts and pleased to be in each other's company. In other words, these moments of shared communion represent the essence of Victor Turner's notion of **communitas**. His interpretation of communitas encompasses quality of experience and deep mutuality; distinguished by what anthropologist James Fernandez refers to as the "undifferentiated experience of communion, [and] openness to the other that recognizes an essential human bond" (Fernandez, 1986: 179). Essentially, "communitas is an experience spontaneous and elementally existential" (Fernandez, 1986: 179). Receptivity to other participants' creativity is a vital part of Poetry of the Wild. Fernandez also notes that participants involved in collective action—or collective *aesthetic* action— achieve consensus, a word that "is etymologically, *con-sensus*, feeling together" (as quoted by Noyes, 1995: 469). The "confluence of feeling" (that is, flow or intermingling of feelings) occurs both introspectively and collectively as individuals share the same experience together (Noyes, 1995: 469). Poetry of the Wild gatherings offer many intense moments of solidarity when time and again we feel that we are not alone within an impervious group of strangers.

When POW poetry recitations are viewed and understood as occurring within performance frames, it further emphasizes the notion of a temporary sense of community immersed in the richness of a specific moment in time and space. The spaces where performance and communion intersect can be seen as "spaces of sociality," which applies anthropologist Michael Jackson's interpretation of intersections of social action together with prescribed moral behavior to the more ludic or playful sites of poetry performance and audience participation associated with POW. Poetry of the Wild's performed events are subject to the "same human impulse to intensify time and space within the community and to reveal mysteries while being engaged in revels" (Abrahams, 1987: 177). Highly crafted cultural artifacts like the poetry boxes with their poetic texts encapsulate the deepest values of a community, which are "simultaneously revealed and made mysterious" (Abrahams, 1987: 177). The fun and the profound, the traditional and improvisatory are characteristic of the gamut of celebratory events from time immemorial, and accentuate the individual and communal impulses behind Poetry of the Wild's enduring success. Openness and receptivity to the way events progress within a certain space-time framework also condition the mood of the crowd and reinforce the shared sense of community-in-the-moment.

As noted earlier, this shared sense of community is essential for the creation of communitas. Evidence of communitas during performance-centered moments indicates an intense comingling and bonding among participants during an event. The resultant intense communion also signals that something is occurring outside everyday life in the guise of this extraordinary communal experience. Another way to consider special or performed experience apart from quotidian or commonplace activities is to examine how differentiated experiences are created and what distinguishes them from day-to-day habitual occurrences. Where does the breakthrough into performance occur? Let's re-examine Victor Turner's notion of communitas, which he links to liminality. The concept of liminality will be familiar from Chapter 1. The given explanation of liminality is that it occurs as a transitional space neither here nor there, "betwixt and between." It exists in between entities, that is, between different states of awareness or consciousness, symbolic domains, different social structures, locations, etc., and according to Turner, refers "to any condition outside or on the peripheries of everyday life" (Turner, 1974: 47). Liminality can characterize performance space as it functions within an arena of heightened invention and creativity where the out-of-the-ordinary happens. In this sense, it is an implicit component in the consummation of the sacred rituals of the Penitentes as well as the celebratory poetry gatherings of Poetry of the Wild. Both are situated in an imaginary stage space of the moment. Occasions that may be more familiar to you that certainly qualify as liminal are weddings and funerals. Christian baptisms are also examples where a transitional ceremonial space catalyzes the transformation from one state to another. Can you think of other examples from your experience?

Framing

Ways of framing performances mark them off as special or distinctive and lift them beyond habitual behavior to a creative zone of intensified performance. These moments are subject to different rules of display and interaction apart from regular social discourse. The 1970s was an era when folklorists paid special attention to the poetics of performance in context. That is, performance was perceived as a dynamic continuum—not just ascribed to unique events on stage (no matter how loosely "stage" was interpreted), but also inclusive of speech acts extending all the way from jokes and storytelling to elaborately staged productions. Consequently, the field of study shifted away from "objects" (that is, plays, ballads, folk concerts, etc.) to process. Process became the unifying factor in evaluation—the common denominator. The quest for understanding creative processes is encapsulated in the following questions: "What is being enacted here?" "How is it done?" "How are the actors and audience relating to the cultural context?" In this way, cultural performance studies evolved to encompass a more egalitarian approach different from the binary model of us, the audience, and, them, the performers, to all of us as participants and collaborators united in action and creativity.

The idea of a performance continuum does not imply that "everything is a performance" for there are ways to distinguish performance from daily habits. On the one hand, there is the recognition and experience of communitas emergent in the performance event; and on the other, various ways to help differentiate performance events from the everyday. One such category would relate to how the event was "crafted," that is, its culturally determined aesthetic dimensions and consciously heightened effects. Competency is an important factor in evaluating the effectiveness of performance where one expects aesthetically persuasive and culturally appropriate expressive actions that transcend simple communication (Webber, 2015: 75). **Ethnoaesthetics** is an internal system of judging competency and aesthetic purpose. "Internal" refers to a set of criteria developed by the people whose work is being judged. Ethnoaesthetics, then, is a means by which a cultural group determines the effectiveness of their own creative cultural expressions vis-à-vis cultural performance and other artistic acts. Another category would recognize the value of boundaries, which frame a performed event. Interpretive frames provide us with a critical space in which to understand and analyze cultural performance and its societal value. The timeless triad of "beginning, middle, and end" usually defines a frame. In storytelling, the onset of a framed event is frequently signaled by the words, "Once upon a time." A popular ending is, "They lived happily ever after." True, these are customary verbal clues, but there are also visual and kinesthetic ones, for example, film credits and the tradition of curtain calls in theatre. Can you think of other familiar performance formulas, which demarcate a "time outside of time," and alert us to expect something different to happen other than the norm of daily speech and predictable human behavior?

Richard Bauman uses the term "**markings**" to designate the boundaries of cultural performance. He notes that cultural performance inheres in these markings. That is, markings or framing elements are fundamental to the identification of cultural performance. Furthermore, cultural performance is demarcated by content "both within and outside the flow of life as lived, as well as its distinct markings of beginnings and endings" (Bauman quoted in Madison, 2012: 170). This description is applicable to the public poetry readings cited above performed in improvised public space but incorporating both the inner "stage space" as well as acknowledging lives being lived "outside" the boundaries of poetry performance.

In New Zealand, Maori often insert sacred elements into secular or civic occasions by commencing with a prayer chant. These verbal performances mark the beginning of a meeting as well as generally closing a meeting with a valedictory prayer. The effect of this type of framing mirrored at the beginning and the end converts the most prosaic occasion into something special, and sets it apart from the usual business activity. The opening prayer calls attention to the specialness of the occasion and creates a feeling of "time away from time" apart from daily routines. The final prayer, which functions as a farewell, offers reentry into the mundane world. Although the content of the meeting would not be considered a cultural performance, the framing elements and the motivation for creating a temporal "sacred space" in which to conduct the meeting are culturally based.

Poetry of the Wild's multiple frames divide into a series of different shades of performance. Poetry celebrations and readings demonstrate the vitality of recitation as a communicative and reciprocal action—a point in time that links the venerable bardic tradition to the in-the-moment vernacular. During poetry events, group participation is also dynamic and perambulatory as people walk together from box to box. Diane Barcelo, an artist participant, described her fascination with the cadence of walking as a group in motion while heading to the next spot being totally immersed in the experience of participation as performance (Barcelo, 2013).

Intensity of the moment enacted through collective performance appears to be one of Poetry of the Wild's dominant themes. As with Penitente cultural performances, it suggests that the meaning of performance is created during the very experience of the performance. According to the philosopher Derrida, "performance itself is constitutive" (cited in Bruner, 1986: 11). Meaning is emergent in the experience of performance. There is no pre-existing meaning nor is the outcome of performance fully predetermined. Poetry readings are both individual artistic performances as well as collaborative experiences of performance inclusive of participants and spectators' feelings, thoughts, responses, and actions. The overall trajectory of a performance's lively and active effects is what Victor Turner referred to as "putting experience into circulation" (cited in Bruner, 1986: 12). In this way, the pleasure is passed on.

Audience

Finally, we need to briefly attend to the notion of **audience** as a vital part of our discussion. In some of the examples throughout this chapter, the audience was actively co-experiencing the performance. In others, audience members assumed a more passive role and to some degree absorbed all that occurred without actively participating in it. Co-experiencing a performance relates to folklorist Barry Toelken's first of four categories of audience types (Toelken, 1996: 139–40) as adapted by Kristin Valentine in her typology of audiences figuring prominently in her study of the Yaqui Easter ceremonial cycle (Valentine, 2002: 286). In Valentine's scheme, the "central audience" includes members of the culture on site, who take part in the ceremony and directly relate to the main actors as well as assuming a more curatorial role in keeping the ceremony on track. Valentine's "bystander audience" is comprised of knowledgeable observers outside the culture who are sensitive and sympathetic to the cultural aims and objectives of the performance. A different, but intriguing, classification is that of "implied cultural audience." Implied signifies those who are present "in spirit," either living or dead. This category embraces the perceived presence of ancestors, which is felt by participants in part as remembrance and in part as homage to those souls who were instrumental in perpetuating cultural traditions. This group of individuals, whether dead ancestors or village elders, absent teachers and masters of tradition, etc., are the final arbiters of the success of a performance. Their implicit judgment has been internalized by the performers and other participants, and provides the critical yardstick whereby the cultural performance is measured. It all boils down to the approval of those absent ancestors, elders, and teachers.

The final type of audience is the "outsider audience." This category encompasses those who know little of the customs and traditions of the performers and their community. Consequently, their behavior is often at odds with what the cultural audience would expect and their understanding of ritual traditions being enacted is nonexistent or very rudimentary. Some are doubters. Others are curious and seeking sensational cultural experiences. If the Penitente communities were not so secretive and reclusive, there would be many of this type attending their Holy Week ceremonies. Both Penitente Lenten observances and Poetry of the Wild celebrations attract audiences that comprise spectators and participants from all four categories. Remember the earlier question about whether an "audience" exists for Las Tinieblas or El Calvario? It may appear, since everyone together is walking around praying and commemorating deceased members of their community, that everyone would be a participant, a member of the "central audience." This is probably true of the majority of those present, but there would also be a few skeptics—perhaps from a mainstream Catholic parish, who might denigrate the Penitente "way" but would still respect the deep spirituality of the Brotherhood. In the past, there are plenty of examples of people spying on Penitente rites and publically reporting the more sensational aspects. The "ancestral audience," of course, would be evoked and activated through the acts of remembering and praying, while the "bystander audience" would attend as respectful and informed religious supporters. How would you apply this audience typology to participants and observers attending Poetry of the Wild? Can you think of other, possibly better, categories appropriate for determining the orientation of audience members in ethnographic contexts?

In the next section, ethnomusicologist and folklorist Tomie Hahn describes her fieldwork experiences following the Monster Truck rallies. She carefully describes the sensory aspects of her experiences and pinpoints the often-overpowering sensations of noise, smell, and physically feeling vibrations rumbling around in one's body. Tomie Hahn's contribution extends the meaning and application of our understanding of investigating cultural performance through the principles and methodology of ethnographic inquiry. She also ponders the presence of traditional folklore elements in an unorthodox community composed of Monster Truck drivers and followers relative to the classic ethnographic concepts of creation, transmission (passing on traditions and lore), temporality, and fluidity.

Terms and Ideas for Study

- Ethnographic practice
- Folk religion
- Fieldwork
- Self-reflection
- Reflexivity
- Participant observer

- Communitas
- Framing
- Ethnoaesthetics
- Markings
- Audience

Questions for Discussions

- Explain how sacred rituals and rites can also be regarded as cultural performance.
- Revisit the Penitente material described earlier, and imagine yourself as part of the congregation audience. Which aspects of Valentine's four areas of "intense spectatorship" would fit your appraisal of the Las Tinieblas ceremony as cultural performance (self-reflection, cultural and historical context, dynamics of performance, and critical reflection)? As you contemplate your understanding of the Penitente performance, be attentive to how the parts are integrated into the whole.

Creative Project

Much of this chapter is concerned with ethnographic practice either in descriptive form or in application. The main objective in this exercise is to begin to learn how to observe what is happening around you and to be able to write about it.

Cell Phone or Public Conversation Exercise

This exercise gives you license to watch and listen to conversations or cell phone users all around you, but you also benefit by perfecting your observational skills and ability to process information quickly—"on the run" so to speak.

1. Observe cell phone users or people talking to each other.
2. Note tone and volume of voice, body language, facial expressions, etc..
3. Note place—is this conversation occurring on the street, in a restaurant, on a bus, etc.? How does the location influence the conversation?
4. Write a brief script (30–60 seconds, approximately one page) based on the conversation(s) you observed.
5. Be prepared to (1) share scripts in small groups. (2) Group selects a few scripts to present to class to be read or enacted by writer or person chosen by group.

Case Study

Arenas of Sense—Monster Truck rallies as cultural performance
by Tomie Hahn

After stepping out of my truck on a large grassy field, I walked toward the arena for the Monster Truck rally. As I approached, I could peer between the bleachers and see nine enormous trucks lined up on the track. They were some of the icons of the Monster Truck world—Big Foot, Towasaurus, Predator, American Guardian, Reptoid. Chills ran through my spine as I approached the chain-link fence; the trucks lived up to their monstrous names. I felt small and awestruck. Nothing could prepare me for the intense sensory experience to follow, not even my voracious reading of books, web pages, or conversations with Monster Truck enthusiasts. The arena event fueled a sensually rich experience more intense than I could conjure: enormous trucks, deafening sound-scape, fanatical crowd, thick clouds of exhaust, and visions of extreme physical force as these 10,000-pound trucks flew into the air and crushed piles of cars or performed freestyle. Monster Trucks are the embodiment of extreme. They are gigantic, twelve foot wide, twelve foot tall trucks—each custom-built expressly for the purpose of thrill-ing entertainment. There's a go-getter style of American dream calling out from the event, a challenge to create a bigger, louder, rougher per-formance instrument.

Extreme sensory experiences like this drove me to interview Monster Truck drivers, builders, and fans to learn more about these cultural performances.[3]

Unpackaging Experience—*Let's get ready to rumm-b-l-e!!!!*

This case study offers glimpses of Monster Truck rallies from several vantage points—including my first-person experiences attending rallies, theoretical perspectives, and interviews with drivers. In closing, I ask: After fieldwork, what next? What knowledge will you transmit after your experience of a performance and being with the community? How does your project, as a response to the cultural knowledge learned, reveal not only the community's identity, but also mirror back yours?

Ethnographers draw on a range of methods to examine and learn about cultural performances. Experiencing events or learning performance practices via participant observation helps a researcher understand first-hand about the performance scene. Each research project necessitates particular methodologies suited to that community and performance. A method that is successful in one cultural setting may not be

---

[3] See T. Hahn, 2006 for perspectives of sensory extremes and extraordinary experiences encoun-tered in fieldwork.

appropriate for another setting. Research methods can be as diverse as locating and studying historical documents, participant observation, interviewing participants, taking field notes, drawing maps, creating media documentation, and so on. A project design that includes multiple methodological approaches offers an array of perspectives on the cultural performance, and often a distinct set of thematic topics will arise from the diversity of "data." The diverse perspectives of a performance provide information about what this particular community finds to be important.

Performance mirrors identity. Elizabeth Fine and Jean Haskell Speer propose, "The power of performance to create, store, and transmit dentity and culture lies in its reflexive nature. Through performance, human beings not only present behavior ... they reflexively comment on it and the values and situations it encompasses (1992: 8)". Observing *how* a subculture transmits, or teaches, their performance practices can help unpackage the various issues of identity embodied in a performance, as well as what defines performance for that community, the meanings the performances holds, and the values held by the community.

The term "transmission" addresses how cultural practices are disseminated and includes the entire teaching-learning cycle. Transmission occurs through sensory channels such as oral, visual, or tactile transmission systems, as well as media (texts or video, for example). Most often, dissemination occurs through several modes simultaneously. Different cultures tend to prioritize particular systems of transmission; some cultures convey knowledge directly from person to person, others through group lessons or group performances, others through a variety of text-based formats, and any combination of these modes of transmission is very common. Noticing how knowledge is transmitted reveals a variety of insights.[4] For example, if a community disseminates cultural knowledge only orally, through a person-to-person system of teaching, what might this reveal? Perhaps the community relies on oral transmission

---

[4] See T. Hahn, *Sensational Knowledge: Embodying Culture through Japanese Dance* (2007) for an inquiry into sensory transmission of culture.

to reinforce community member bonding, or because the transmission upholds a hierarchical social structure, or because the knowledge transmitted holds sacred, powerful, or proprietary information not intended for non-community members. In this way, transmission regulates how knowledge is passed on. What other reasons can you imagine? How about other methods of transmission, such as text, or media (such as video, audio, web-based media)? How might mediated transmission practices expedite learning? Uproot existing power structures? Or hinder learning?

How does a subculture inform community members about the necessary attributes and activities included in their performances? "Attributes and activities" might be how to behave during the performance; the sequence or ordering of the events; how time unfurls; organization of space, environment and architecture; the variety of sensory cues that express a performance such as the look of the event, how it sounds, feels, tastes, moves, or smells; participants present, or excluded; objects employed; aesthetic concerns; and so on. After observing the details of performance attributes and activities, several overarching themes will arise that impart larger concepts of cultural identity.

In short, what are all of the characteristics of a cultural performance that community members identify as fundamental features of the experience? Should one of these characteristics be missing, how does the community react? Is the missing feature considered so minor that no one notices? Or only insiders to the tradition notice? Or is the missing characteristic so fundamental to the identity of the event that the community does not recognize the performance without it? During an interview, Monster Truck builder-driver Robbie "Flying" Dawson told me an interesting story about identity:

> I was in a parade at Disney World one time, and it was a Father's Day Parade, right down main street of Disney World. So of course, the Father's Day Parade had the biggest tow truck they could find, a Monster Truck, the biggest motorcycle, all the BIG things, all men's stuff, all for Father's Day, all tough guy stuff, all sponsored by Binford Tools.

> So when we got there with our Monster Truck they said, "You know, it's the Father's Day Parade in the middle of Disney World." (And we said)

"No problem we built an exhaust for it to quiet it down." Well the guy came out—"Mickey" is his name, honest to God truth [chuckles]. Yeah, Mickey came out, "You guys ready to go?" We said "Yeah!" We started the truck up and he was like, "Uh, that's awful quiet." And we said, "Well, we thought you were concerned about that!" And he goes, "Well, that's too quiet—*take it off!!*" (laughs). So they needed to take the exhaust all back off again… just, just so it could be loud. (Interview, September 10, 1999, Sturbridge, MA)

Dawson's story, delivered with a grin and a chuckle, testifies that a Monster Truck is not a Monster Truck without all characteristics of its larger-than-life monstrous identity present. There seemed to be a mis-communication about the intensity of the Monster Truck sound for the Disney World engagement, and Mickey's confused response quickly exposed that the loud engine sound stood as an identity marker. I recall Dawson scratching the back of his head after telling me this story, and he went on to say how the team had specifically engineered dampening systems to bring down the sound for the parade. Community expecta-tions of the extreme Monster Truck identity included its distinct, lush sensory personality. When audiences' and participants' expectations fall into place during an event, then the cultural performance is recognizable to the community. In this case, the intensity of the soundscape needed to meet expectations.

In the Monster Truck arena, how can we imagine "community"? In the opening to Chapter 2, Suzanne MacAulay asks, "How does community emerge from performance?" Monster Truck rallies, as well as their appear-ances at state fairs, parades, or even movies, draw crowds that share the experience. If the individuals attending the shows never see each other again, can we designate the audience as a community? Since audience members attending Monster Truck rallies share similar performance expectations and often attend events annually, we would consider the participants and audience members a temporary community. From my experience attending rallies, talking to drivers, builders, and fans, I believe the thrill of the Monster Truck event draws the community together. The monstrous identity embodied in a sensually extreme performance—the sounds, feel, smells, movements, and sights—brings crowds in. Danger lives on the edge. The anticipation of an *un*expected incident arises *as* an expectation of a wild rally for this community. After all, a Monster Truck might roll over while doing a wheelie, or it could land close to the bleachers after a jump, or some unforeseen thrill. Historically, audiences packed arenas to see powerful animals, machines, and people demonstrate their skills of physical control as cultural performance: gladiators in coliseums, bullfights, boxing, cockfights, tractor pulls, ox pulls, and other public spectacles showcasing might and dexterity. In the 1930s, auto thrill shows, touring across America, often showcased at county fairgrounds. Sometimes these were auto stunt shows where the theme of "man vs. beast" translated to "man vs. machine," and continues today with a variety of vehicles, such as motocross, motorcycles, race cars, demolition derbies, and so on.

As an American phenomenon, Monster Truck events stage the essence of a "Made in America" identity—each truck created from the bottom up—embodying American-style individualism. Performances display a daring and brash, often irreverent, iconic identity through the spectacle of the rowdy contest. Monster Trucks embody the fantastic, gruesome, and awesome as their outward appearances are designed to represent superheroes, cartoon and other larger-than-life characters that come to life via performance. In this way, the competitions display the fantasy of warrior machines in an oversized sandbox. Yet, as driver Robbie Dawson conveyed in his story, Monster Truck identities are not only embodied in their gigantic look, they need to display the magnitude of extreme in all sensory modalities.

Dawson emphasized how the names of Monster Trucks and truck manufacturers project the Made in America brand and loyalty:

Names like American Guardian… these home brewed names say they are American made, and all of that, where they're from, you know? For instance, Carolina Crusher… well, Carolina Crusher isn't going to make people in Quebec necessarily real rowdy, you know? (cracking up) Then there's Keystone Crusher, New Jersey Outlaw, USA 1. So it's like apple pie, (laughs) you know, it keeps that home base. Guatemala Masher and Canadian Crusher—you don't see any of that, it's all American stuff. It's all American industry of Chevrolet, Ford, Dodge, out there—there's no

Toyotas out there, there's no Datsuns and Nissans and what not. And that classic way of thinking, it's big, they're the BIGGEST trucks. Those are BIG pickup trucks! You know, it's that American way of thinking. Proud, proud, cocky Americans. (Ibid.)

Setting the Scene

Rallies traditionally open with American heavy metal band Quiet Riot's song "Cum On Feel the Noize," forecasting an experience everyone shares during the event—participants physically feel the trucks rumble their chest cavities when they drive by. No kidding. After the emcee makes a few general announcements about the arena, such as safety precautions, location of refreshment stands, or merchandise booths, he directs everyone to rise, face the American flag, and sing the "National Anthem." Depending on the venue, the audience sings the anthem with a recording or a guest singer. Soon after folks are back in their seats, the emcee blares out the now famous line *"Let's get ready to rumm-b-l-e!"* over the crackling PA system and begins to introduce the trucks and drivers in the day's lineup. Then we hear "Gentlemen, start your engines!"

The emcee narrates the entire event, everything about the trucks, drivers, audience, and general arena. For the opening lineup, the emcee introduces the drivers of each Monster Truck, as well as the truck and driver's well-being as the rally picks up intensity. For example, at one rally I witnessed Grave Digger hit and fly over a pile of crushed cars and land on one wheel, then continue into a "rollover." The emcee enthusiastically narrated the entire incident from the time "Digger" revved up behind the scenes to when the emergency vehicles arrived. The adrenaline-charged run started with the emcee's stylized sing-song voice, then he reported Digger crushing and soaring over cars with a more forceful voice, but as the truck landed and rolled, the quality of his frantic, high-strung voice mirrored what we witnessed—dust, smoke, a rocking sideways truck. As the emcee's voice intensified, the audience did as well, until they fell silent during the rollover. Digger's run, including the emcee's narration, and the audience response was a singular sensory phrase of smaller events. It is a phrase that is composed in a general manner: driver begins the engine, drives with force toward a stack of cars, and then "something" happens.

The phrase, unlike a pianist playing a musical phrase of a Chopin Nocturne, is indeterminate from the point the truck hits the pile of cars. All of the variables of the truck's run, as well as the arena space, the quality of the dirt, and the stacking of the cars, factor into the how the Monster Truck will "fly" and also land. The heightened commotion and potential for unexpected chaos drive crowd expectations toward a drama of shared experience. Extreme. Larger than life. Imagine 10,000 pounds of metal flying in the air, then landing. By the way, in this run Digger suffered a tire blowout and a crumpled body, and luckily the driver suffered no injuries. In the Monster Truck tradition, the driver climbed out of the Digger's window and waved to the cheering audience. A communal sigh of relief rose through the crowd.

During an interview with Scott Pontbriand, driver of "Undertaker" at that time, he described taking a Monster Truck airborne:

> Well, you know you work on the truck for, hey, forty hours making sure everything's ready to go, the bolts and everything. When you get in the truck, as soon as you're in there … you just kinda, I don't know, I kinda zone out into my own little world and I'm at one with the truck. You know, there's not a part on the truck that I'm not aware of at any given moment when I'm in it. I mean, you become one with it, you know?

> …When you're flying up in the air, you know, *Ra-a-a-aa!!!* (making a motion with his arms outstretched skyward) You get up in the air and it's like, you know there's times when you're up there and it's like, "Okay, I know I just jumped, but when am I going to land? (laughs) Am I going to land?" You get that *wonder* while you're up there and wondering the outcome and, I know pretty much as soon as the rear wheels leave the cars I know pretty much what's going to happen. I know what the truck's going to do at that point. And it's a RUSH! (laughs) You know? … yeah, it's good, that's what drives you to do it, yeah. And like I said, every jump is different, every time is different. (Interview, September 10, 1999, Sturbridge, MA)

Pontbriand's story recounted his experience of a jump, yet I found his storytelling a cultural performance itself. In a sense, he narrated the phrasing of a jump much like an emcee, yet his story was delivered from his perspective inside the truck, driving the truck skyward. He testified that, even as a driver, he wasn't sure what the outcome of the run, the phrase, would be until he was in flight. What is not reflected in the interview transcript is Pontbriand's spark of energy during his "flight" story. He sat on the edge of the sofa, face lit up. He seemed to be reliving the moment of flight by actually *performing extreme* before me in the interview. The story raised adrenaline. I was taken off-guard, not expecting such a moving or exhilarating story. Here we sat in a log cabin on what had been an old hog farm in Massachusetts, talking about giant trucks taking flight, and suddenly it sounded like Zen and the art of Monster Trucks! Reliving the flight in his mind, he seemed enthralled with the experience and conveyed that sensibility to me. Pontbriand's delivery of his aerial experience included a suspended moment, "that *wonder* while you're up there," that revealed how jumps include transformative moments out of the chaos.

Vehicles of Transmission

The observation of performances, identifying transmission practices, and conducting interviews with participants offer a range of cultural insights concerning issues of identity and community. How are cultural practices passed on to community members? How do performances create and support community? Finding methods that help us notice the attributes and activities that align (or contrast) with the subcultures' principles or beliefs, such as ethics, morals, aesthetics, political values, spiritual beliefs, leisure and entertainment, to name a few. Often the significant attributes of a performance, those features held strongly by a community, are mirrored in the very structures of the performance as well as the transmission process. How does an audience learn about the Monster Truck scene, including the specifics of the event program and how to interpret the rally? For one, no one can ignore that the emcee literally narrates the event, blow-by-blow, from beginning to end. The loudspeakers must transmit the emcee's voice loudly over the ruckus of the trucks and cheering crowd. Since the emcee's vocal quality is highly stylized, it stands out above the din of the crowd and truck commotion. The emcee transmits to the audience where they need to turn their focus during a rally while also including other information such as insider traditions, instructs behaviors, and even announces the legends of individual

Monster Trucks during the performance. The emcee needs to keep up the banter between runs, when there might be lulls, or a delay, such as when a truck needs extra time to start its engine and take its place. In this sense, the emcee serves as the narrator, instructor, as well as the orchestrator of the evening, because the audience needs to keep entertained throughout the event, despite lulls or emergencies. In every rally I've attended, the emcees direct the audience to cheer at certain times, "Everyone give a big shoutout for American Guardian!" or "Who's your favorite?" with a chanted response from the audience "Dig-ger, Dig-ger, Dig-ger..." or the emcee will cry out "*W-h-a-t?* I can't hear you!" New audience members also learn from noticing seasoned rally attendees. There is never a shortage of devoted kids instructing their parents (and strangers sitting on the stands next to them) how to behave, what to expect next, the history of particular trucks, or the details of the last time they saw a race or freestyle.

Suspense ... What Next?

Project design is tricky for ethnographers. Prior to conducting fieldwork we need to make decisions about "data collection" and determine what research methodologies and types of media would support the particulars of the proposed project. However, the conundrum is: How can we know what we will find before getting there? Even if an ethnographer has visited the field site previously, there is no guarantee that the next visit will mirror the experience. We need to be prepared yet also flexible in our project designs. The conundrum continues as we realize that our prior expectations might not align with our experience and findings while conducting fieldwork. Of course, we cannot force the information that we collect into our previously anticipated vision and theoretical structures. The challenge is to keep our awareness open to a range of possibilities that may arise. Most importantly, allowing the thematic topics to arise from what we collect, such as experiences, interviews, artifacts, audio, or video. Although this aspect of ethnographic research may appear straightforward, it is not. After investing time and energy into examining a particular cultural performance—writing grants, reading books and articles—it is difficult to take off the blinders and note the themes that truly arise from the materials gathered.

Before and after learning and collecting information about a subculture, whatever the research methodologies employed, ethnographers consider how they want to display the information. What about "the product"? In other words, after research—*then what?* Will the ethnographer write an article or book, create a website, a film, or DVD? Clearly, we cannot travel back in time and space, re-experience cultural performances, or shoot film if you did not have a camera the first trip. Again, project design is tricky because we have no idea what encounters we may have after arriving. We may intend to create a film about a cultural performance, only to find out film is considered taboo. Collecting information in the field carries ethical and other considerations that affect the choice of the display medium. Also, *how* ethnographers interpret what they collect may alter their decisions concerning the display of cultural knowledge. What is displayed and what is edited out? Here I return to questions I posed earlier: After fieldwork, *what next?* What might you create with the cultural information you collect and learn from a community? Can you be inclusive and collaborate with the community in what you create? How does your project, as a response to the cultural knowledge learned, reveal not only the community's identity, but also mirror back yours?

If you create a written text to convey knowledge, what voice(s) do you employ? A reflexively written text strategically includes the identity of the ethnographer to reveal the identity of the narrator. Textual reflexivity provides a challenge for authors, as it requires a balance of identities to convey the narrative. Too much of the author's inner voice seems narcissistic, yet too little leaves readers wondering about the narrator's identity. Ethnographers, not limited to writing a single tome of their fieldwork, often create a variety of works in response to their experiences in the field. Circling back to concepts of transmission, I posit that our work serves as transmission. What we create needs to reflect a sensibility that profoundly engages with the community's concerns, aesthetics, and beliefs, as the mediums that we select to transmit our research exist as extensions of the communities and cultural performances we study.

I find that most experiences I encounter in the field provide deeply rich knowledge that influences and moves me. After research and conducting fieldwork, I take time to sort, re-evaluate, and synthesize the varied cultural information. Allowing the themes to arise from the cultural "data," I stand back and contemplate the topics and how I can best convey the ideas and emotions. I ask myself: How many ways can I express what I learned and experienced? For example, theoretical texts provide a wealth of knowledge, an academic record, scope of a project, methods, and its theoretical topics. However, words can also fall short of transmitting the qualities of the experiential and emotional encounter. I experiment with diverse forms for expressivity, such as drawing, sewing, writing a poem, or writing vignettes. Each expressive medium enables diverse interpretations of the field experience. Curiously, this process of inquiry is cyclic, as my experimental explorations imbue new qualities and insights into my scholarly research and the scholarly examination inspires new creative explorations. In this way, the "what next?" query moves the inquiry forward. Consider how you might convey a sensory experience, whether from a field site, or even an everyday experience. How might you communicate it to others?

In closing, I offer a vignette drawn from my Monster Truck fieldwork as an example of a text inspired by an interview quote and attending a rally.

Flying Monsters

With a glow of neon in his eyes the Monster Truck driver flashed, "It's the RUSH ... that's what drives you to do it." Earlier, he sailed a 10,000 pound, twelve-foot high, twelve-foot wide truck over twenty feet in the air. The rumble of his engine stirred my body. Immersed in sensory overload—thick clouds of smoke, overwhelming noise, visions of extreme physical force. Inhale 1... 2... arousing a wonder of flight, 3... crumpling cars like potato chips. Exhale 2... 1.

References

Dawson, Robbie. Interview with the author, September 10, 1999, Sturbridge, MA.

Fine, Elizabeth and Jean Haskell Speer. *Performance, Culture, and Identity.* Westport, CT: Praeger Publishers, 1992.

Hahn, Tomie. "'It's the RUSH': Sites of the Sensually Extreme." *The Drama Review* 50.2, 2006: 87–96.

Hahn, Tomie. *Sensational Knowledge: Embodying Culture through Japanese Dance*. Middletown, CT: Wesleyan University Press, 2007.

Pontbriand, Scott. Interview with author, September 10, 1999, Sturbridge, MA.

Part II

Place and Space

3

The Architecture of Performance Space

Image 4 *Tiger's Nest* © Kevin Landis

Deep in the Paro Valley in Eastern Bhutan there is a turn-off from the main road leading to a driveway that winds through the forest and up to a small parking lot. There is a trail there, next to a stupa (a Buddhist shrine) and a brook with a gurgling waterfall. The hillside is covered with masses of pink and white rhododendrons. The trail is the beginning of the now famous trekking route to the Taktsang Palphug Monastery, better known as the Tiger's Nest, which sits on a cliff, jutting out 3,000 feet above the Paro Valley. But before you think about the building itself, consider the journey to get there. From the parking lot one commits to a strenuous two-hour hike through verdant forests and up a steep gravely path. The route is often populated with monks in orange robes making a pilgrimage to the most holy site in Bhutanese Buddhism. Some people ride atop the mules that make their way up and down the mountain all day long. The path creeps up a ridge crest, with views of Paro town on one side and the vast Himalayas on the other. The air is crisp and, at 10,000 feet, breathing is difficult.

Eventually, the traveler comes to a promontory where a little cafe has been constructed for weary hikers, and it is here that one first gets a view of the Tiger's Nest, emerging from the mists on the other side of a deep gorge; it could be Shangri-La or Brigadoon, a mystical place that seems to hang in a temporal limbo. Why is it here? It is the confluence of man-made devotion to spirituality and a natural site that is otherwise devoid of human touch. It clings, impossibly, to the side of the mountain over the cave where the guru Padmasambhava was said to have meditated thousands of years ago. The red roof and brightly adorned façade look at once jarringly out of place, precarious and strangely beautiful; the entire image is framed with multi-colored prayer flags, flapping in the Himalayan breeze. The route continues around the side of the gorge, the trail narrow, rocky and slippery from the springs that spill onto the path. At last, straight ahead, the entrance to the monastery and after the exhausting journey, the traveler feels as if he has truly arrived. Step inside and one finds monks in prayer, the sound of horns and the rattle of the prayer wheels. The air is thick with incense, mixed with mountain mist and the ever-present smell of pine.

In the first chapter, the British director Peter Brook was mentioned, and his important book, *The Empty Space*, was folded into our conversation about the necessities of theatre. In the opening pages of his study, he established the

empty space and the presence of the performer and spectator as the only elements needed to create an act of theatre. The empty space represents, then, the simplicity of the performance event and stands as a beautiful reference point for all performers wishing to return to the roots of performance. In that definition, Brook focused our attention on the essentials of performance creation. He seemed to be telling us that all that is needed—the basic building block—is the space and presence of a performer, and someone to witness.

In this exploration of cultural performance, we have moved from that simple audience/performer dialectic to a discussion of community creation and interaction. We move now to the locations of performances and the implications that these locations have on performative aesthetics. How might a mountainous terrain affect an outdoor wedding? How do ancient cultures use gathering spaces to inform the nature of their rituals? As we saw in our first section, it is clear that performance is far more than the narrative elements of the performance event; more than simply a story that has a thematic beginning, middle and end. But we could also turn this around and say that we may see many elements of the performance *in toto* as creating or contributing to a performance structure. While not yet identified, we have been thinking about several ideas from the beginning: structure, geography, location, architecture. In this chapter we will try to come to a more complete understanding of the importance of these concepts.

Structure may be appropriately seen as an overriding term that can help us analyze locations of performance, and as with everything in cultural performance, it can be defined and understood in myriad ways. It can certainly point to the way a performance is set up, meaning the textual or thematic attributes that define it as a contained unit of behavior or experience. The structure of a play may simply be the plot. But, we encourage you to look at structure both more broadly and, more literally, to include the structural framing that is used to define a cultural performance. Particularly, we will assess architecture—the actual physical structure of performance and actions that go in to creating considered physical space. You might think of the geographic location, the actual building, the stage, the platform or the city in which the performance takes place. But we will look deeper, too, and see architecture and structure more theoretically and assess how the cultural creator has chosen to arrange or manipulate his space to fulfill the needs of the performance and community.

The theatre scholar Una Chaudhuri writes in *Staging Place*, "… the theatre grounds its meanings in that essential element of all theatrical presentation: space" (Chaudhuri, 1997: xi). Again, let us take a moment to identify the nuances of terms, since Chaudhuri rightly considers these spatial concepts essential. In recent years there have been many excellent studies written about the places of performance and how those places are used. While the words "place" and "space" are often used interchangeably, some difference is compelling to consider. Geographer Yi-Fu Tuan writes, "What begins as undifferentiated space becomes place as we get to know it better and endow it with value" (Tuan, 1977: 4). Though his seminal study deeply considers these concepts, for our purposes, let us see **space** as broadly defined—territory, landscape, fields, valleys—while a **place** is more specified and filled with cultural meaning. In this chapter we will build from that simple empty space and explore several examples of theatres and cultural performances that blend community connectivity with architectural and situational intentionality in an effort to create a rich experience: to create a place. Throughout, you will note that the intentional place of performance greater connects the community of participants to a (hopefully) transcendent relationship to the ritual-making process. Sean Edgecomb offers a vivid case study at the end of the chapter about the gay underground in the West Village of New York and discusses the ways that both the urban physical architecture and the architecture of play structure influenced and guided the "performance" of the gay rights movement.[1]

Investing the Space

Before we enter the architectural place of performance, we have learned that it is wise to take a moment to consider the journey to that location and its implications. If we accept that Tiger's Nest Monastery is a place of cultural performance, it makes sense that we come to terms

---

[1] Marvin Carlson's excellent study *Places of Performance* (1989) has been consulted extensively here but it should be noted that there are many superb works, both practical and theoretical, that unpack the importance of the theatre building and the place of performance. See Leacroft (1984), Chaudhuri (1997), Fuchs and Chaudhuri (2002), Fisher-Lichte (2008), and Camp (2014), among others.

with the fact that so much was made of the journey to the actual site, from the sound of the wind, to the description of the hiking conditions to the presence of donkeys. There is an important aspect that must be addressed here, and is well captured by dance scholar Victoria Hunter: "The site-specific audience member does not approach the performance and the site in an arbitrary, passive manner, arriving instead armed with a wealth of personal and contextual information serving to inform their experience of the site and the performance work" (Hunter, 2005: 377). Much of the acceptance of the space as a place of performance and cultural building comes from the collected ideals and experiences of the viewer. This was comprehensively discussed in Chapter 2 in reference to experience *in situ*, and will continue to be reiterated. Understanding this concept is a critical underpinning of our discovery of cultural performance since we, as the viewers of the cultural event, necessarily help create the performance through our needs, emotions, and life experiences. We may say the same thing about the actual building and location and our journey to that space. The building is no longer arbitrarily "happened upon" but rather, as Hunter asserts, is already invested with the specific experiences of the viewer. Imagine the difference in experiencing the monk's music having *not* completed the steep trek to the Tiger's Nest. What would be missed? The relief that comes at the end of a hike. The met expectations of seeing a building you had been told about or seen in pictures on the internet. The warmth of the room as you enter it from the cold outside air.

When one mentions **architecture of performance** we rightly think about the building, its construction and the physical attributes of the performance place. It is good to remember that while experience of all forms of a performance event are affected by each viewer's unique gaze, the way a building is created and situated performs upon the audience. In this way, investing in space is multi-directional. Theatre historian Marvin Carlson has outlined this relationship: "The entire theatre, its audience arrangements, its other public spaces, its physical appearance, even its location within a city, are all important elements of the process by which an audience makes meaning of its experience" (Carlson, 1989: 3). We actively think about where we locate our places of performance and take into account how that location will affect our audiences.

In the history of theatre, there are many examples of artists who built their theatres or performance venues in locations that were difficult to access. Tadasha Suzuki, the famed Japanese director, has located his studio for performance in the village of Toga, in the mountains of eastern Japan. The Duke of Sake Meniengen, considered by many to be the first theatre director, presented in a small duchy in the middle of the German Empire. As astute students of performance, culture and art you must embrace the need to ask why such choices are made. In these two cases we can see that the performance and a performance building benefit from the emotional and spiritual cachet of **pilgrimage**, in a way much like the Bhutanese story that began the chapter. Similarly, Richard Wagner is an excellent example of this geographic investing of space and his theatre and style of performance demonstrate elaborate considerations of cultural performance. Wagner was perhaps the most famous opera composer of all time and so you might be surprised to know that his opera house—his temple to art—was located in a small town called Bayreuth, outside of the big German cities of Berlin or Munich. While there were many reasons for this choice, the remoteness of the location was seen as an advantage, and now Bayreuth and its festival are aided by the location and its cachet of pilgrimage. Consider the buildings of entertainment in your community. You might think of a theatre, a baseball park, a stadium, or a concert hall. It is not unusual for people to invest these spaces with enormous mythological significance—perhaps making trips to Fenway Park or Wembley Stadium. You may quickly see that there is something almost religious in this fetishizing of the architecture of performance.

An Empty Room to a Stage

Let us take a step back. As we know from Brook, the elaborate considerations and grand buildings described above are not actually necessary. The simple space is the primary building block of our architectural understanding of cultural performance and the very act of performance, and the travel to the building of performance, invests the space with a spiritual and/or religious authority. But so too does the immediate relationship that takes place once the viewer has entered the site. Think again of that moment when one enters the Tiger's Nest Monastery and a co-presence is established. Now, this empty space is a gathering place, an architecture of communal experience, where members of a community are expected to engage and share. Donald Kaplin writes, "Consider a prospective member of a theatre audience entering a theatre. He is about to occupy one of the two major spaces inside the theatre, and he is joining others who will share this space with him" (Kaplan, 1968: 107). The empty space is thus invested with presence, a communion between viewer and performer and this is a central aspect of the creation of cultural performance.[2] It is not surprising then that when we talk about the physical structures of performance spaces, we often do so with an acknowledgment of the spirituality of that space. Cultural performance buildings then often become deeply symbolic pieces of architecture, far more than simply an empty space. The place of performance then becomes the church of the cultural engagement and the performers the conduit between the viewers and the spirits or gods.

Many cultural anthropologists have assessed this idea of community being defined by these very simple parameters. In his book *Culture and Space*, Jöel Bonnemaison looks at gathering spaces on the South Pacific island of Vanuatu and defines them as "dancing places." Here, in these physical places of gathering, communities establish their cultural crossroads, their roots. Bonnemaison asserts that the islanders believe that sacred powers appeared in certain locations within a community and then expanded by way of roads in a spoke-like pattern away and to the dancing place. He writes, "In the final analysis, spatial systems rather than social structures bring the islanders together to make them a 'society'" (Bonnemaison, 2005: 64). Simply put, the location of performance is *the* central component in creating community cohesion. That is a remarkable statement, though as we unpack that further, we can see that it is indeed true in other cultures as well. Communities establish their sense of togetherness through an architectural relationship to a constructed place of ritual and performance.

---

[2] For *presence* see Schechner and Appel (1990) and Valentine (2002).

The Seeing Place

To see a clear example of the intersections of theatre, performance and spirituality in the western traditions, one need not look further than the origins of theatre in the performances and celebrations dedicated to the gods of Ancient Greece. The Theatre of Dionysus, often cited as the first major theatre of western tradition, blended the sense of **ritual space/place** that we have discussed already, with an architectural intentionality that encouraged community and spiritual communion. The Greek theatre scholar Peter Arnott describes a theatre complex that developed as a community gathering place, a theatre that was entirely presentational and not "adorned" like many of the performance spaces we know today. Again, the foundations of western theatre are here described as architecturally minimal—only the bare necessities to facilitate a gathering. So, in a way, we may see this early Greek performance space as a simple step up from the empty space. In fact, some suspect that early theatre stages were derivatives of threshing circles, places where grain was collected and separated. If true, it establishes the early architecture of western cultural performance as rooted in the simplicity of daily community tasks and chores. As we know, architectural development occurred in the western theatre and eventually evolved into the grand theatres that we see in major metropolitan centers today, replete with gilded ceilings, frescoes, plush red seats, and enormous stages with hydraulic platforms. But if we see the Greek theatre as a starting point, we can identify the essential elements that facilitate the tenets of performance that were discussed in the first chapter, *location, audience/performer relationship*, and *skills/product*. In this case, the location is significant and can be read as symbolically important.

The early theatres in Greece were generally built, for convenience, on a sloping hillside so that an audience of community members could sit in seats, easily arranged in the appropriate geographic locale. As theatre became recognized as an essential facet of community ritual and connection, theatres became central architectural features of Greek cities. The famous Theatre of Dionysus, proudly arranged on the side of the Acropolis in a semi-circular arrangement, contained a small "stage" or presentational place that was empty or, perhaps, containing a small building (called a *skene*, the source for the word *scene*). Beyond was the city of

Athens. It is said that this early incarnation of western theatre included an animal sacrifice before the performance, a performance dedicated to Dionysus, the god of wine and revelry. In fact, there may have even been seats in the front row reserved for priests. The intersection of the spiritual and performative are thus fused from the beginning.

Let us assess this very simple architectural arrangement a bit more. Marvin Carlson notes, "… we need only recall that Greek theatre, like its successors, was essentially a structure for the encounter of two spaces—that of the public and that of the actors" (Carlson, 1989: 62). From a structural standpoint, the community gathering space served one essential function, to connect spectator and performer, a place for community. In fact, the word for theatre comes from the Greek word *theatron* or "place for seeing." Nothing elaborate. A place for an experience—seeing something unfold, usually in a location that could easily accommodate that encounter of two spaces.[3] Though perhaps a romantic notion, it is noteworthy that we may trace the evolution of western democracy to Athens in the fifth century BC, the same time and location that we identify as the birthplace of western theatre. The centralized location of these places for seeing a performance within an urban center correlates with the rise of democratic principles of community engagement in the development of societal structure. And the Theatre of Dionysus is certainly not unique in this respect. If one looks at maps of the Roman theatre at Orange in present day France, one sees an enormous structure, placed centrally in the city with convenient roads in spokes that spread out much as in the descriptions of the dancing places of Vanuatu.

Carlson's study on the architecture of performance is superb, expansive, and perhaps definitive in the field of theatre studies. For our purposes here, however, it is important to simply recognize the ways in which culture is so often created and developed around a shared spiritual ethos, in a specific geographic location, facilitated by a physical structure that deftly merges its people with their expressions of identity. With the Greek theatre, we see just that. Stories about the gods, performed at the Acropolis

---

[3] Many sources on Greek theatre architecture are here consulted and give detail on the buildings created by these ancient civilizations. See, Arnott (1962), Brockett and Hildy (2003), Ley (1991).

by a community for the community. The theatre building, a place dedicated to cultural performance, then becomes a central civic monument.

House of Theatre, House of Worship

Continue to keep in mind the connection between religious institutions, cultural performance and the theatre. It is often said that western theatre was twice born in religion. Indeed, after a long period in which organized performance disappeared, it made a resurgence in the Middle Ages out of the practices of the Catholic Church as a way to share the stories of Jesus Christ to the community of the faithful. Here, too, we see the church building itself as the fulcrum of community, an architectural structure that housed cultural performance located, often, in the center of a medieval town. Again, Carlson aptly notes, "The church or temple has perhaps the closest systematic architectural relationship to the theatre, since it involves the meeting of a secular celebrant with a sacred celebrated ..." (Carlson, 1989: 129).

Since we have now seen that the temple, shrine, or "dancing place" can be understood as a place of cultural performance, it is necessary to also acknowledge that the decoration of such places serves to assist the stories of those cultures. The Sistine Chapel in the Vatican City is an appropriate example. The altar of the church, as in most churches, is dominated by a large image of the crucified Jesus. In addition to the statuary images of Jesus, the walls are covered in the famous frescoes by Michelangelo. As the churchgoer enters the building, she is met by a striking painting of the Last Judgment, depicting Jesus condemning some to hell and accepting others into the kingdom of God. In addition to the images of Jesus are the likenesses of other saints and Biblical heroes. The Tiger's Nest Monastery is painted with rich colors, has a gold roof, and the inside is an amalgam of textures and spiritual references, including statues of Buddha. At the Cathedral of Notre Dame in Paris, the facade is covered with statuary of saints and kings. In a time of illiteracy, the images taught lessons to those who could not acquire the same knowledge from reading the Bible. The images act as decoration, literally giving a face to their religion and place of worship.

Whatever the intentions of the specific decorations, as we move from an empty space to adorned places, we may see them as active elements, props, and "set dressing" that help the cultural performance. Most notably perhaps, the images often remind ancestors of the life and power of the people they respect and worship. They become icons of the religion and the society that creates them. Architectural adornment to facilitate cultural performance is certainly not unique to any one faith, performance tradition, or society. You should think of places of civic engagement in other communities too and consider how they facilitate the development of stories.

If we acknowledge the ritual performance of spirituality and religion to be tightly stitched to what we define as theatre and theatre architecture, we may ask why some cultures so highly decorate these spaces. If an audience is sitting in the dark, watching a performance of *King Lear*, why is there any need for architectural flourishes? The easy answer to this question is that the need for theatre to be enjoyed in a dark space is a relatively new notion. Remember, in the scope of history, the advent of electricity is recent and for an audience to fully appreciate the spectacle of performance, the best light source was the sun. William Shakespeare's Globe Theatre in London was outdoors and the performances were given during the daylight hours. Everything was visible. The audience, sitting in a semi-circular space, could see each other as easily as they could the actors on the stage. Indeed, the roof of the stage house was elaborately decorated with stars and astrological imagery and referred to as "the heavens".

While Greek theatre forms a foundation of western drama, you are encouraged to look at other cultures beyond just the ones described in this book. Japanese Noh Theatre, for example, is identified by a main playing space, a bridgeway, and a painting of a pine tree. The architectural detail of Indian Sanskrit theatre, Peking Opera of China, and myriad others provide rich opportunities for analysis and study as you uncover the architectural nuances of cultural performance. Since the English word theatre comes from the Greek for "seeing/viewing place", we should consider all that we see as elements of the creation of a cultural performance. The architecture of that formerly empty space gives way to a colorful aesthetic of storytelling and community.

Ambulatory Architectural Experience

In this introduction to the ways in which structures assist our understanding of the way we perform our sense of culture, we have focused on specific physical space: a circular stage, an amphitheater, a church, a monastery on the side of a cliff, statues, and painting. When we talk about architecture of performance, we need to include the many ways that our physical surroundings influence reception of performance. Chaudhuri describes the importance of the location of a performance event: "Who one is and who one can be are... a function of *where* one is and how one experiences that place. From the experience of place as one-dimensional and fully determining, to the experience of place as multi-dimensional and creative, the stages of modern drama recount an ongoing *experiment* with place" (Chaudhuri, 1997: xii). While Chaudhuri writes of the "modern drama," we have read enough at this point to understand that location has been considered as long as performance and cultural performance have existed.

Let us take a bit of a theoretical leap and see how some contemporary societies and performance situations use entire collections of structures as a form of performance. Indeed, in the following examples, "experiment with place" is the essential building block of performance creation. Consider the description of a recent performance:

There is an old farm in western Massachusetts that lies along the winding state route 116, just south of the village of Ashfield. The property is about 100 acres and is bordered by a gurgling creek and a forested hillside. The former Fitzvale Dairy Farm shows some signs of its past life—the occasional cow grazes in the fields, there is a crumbling silo, a barn, and various collected farm equipment. It is no longer a farm, but the current owners, Double Edge Theatre Company, maintain that it is now a place of "cultural growth," a location where theatre intersects with ritual and community making and becomes an urban/ suburban amalgam of performative signification.

One breezy summer evening, an audience of 100 or so people from the surrounding communities arrived at a tent that was erected in the center of the farm, just next to the vegetable garden. After several minutes of discussion and "catching up" with the members of the company, the group was led to the old silo, where a trapeze was erected over a golden apple tree. Actors, mingling among the audience, performed original music as a trapezist playing the folkloric firebird, defied the king and plunged down into the magic tree. The next scene unfolded at the creek, where an ethereal figure sang folk songs to spectators on the opposite bank. As the New England twilight gave over to flashes of fireflies, actors, in masks and homemade costumes, guided the audience up the hill to an open field. Characters and spectators blended, both the farm and a Russian folk world existed as overlapping realities.

As darkness descended, the performance moved to a garden festooned with trapezes and enormous horse sculptures that seemed to have jumped out of a painting of Marc Chagall. The moment inspired awe in the audience, heightened perhaps for its being in a place of growth—the company's vegetable patch—surrounded by theatrical figures sprouting from the sunflowers, kale, and squash.

When the sun went down the performance resituated itself inside the main barn theatre. At the entrance to the barn, the door covered by an enormous backlit screen showed a shadow play. Sounds from the other side of the door and the mysterious objects playing on the screen enticed the audience to enter the world of the story unfolding inside. There, several vignettes from a folktale were performed. Acrobats flew on silk streamers over the audience members' heads.

After twenty minutes in the barn, the audience was again led outside, this time to the other side of the farm, where several rows of benches were set up at the pond's edge. In total darkness except for a few theatre lights on the far shore, performers began to play with fire and water and their own acrobatic exuberance, creating scenes out of the elements and the specific geography of the farm. Moments later, the audience was led on a forest path decorated with paintings illuminated by candlelight. Actors clung from the branches, sang, and told stories of folklore.

The performance ended on the far side of the pond. Watching from the base of the hill that rises from the west side of the property, spectators saw an actor with enormous, blazing wings run up the hill and disappear behind the trees. As the music reached a crescendo, a fireball slowly rose from the trees at the top of the hill. At least 300 yards from where the audience stood, the fire climbed into the air and vanished in the night sky.[4]

If you can close your eyes and imagine the performance described above, you can begin to envision the potential for majesty that can occur when location and architecture seamlessly intersect with cultural creation and performative sensibilities. As we have seen with our several examples in the chapter, the transition from cultural expression to theatrical performance can occur when geography, audience experience, and performance architecture fuse into a whole experience. Here, it is well to think about how the Double Edge company uses the symbols and the physical reference points of the farm and the roving nature of the experience to create performance.

This brings us to a critical concept when analyzing structures of performance. All of the physical/visual attributes that we have described may fall into general categories of "symbols and signs." It is important to know that there is a complex and fascinating field of study called **semiotics** that analyzes the nuances of signs and their cultural significance. Let us just look at a couple of basic examples from our small case study.

The actual barn on the Double Edge farm has no inherent or innate meaning; that is, it is simply a structure composed of wood planks, nails, and a shake roof. The semiotic questions arise when we, as viewers, invest the structure with cultural meaning and, in this case, the actors and performers are counting on us to do just that. Just as the Acropolis and its location would have provided the Greek theatre with layers of cultural significance, so too does the Ashfield community's understanding and memory of the Fitzvale Farm as a location of growth. A barn is no longer simply a barn. It is a place that raised chickens and cows, stored food for the winter, and existed as critical fulcrum in its society. With that in mind, using the same barn as a location for performance, layers of significance are applied onto the performance that the community is

---

[4] For more detailed analysis of Double Edge Theatre consult Landis (2009).

gathered to see. "An architect has an intuitive grasp, a tacit understanding, of the rhythms of a culture, and he seeks to give them symbolic form" (Tuan, 1977: 164). Like the architect, the artist/performer/cultural creator, too, understands the symbolic weight of the locational choices that she makes, making the architecture and the experience of the architecture critical components of the cultural performance. When members of a theatre company assert that they are creating a "living culture" you can now easily understand what they mean. They see that their roving audience is programmed to attempt to makes sense of the geography and architecture that surrounds it and use that knowledge and experience to strengthen cultural bonds.[5]

You might appropriately be thinking that it is impossible to always know how each spectator will process and understand the semiotics of performative architecture. This is always true and theatre, just like any cultural expression, both relies on shared cultural memory and individual creation of meaning. The theatre scholar Erika Fischer-Lichte succinctly confirms this: "The performative space always also creates an atmospheric space... spatiality results not just from the specific spatial uses of the actors and spectators but also from the particular atmospheres theses spaces exude" (Fischer-Lichte, 2008, 11). In this, Fischer-Lichte illuminates the creation of **atmospheric space**, perhaps a hazy concept, but a useful term that we should contend with. Atmospheric space implies a location that is made up of more than simply the architecture of the immediate moment but a space that is made electric due to feelings, histories, memories and multiple viewpoints. Spaces exude atmosphere. You can certainly sense this when you enter a sacred space in your life. There often is an ineffable sense of importance that lingers in the air. Indeed, cultural performance is a palimpsest (a layering, with shadows of the past just underneath) of many associations such that definitive symbolic meaning can never be pinpointed. In this mini case study we can see that the buildings at the Double Edge farm intersect

---

[5] While not detailed in this book, you might consider researching clothing worn in cultural performance, from the vestments of a monk to a headdress of a shaman. Like the adornments of the architectural place, clothing is a richly nuanced element of cultural storytelling and an active semiotic component linked to a sense of place.

with a multitude of unique views of a performance based on individual context.[6] You are correct to be now thinking that we are far away from the simple understanding of theatre and cultural performance as an empty space. Though that framing of performance is elegant, we can see that any empty space is far from empty in that it necessarily carries with it a host of signification.

The Urban Stage

There is a French performance company called Royal de Luxe. A few years ago I was visiting the city of Reykjavik, Iceland, and quite literally happened upon one of their performances. As I turned a corner on an afternoon stroll, at the end of the street, walking my way, was a three-story-tall puppet in the image of a little girl. It was controlled by a group of puppet masters in beautiful red jackets, some on the street and others sitting in roosts in the scaffolding system that kept the girl upright. The Little Girl Giant was at once inspiring and terrifying as she lumbered slowly down the street. For me, the performance was completely unexpected and astonishing in that it was in the middle of a European capital.

I later discovered that Royal de Luxe was well known for its mechanical marionettes, and, importantly, their placement in urban centers. Indeed, as we continue to analyze the architecture of performance we must recognize that not only does a city often develop out of areas of cultural performance creation, but some of the most exciting cultural performance that we can witness occurs when the participants create in tandem with their urban environment, a location packed full of culturally meaningful signs. As we saw with the Double Edge example and with the assessment of the Penitentes in Colorado, place is defined by the geography, the buildings, and the individual responses to those elements. Increasingly, we see the audience immersed into the performance—helping create the stories that they see by the very nature that they decide what they see

---

[6] Victoria Hunter uses the term *contextual trajectories* to describe the various viewpoints that an audience brings to a performance (Hunter, 2005: 377).

and assign value to—what Leslie Hill calls the creation of "spatial stories" (Hill, 2006: 102). To explicate this idea further, perhaps you can see that the performance of the Little Girl Giant in Reykjavik was a story that was created from the environment in which it was received. The impact was more powerful for being "out of place" in an urban environment. The spatial story was rich and nuanced.

Contemporary theatre has seen a great interest in creating drama in the urban environment, since the architecture of the "man-made" space of the city necessarily increases and enriches the spatial stories that are developed. But it would be unwise to see urban architecture and its implications as new in an understanding of cultural performance. In this chapter alone we have seen how Greek theatre practitioners used the urban environment to influence the building of their cultural performance. Likewise, the Middle Ages saw performances of cycle plays (plays about the life of Christ) that lasted all day long and moved around the villages in which they were created. This is powerful symbolism, since viewers could locate the life of Jesus within the urban environment that they called home. As the world urbanizes, we have to resist the temptation to locate cultural performance solely in rural locations and limit it to clearly religious experiences. It is, in fact, everywhere. Cities, with their parades, festivals, civic gatherings, and street entertainment, are the most elaborate sites of cultural performance (Garner, 2002: 101). We use our cities and our towns as stages for our expression of self. While we have seen how some theatre buildings are urban landmarks, we now have to consider how the urban environment is itself a theatre space.

It is good to return to the defining term of this book, *cultural performance*, and re-contextualize it vis-à-vis the architectures that we have been exploring. How, you might ask, is Royal de Luxe a cultural performance? While it doesn't seem to have an obvious religious or spiritual value, the placement of performance in the city allows the community of observers to think about their relationship to the place of performance: demands that the audience and performers consider their presence in the urban environment. Rather than going to a theatre to take oneself out of the everyday, these sorts of performance locate the experience in the middle of the place in which we live. Suddenly, our sense of concrete reality— our *home*—coexists with our sense of the imaginative. Think about how you relate to the city in which you live and the ways in which your every-day experience of your city or town is a performance of your culture. You might ask yourself how the spatial arrangement of your city, its streets, its buildings, its artistic decorations, can affect the way a performance may be created and received. Certainly, a parade on Long Street in Cape Town is entirely different than the same parade dropped in the middle of the Fitzvale Farm in Ashfield, Massachusetts.

A final example of art in the urban milieu might help illuminate the complex relationship we, as human beings, have to the places that we call home. Perhaps one of the great post-modern examples of cultural perfor-mance is Disneyland, the make believe amusement park created in the 1950s that spawned the development of other, similar parks around the world. By this point, we can all see how Disneyland, with amusements, people dressed in costumes, recreating scenes from animated movies, can certainly be considered a performance location. But look even closer, as many scholars have before, and you uncover a complex cultural perfor-mance with urbanity at its core. The center of the original park in Los Angeles, California, is an "attraction" called "Main Street USA." You can see something of this sort in most amusement parks, in fact: a main street that becomes the central artery of the park, a recreation of a small town, with shops and streets branching off, leading to other attractions and precincts. As Matthew Wilson Smith has written in his excellent study on urban spaces, "In Disney parlance, Main Street is the 'center stage' of Disneyland, the route through which one must travel to enter the various mythic zones that spiral off in all directions" (Smith, 2002: 267).[7]

This is a complex idea, but one you should revel in. An amusement park is a beautiful encapsulation of many of the topics that we have dis-cussed throughout the book. It seems to qualify as a cultural performance since it so clearly expresses the needs of the community that creates it. The park highlights the values of the community by recreating an idealized

---

[7] Much has been written about Disneyland, especially in the context of its presence as *simulation*. While here we are focusing on the considerations of architecture and urban environments and the ways that theme parks recreate our urban precincts, you are encouraged to read some of the excel-lent scholarship on these curious forms of performance. Chief among these is Jean Baudrillard's well-known study *Simulacra and Simulation* (1994) and much of the work done on the subject by Richard Schechner (2006).

imitation of its home; the streets emphasize travel, pilgrimage, and personal discovery. Indeed, many people travel great distances, almost ritualistically, to bring their families to such parks. Alexander Moore has written about this and the ritual connections between Disneyland and its followers. He aptly notes that in the Magic Kingdom it is fantasy, not religion, that "reigns" (Moore, 1980: 211). But here the differences between religion and fantasy are insignificant, for they both serve the purpose of connecting a community and, in their outward expression, create culturally rich performance spectacles.

We can learn from the example that it provides: that cultural performance, at its core, is a way to represent the ethos of its community. Increasingly, traversing an urban landscape and assessing how the city represents our culture are some of the most exciting ways we can look at cultural performance. In the case study that follows, theatre scholar Sean Edgecomb addresses the way gay culture in New York City's West Village used the specific urban environment to influence the dissemination of its unique cultural expression. You will also see the multiple ways that structure, design, and architecture can be used to craft an experience of performance.

Terms and Ideas for Study

- Empty space structure
- Space
- Place
- Investing space
- Architecture of performance

- Pilgrimage
- Ritual space/place
- Semiotics
- Atmospheric space

Questions for Discussions

- What are the locations of performance in your community? How did they come to be?
- Select a building of performance in your city or town and identify the symbolic elements. How are the particular signs and symbols important to the audience and participants?
- Describe the *atmospheric space* of a performance location that is important to you. What are the elements that give the space atmosphere?

Creative Project

In small groups, design a simple place of performance. Consider ways that you can use location to greater illuminate the story about your community that you want to tell. You are encouraged to consider physical location as well as atmospheric space. What are the ways that you can affect the audience's feeling of the place? Create a ground plan that includes images and references to the physical architecture of the place as well as the atmospheric space.

Case Study

Architecting Queer Space: Charles Ludlam's *Bluebeard* in the West Village

by Sean F. Edgecomb

> "'You have some queer friends, Dorothy,' she said.
> 'The queerness doesn't matter, so long as they're friends,' was
> the answer."
> — L. Frank Baum, *The Road to Oz* (1909: 3)

Introduction: Queering Architecture

Charles Ludlam (1943–1987), director, playwright, actor, and founder of the Ridiculous Theatrical Company, acted as a kind of queer architect to transform preexisting urban spaces through cultural performance in the age of Gay Liberation (the late 1960s through the early 1980s). Ludlam specifically stated, "I think of myself as an inventor of plays. The wright in playwright is worker, maker: one who works in wood such as a shipwright. My [gay] plays are wrought as much as written" (1992: 3). Just as ships are built through skills that have been passed down through time, Ludlam is suggesting that through the process of creating a fully produced play from scratch or "inventing," he is adeptly fashioning something new and queer through the continuance of preexisting theatrical traditions and thereafter the inversion of them.

Using Ludlam as its main subject of inquiry, this case study interrogates the notion of how spaces might be architecturally transformed, retransformed or *queered* via the cultural performance/communal performativity of people who identify as queer. It also considers how a queered space may in turn act as a nonhuman participant in helping to assemble and assimilate people toward a collective goal (community, desire, or civil rights). My own understanding of queer space is, in part, inspired by queer blogger as self-professed "gender explorer" Jasper Gregory's notion of the term as "a field of possibility in a social space." Gregory's "field of possibility" connects back to the potential for the aforementioned collective goals to be pursued or even achieved (2009).

To better understand how cultural performances like Ludlam's can be pinpointed as a seed for the growth of queer spaces that have the power to "*show ourselves to ourselves* in ways that help us to recognize our behavior… needs and desires," I introduce the use of architect as a verb, as in *to* architect (Turner, 2001: 122). When you think of architecture, you probably envision some of the world's most iconic buildings and their creators, but the queer architecture I'm discussing is more about the construction and adaptation of social constructs in relation to preexisting spaces that are *re*envisioned through a queer lens. Ludlam *architected* two distinct productions of his play *Bluebeard: A Melodrama in Three Acts* (1970) at two locations in the West Village: the gay bar Christopher's End and the more formalized version when the play transferred to The Performing Garage. It is recommended that you read the full script of Ludlam's *Bluebeard* before continuing on to the analysis.

A Pause for Critical Reflection: What Does Queer Mean?

You have probably encountered the term queer before reading this case study, whether used conversationally or theoretically. Although the preceding case study on Charles Ludlam's play *Bluebeard* can be read as an example of how queer architecture and architecting strives to help you to better understand how queer*ness* can be applied to ethnographic performance or performance space, it may *still* feel innately complex and confusing. This is perfectly normal; in fact one of the greatest strengths of queerness is its inability to be singularly defined. As an umbrella term, queer can be applied in a number of ways even beyond the LGBT community: as a positionality (or how your environment, culture, nationality, race, gender, class, or other circumstances might affect your perspective) to understand ones desires, a way of operating with a sense of autonomy in the world, as a political stance against heteronormative social structures, or even as a theory. Queer theorists Lauren Berlant and Michael Warner define the notion of heteronormativity as follows: "Heteronormativity is more an ideology, or prejudice, or phobia against gays and lesbians; it is produced in almost every aspect of the forms and arrangements of social life: nationality, the state, and the law; commerce; medicine; and education; as well as in the conventions and affects of narrativity, romance and other protected space of culture." (2003: 173).

Originally meaning peculiar, queer became a derogatory slang for homosexual men sometime in the late nineteenth century. About one hundred years later in the 1980s, however, scholars of feminism and gender joined as activists to reclaim the term as a call to agency and action. At the time of this reclamation the term was malleable and fluid, but largely associated with gays and lesbians. Some of the original scholars who introduced the notion of queer theory include Teresa de Lauretis, Judith Butler, Lauren Berlant, Adrienne Rich, Eve Kosofsky Sedgwick, Michael Warner, and David Halperin. A grassroots group called Queer Nation distributed the following flyer at the New York City Gay Pride Parade in June, 1990: one section read:

> Ah, do we really have to use that word? It's trouble. Every gay person has his or her own take on it. For some it means strange and eccentric and kind of mysterious [...] And for others "queer" conjures up those awful memories of adolescent suffering [...] Well, yes, "gay" is great. It has its place. But when a lot of lesbians and gay men wake up in the morning we feel angry and disgusted, not gay. So we've chosen to call ourselves queer. Using "queer" is a way of reminding us how we are perceived by the rest of the world. (Queer Nation, 1990)

This brief extract demonstrates how queer is used not as an identity, but, as mentioned earlier, a lens to invert the way the world is viewed by a collective group identifying *as* queer. Oftentimes queerness is made visible through the process creating queer spaces. I'm defining queer spaces broadly as open sites for being and doing where a tolerance for difference, fluidity, and ambivalence may be encountered and expressed. Such a space, whether physical or theoretic, is not strictly defined by alternative sexualities (including LGBT), but is very often a product of them. This corroborates Aaron Betsky's argument that "[In a queer space] we can continually search within ourselves as we mirror ourselves in a world that has body, a desire, a life. Queer space queers reality to produce a space to live" (1997: 193). As you have read, Ludlam's diverse performances and the spaces in which they took place are demonstrative of theatre as a mirror, reflecting then deflecting oppressive and heteronormative ideologies back onto the world through inversion (think of it as a more sophisticated and ribald application of the phrase "I'm rubber, your glue, whatever you say bounces of me and sticks to you"). So although queer in the context of Ludlam is most often associated with people who express alternative sexual desire, gay, lesbian, bisexual, or trans, queer can productively be applied to any individual who lives outside the normative constraints of culture's hegemonic (or dominant political and social) expectations. These expectations typically revolve around structures of normality and patriarchy, such as the expression of distinct and limiting gender roles as performed through contracts like marriage, reproduction and the legal distribution on property.

Getting Ridiculous

Ludlam's Theatre of the Ridiculous was a distinct genre created by a group of gay men and their friends in an attempt to express a feeling of queer camaraderie and togetherness using encoded language, camp, and, more specifically, by inverting heteronormative stories (everything from canonical novels and plays to "B" movies to contemporary advertisements), socio-cultural traditions (like romance, marriage, reproduction, and mourning), and stereotypes (particularly the heterosexual perceptions of gays and lesbians) to the point of ridicule. Making fun of traditions in this way is an effective tool because it allows the audience to see from a potentially different and unfamiliar perspective, which might, in turn, encourage understanding toward empathy. Though the intention of the Ridiculous theatre form was not inherently political, it gained its initial traction and subsequently a lasting legacy by creating queer spaces of ritual that instigated indirect political organization, action, and the formation of queer spaces with more visibility. Ludlam stated explicitly how the Ridiculous could be used as a tool of queer empowerment:

> One of the greatest weapons that people use on you to get you to conform is ridicule. So you don't dare do anything that people will laugh at. It's a way that society exerts pressure on you. However, if you take the position that you are already going to be ridiculous, they are powerless. They ridicule you? They're doing what you want them to do. (Ludlam, 1992: 130)

The forging of a queer performance that was worked around a core of ridicule (or what Ludlam might have referred to as ridiculousness) largely resulted in a collective feeling of shared experience, kinship, and togetherness. As you have read throughout *Cultural Performance*, togetherness can be a key factor in generating spaces for cultural performance. This provided an alternative to the heteronormative and biological family structures that Ludlam and his queer contemporaries were eschewing. The Ridiculous also provided a physical space that felt safe for queers to dance, socialize, flirt, express physical affection, or even hook up without fear or backlash. This was an effective antidote to feelings of shame, isolation, and oppression that plagued closeted gays and lesbians in a period when same-sex desire was considered both a mental illness and a criminal act. As you will see, this particular study is primarily concerned with gay men during the period of gay liberation after the Stonewall Riots (June 28, 1969); this does not, however, foreclose the possibility and necessity of understanding queerness as it applies to other individuals, groups, or particular communities.

Bluebeard: A Melodrama

Ludlam's three-act play *Bluebeard* was the product of his desire to create a more serious play (in form and structure not theme) after years of writing epic dramas that were grandly episodic, lacking linear plots, and very difficult for an audience to follow (these early epic plays included *Big Hotel* (1967), *Conquest of the Universe/When Queens Collide* (1968), *Turds in Hell* (1969), and *The Grand Tarot* (1969)). The structure of *Bluebeard* is inspired directly by Eugène Scribe, a French nineteenth-century play-wright who codified a form called the well-made play, or in French *la pièce a bien faite*. The construction of the well-made play follows a rather technical formula that is dependent on an arch that includes the build-up of suspense, a climax, and final resolution. *Bluebeard* perfectly demonstrates Ludlam's role as a wright or even architect, starting with a foundation drawn from Scribe and then completely inverting it through campy queer humor and encoded messages intended for a queer audience.

The pastiched structure of *Bluebeard* juxtaposes several sources: Charles Perrault's fairytale of the same name, the opera *Bluebeard's Castle* by Bela Bartók, H.G. Wells' novel *The Island of Dr. Moreau*, *The Rivals* by Richard Brinsley Sheridan, and references to the "B" horror films of Ludlam's childhood and fits them into Scribe's formula. Taking place in the lair of the mad-scientist Bluebeard off the coast of Maine—"the House of Pain"—the plot follows the titular cobalt-bearded anti-hero as he seeks to invent "a third gentler genital" through human testing, a clear metaphor for homosexuality. In a scene influenced directly by another classic source, Christopher Marlowe's *The Tragical History of the Life and Death of Doctor Faustus* (c. 1592), our Bluebeard laments:

BLUEBEARD:
Love must be reinvented, that's obvious.
Sex to me is no longer mysterious.
And so I'll swear that while my beard is blue,
I'll twist some human flesh into a genital new. (Ludlam, 1989: 119)

Rick Roemer expands on the importance of the encoded themes to gay men at the time of the play's premiere:

Thematically [*Bluebeard*] works on a number of levels. First, the very need to create a third sexual being indicates Ludlam's frustration with the level of bigotry against homosexuality. A gay man is not sexually attracted to women, and if society makes it difficult, if not torturous and impossible, to be true to one's homosexual desires, then that society has forced the logical, if not absurd, solution of a third type of genital organ onto the homosexual community. As ludicrous as this may sound, it must have seemed equally ludicrous to Ludlam, and to many other gay men as well, to feel so maligned by the straight world for merely being sexually attracted to other men. Indeed, how difficult it is to develop and maintain a "normal" relationship in a society that constantly tells you how abnormal you are. (2010: 93)

Roemer's analysis highlights not only why *Bluebeard* spoke so clearly to its gay audience through its symbolism during a time of oppression, but also intuits how the gathering of such a like-minded group could result in unification and the formulation of queer spaces. James Bidgood, a contemporary filmmaker and queer artist to Ludlam, recollects how circumscribed these plays could be, commenting "They were very strange plays… if you were really straight and watching them you would have trouble following them" (2006). While this kind of encodedness potentially helped to forge and protect a queer audience, it also produced a kind of exclusivity that helped to create a spirit of belonging and communitas, what Benedict Anderson coined an "imagined community" (2006: 6). Although the queer message of *Bluebeard* remained consistent, I suggest that its queer dynamic changed depending on the space in which it was performed and how the audience and actors changed that space.

Christopher's End

In March of 1970, *Bluebeard* premiered at the LaMama Theatre in the East Village, one of the most important theatres in New York City supporting new artistic voices and avant-garde performances since 1961. Although it was scheduled for a four-week run, Ludlam and LaMama's founder and manager, Ellen Stewart, had an argument over royalties and the run was cut to only five performances with no reviewers from the press invited. With a fully fleshed-out production and no theatre in which to perform, Ludlam had to get creative; he had to find a location in which to architect a queer space for his play.

At the end of Christopher Street in the West Village, the epicenter of gay life in New York in the 1970s, was a down-at-heel bar provocatively named Christopher's End; this was where Ludlam moved *Bluebeard* in late April of the same year. By placing boards to lengthen the bar into a larger stage and hanging hastily painted drops, Ludlam transformed a space that was already used for a queer performance of desire, what Betsky deems "a space of spectacle [and] consumption," and transformed it into a space where that queer desire was reflected in the live theatrical performance of *Bluebeard*. This reflection was achieved by inverting a story that appeared to be about heterosexuals on its surface, though it was really about a same-sex yearning. Moreover, the bar and its patrons can be considered key contributors to the architecting of the performance aesthetic. Erving Goffman suggests that "A performance may be defined as all of the activity of a given participant on a given occasion which serves to influence in any way any of the participants" (Schechner, 2006: 26). Through Ludlam's careful drafting as architect, Christopher's End was transformed into a non-human participant that enlivened and streamlined the overall cultural performance of *Bluebeard* as a site of queer ephemerality. While the play could be repeated as a kind of ethnographic ritual, the unfolding of performance process would never be the same due to variable participants (including the bar and its patrons), even if the end goal of a larger communal bonding through inversion remained the same.

The prime example of such queer inversion takes place in Act II Scene III of *Bluebeard* when our mad scientist seduces the obese character of Miss Cubbidge, played by company member Lola Pashalinski. In the script Ludlam notes: "follows a scene of unprecedented eroticism in which Miss Cubbidge gives herself voluptuously to Baron Von Bluebeard" (1989: 135). The purpose of this scene, a satirical inversion of heterosexual copulation performed in the most absurd way possible, is a histrionic thumb biting at cultural opinions that deemed gay sex as unnatural. The pornographic spoof used physical awkwardness as its punch line to push the audience outside of their comfort zone as far as possible—like when Bluebeard pulls his hat out of Cubbidge's vagina. The juxtaposition of ribald humor with the underlying radical message resulted in a powerful product that famous Brechtian actress Lotte Lenya deemed "very pure" (Ludlam, 1992: 25), the result of all elements coming together as architected to create a queer space.

In an early study of queer space, Jeffrey Weeks notes the fundamental role of the gay bar, as it "encouraged an identity that [is] both public and collective, and [have] become seed beds for a collective consciousness[…]" (1985: 6). Just imagine watching the performance amidst the fun and seedy atmosphere on the bar, heady with the scent of cigarettes, poppers, and beer embodying a feeling of escape from the outside world, a sanctuary where the LGBT community could live their lives openly without the fear of oppression or attack. Because Christopher's End was also a spot for cruising, its environs magnified the hyperbolized sexuality of the performance, with its denim and leather-clad crowd delighting in its camp send up of gay sex. Scholar Gregory W. Bredbeck highlights the exclusivity of the event, noting that it "play[ed] solely to the urban gay men populating some thirty blocks that [made up] Ludlam's world, The West Village of Manhattan" (1996: 78). The major exception to Bredbeck's observation was in the throng of reviewers who rushed to the bar after being denied entry at LaMama. The critics were enamored of the performance, no doubt invigorated by the unique energy of the space as architected fortuitously by Ludlam himself. The informality and bawdiness of the bar only liberated the actors to a more heightened level of performance. One way to think about this queer space is as a closet. You have probably heard the phrase "being in the closet," in reference to a gay or lesbian individual who had not disclosed their sexuality. In this sense, a closet is usually considered a place to hide from homophobia, social pressure, or feelings of shame. Ludlam's closet, on the other hand, was not a place for shame, but rather a carnivalesque space to play out fantasies. Rather than coming out of this closet, he was inviting others in. Ludlam spoke to the empowering nature of this experience, declaring "Gay theatre encourages those who may not have the strength to stand alone against the cultural traditions which seek to denigrate and trivialize their profound human needs" (1992: 254). This was a period in American history, after all, when socializing publicly with the gay community could be read as a radical act. Though the majority of the reporters were heterosexual, the opportunity to engage with this queer performance in a queer space allowed them the opportunity to liberate themselves through queering, providing the unique experience to better understand LGBT individuals and generate compassion through communion.

Rave reviews came in from newspapers across town including *The New York Times, Wall Street Journal, Women's Wear Daily*, and *The Village Voice*, with queer artist and Stonewall veteran Thomas Lanigan Smith declaring the performance akin to "attending Easter Mass at the Church of the Holy Sepulcher" (Kaufman, 2002: 124). Smith's description highlights the heightened state of emotion that he derived from the performance, but also connects back to the notion of religious ritual as a kind of proto-cultural performance as previously discussed in this book. In all likelihood it was the combination of Ludlam's brilliant writing and acting paired with the intimacy of the experience within the space of Christopher's End that made his stars align; that summer the play would be awarded an Obie and it received an invitation for a longer run at The Performing Garage, also located in the West Village. The transfer provided an oppor-tunity for Ludlam's troupe to intersect with communities beyond the gay men that populated the tail end of Christopher Street.

The Performing Garage

In 1967 director Richard Schechner founded his experimental theatre company, The Performance Group, and a year later opened a new space called the Performing Garage. The space was distinct, taking the form of bleachers and platforms surrounding the stage, a large and poten-tially immersive area that had formerly served as a flatware factory. This allowed the audience and actors to interact more, in a space that could be easily transformed or adapted depending upon the needs of the show in production. Beyond its unique layout, the location of the Performing Garage in the West Village would also help give rise to the off-off Broadway movement, loosely defined as the experimental theatre that developed in lower Manhattan in the 1960s and 1970s, far from the public visibility and immense budgets of the Great White Way. Historian George Chauncey explains how the West Village evolved into a queer space even before Ludlam's time: "The Gay History of Greenwich Village [presents] a peculiar social territory in which the normal social constraints on behavior seemed to have been suspended and where men and women built unconventional lives outside of the family nexus" (1994: 244). Whereas Ludlam's performance of *Bluebeard* at Christopher's End was shaped by its location in a protected space that was intended as exclu-sively gay, the aforementioned reviewers expanded its sphere of influ-ence. *Bluebeard's* relocation was directly related to this event as Schechner was, at the time, the theatre reviewer for *The Village Voice*. This happy coincidence resulted in the invitation for Ludlam's troupe to use the Performing Garage for a summer run of the play. With the reputation of the Performing Garage already steadfast as a place to see innovative work, largely due to Schechner's production of *Dionysus in 69*, which premiered two years before, the space helped to expand the audience from gay men to a more diverse group of individuals who might be better positioned as queer. Ludlam stated explicitly how he viewed his theatre and audience as more inclusively queer:

> "Queer theatre" embraces more variation and the possibility of something being odd or peculiar rather than just simply homosexuality[…] Homosexuals, just as women, are not politically one group. They are communists and they are extreme right wing, they are fascists, there is every kind of opinion. Gay becomes an ineffective category, whereas "queer" is a little more of a splash of cold water. There is more room for more people in the queer category. (1992: 229)

Ludlam's ideas about queerness and queer people prophetically paved the way for more contemporary attempts to define the term, perhaps most closely echoed in Jack (formerly Judith) Halberstam's theory of a queer temporality where "[queer] participants […] believe that their futures can be imagined according to logic outside of those [heteronormative] paradigmatic markers of life experience" (2005: 2). In other words, the queer architecture of space may also alter the way time is used or recorded by its participants within that space.

Drawing upon the "unconventional" climate of the West Village, Ludlam worked from his own queer blueprint in much the same way as an architect relies on their own carefully prepared renderings. The success of the performance of *Bluebeard* at the Performing Garage was largely impacted by the merging of Ludlam's gay fans (who followed the play) with Schechner's patrons, setting off a domino effect of potential intersectional relationships to bring visibility to the play. One way that this is demonstrated was in the tours that the Ridiculous Theatrical Company was invited to partake in following the Performing Garage performance, exposing new audiences to *Bluebeard* in American colleges and their theatres in Europe. Admittedly, Ludlam may have had less control in architecting the physical spaces in which his touring shows were performed, but the selection of the tour sites demonstrates a clearly crafted plan to spread the Ridiculous to new audiences. While the economic and popular success of these traveling shows varied, the performance of *Bluebeard* in diverse places and spaces provided the unique opportunity for audience members to get a glimpse of what was taking place in the gay urban center of New York. This may not have found appeal for all in attendance, but the potential for exposure and epiphany for even one queer person connects back to Gregory's notion of "possibility" (2009).

Just because a space already has a queer reputation (like Christopher's End or even Schechner's Performing Garage as a site for individuals that embrace life choices that lie beyond the confines of the normative to congregate) it can still be queered further and in different ways. Although *Bluebeard*'s original intent as a metaphor for homosexuality remained throughout its run at the Performing Garage and the other touring and repertory versions, the power of its message could be extended to promote inclusivity and empathy to a larger group in solidarity with its ability to transform both space and audience through a queer architecture.

Queer Space

At the Queer Space Conference held in New York City in 1994, the organizers posed the question: "Is [queer space] even physical space that is in question, or is it the space of discursive practices, texts, codes of behavior…?" (1994). Betsky fortuitously helps to answer this inquiry: "By its very nature, queer space is something that is not built, only implied, and usually invisible. Queer space does not confidently establish a clear, ordered space for itself… It is altogether more ambivalent, open, self-critical, ironic and ephemeral" (1997: 18). Betsky clearly lays out the notion that queer spaces are, in fact, *queered* spaces, like Christopher's End or the Performing Garage, preexisting sites that are transformed, adapted, or reshaped through a lens of queerness, resulting in spaces becoming places of belonging for like-minded and often oppressed individuals and their allies.

Queer spaces like those just discussed are of a particular time and place, but this does not negate them from having a continued (if altered) presence in the urban milieu. The Performing Garage continues to house the Wooster Group (the offshoot of the original Performance group) as well as a number of other avant-garde performers making queer work.

Christopher's End, on the other hand, shuttered its windows and doors and shut down decades ago, but the ghost of its past, along with other key sites such as the iconic Stonewall Bar and the Stonewall Memorial, continue to inform Christopher Street as a space that embodies a sense of an LGBT history and continuing heritage. In fact, because of this multi-layered history, Christopher Street continues to adapt and metamorphose into a site for a contemporary queer community to gather for events of cultural performance, like an immense vigil held in honor of the LGBT men and women who were killed in the homophobia-fueled hate crime at the Orlando nightclub Pulse on June 12, 2016. This gathering resurrected the notion of taking back a queer safe space that has been taken from the community through a violent act terror.

As theoretical as they are physical, queer spaces adhere to "ambiva-lence," because they lie between the normative and the anti-normative, forging a way of being and doing that refuses to be pinned down or labeled. In a recent *New York Times Magazine* opinion piece, journalist Jenna Wortham went as far as defining queer as a "shimmer of multi-tudes," in an attempt to give shape to its seemingly amorphous existence (2016). Because of such amorphousness, only by applying queer as a tool with which to read cultural phenomena, like Ludlam's architected perfor-mances, are we able to even begin to see how queerness might manifest and what it looks like. Although queer is often used as a label (and I'm sure you that you can brainstorm a list of ways that it has been applied in this vein), its meaning lies closer to that which will not be controlled by hegemonically constructed rules of identity-making.

Ludlam's performance of *Bluebeard* is the prime example to incite further conversation about how queerness can be read as that which is ambivalent, implied, open, ironic, ephemeral, and I would add timely and contradictory, setting the model for decades of queer performance to follow and then queerly deconstruct. In other words, the queer per-formances that you might encounter today are arguably all rooted in this period of sexual liberation as an artistic genesis, the origin of a queer architecture. Because queerly architected spaces are as dependent on the individuals present as their physical structure or environs, they are tem-porary and moreover empowered by a constant state of flux.

References

Anderson, B. *Imagined Communities: Reflections on the Origin and Spread of Nationalism*, Revised *Edition*. London: Verso, 2006.

Baum, L. F. *The Road to Oz*. Chicago: Reilly & Britton, 1909.

Berlant, L. and M. Warner. "Sex in Public." In *Queer Studies: An Interdisciplinary Reader*, edited by Robert J. Corber and Stephen Valocchi. London: Blackwell Publishing Ltd., 2003.

Betsky, A. *Queer Space: Architecture and Same-Sex Desire*. New York: William Morrow and Company, Inc, 1997.

Bidgood, J. Unpublished interview with the author, 2006.

Bredbeck, Gregory S. "The Ridiculous Sound of One Hand Clapping: Placing Ludlam's 'Gay' Theatre in Space and Time." In *Modern Drama* 39, 1996: 64–83.

Chauncey, G. *Gay New York*. New York: Basic Books, 1994.

Halberstam, J. *In a Queer Time & Place: Transgender Bodies, Subcultural Lives*. New York: New York University Press, 2005.

Kaufman, David. *Ridiculous!: The Theatrical Life and Times of Charles Ludlam*. New York: Applause Books, 2002.

Ludlam, C. *Ridiculous Theatre: Scourge of Human Folly: The Essays and Opinions of Charles Ludlam*, edited by Steven Samuels. New York: Theatre Communications Group, 1992.

Ludlam, C. *The Complete Plays of Charles Ludlam*. New York: Harper & Row, 1989.

Roemer, R. *Charles Ludlam and the Ridiculous Theatrical Company: An Analysis of 29 Plays*. McFarland: Jefferson NC, 2010.

Schechner, R. *Performance Studies: An Introduction*. New York: Routledge, 2006.

Turner, V. *From Ritual to Theatre: The Human Seriousness of Play*. Cambridge: PAJ Books, 2001.

Weeks, J. *Sexuality and Its Discontents: Meaning, Myths and Modern Sexualities*. London: Routledge, 1985.

Web Pages Consulted

Gregory, J. *Jasper's Wardrobe: Oakland Postgender Application*, "What is 'Queer Space?'" (January 21, 2009), accessed June 5, 2016, https://jasperswardrobe. wordpress.com/2009/01/21/what-is-queer-space/.

Queer Nation, "Queers Read This," (June, 1990), accessed June 5, 2016, http:// www.qrd.org/qrd/misc/text/queers.read.this.

Storefront for Art and Architecture, "Queer Space," (June, 1994), accessed June 5, 2016, http://storefrontnews.org/programming/queer-space/.

Wortham, J. *The New York Times Magazine*, "When Everyone Can Be 'Queer,' Is Anyone?," (July 12, 2016), accessed June 13, 2016, http://www.nytimes.com/2016/07/17/magazine/when-everyone-can-be-queer-is-anyone.html?_r=0.

4

Topography of Performance

Image 5   *Las Posadas* © Suzanne MacAulay

"I nga rua o mua"
(Our past is our future and is also our present)

Out of the dark, Maori came paddling downriver toward the sea. The canoes were from Pipiriki, from Hiruharama, from Koriniti and Parikino until at First Light they finally reached their destination along the lower reaches of the Whanganui River. Like spectral chaperones, cars and trucks laden with supplies and equipment moved stealthily through the night, traveling the land route along the river, keeping the canoes company. The motor caravan was also intent on eventually meeting up with friends, allies, and kinfolk on the banks of the river near the town center of Wanganui[1] not far from the delta where the river flows into the Tasman Sea. Their destination was a city park. Their goal was to occupy that park and claim it as part of the original nineteenth-century Treaty of Waitangi land settlement that was never honored in the past by New Zealand settlers and their descendants.

Topography is referred to in the context of this chapter as a scheme for conceiving the different shapes and configurations of the relationship of performance to elements of the physical and cultural geography of an area. These include land formations like open space, valleys, rivers, and mountains as well as abstract formulations like place and space. Our first example shows how indigenous Maori use cultural performance to maneuver a state of political disenfranchisement to one of power vis-à-vis their takeover of a city park. The discussion then leads into a concern with the dynamics of cultural intervention and spatial tactics. By using Maori performance actions, we will trace how these strategies catalyze and unleash potent forces of social deconstruction and reconstruction arising from cultural clashes (some materializing in performance), crisis, and reconciliation. In the first part of the chapter, we will also learn about

---

[1] Maori pronounce Wanganui (town) with a soft initial *wh* sound. The river is referred to as Whanganui, which phonetically spells out the local indigenous pronunciation. Maori regard it as *Te awa tupuna* (the ancestral river from which they are descended). It is respected as one of their great national treasures, *taonga*. Up until recently, New Zealanders called the town Wanganui. To be consistent, the town has now been changed to Whanganui, which respects Maori as *tangata whenua*, First People of the Land. Throughout this chapter, Wanganui is used, alluding to the name in effect during the 1995 occupation.

the role of cultural performance as a political tool. We will explore the dynamic cultural and political transformation of civic space into sacred space and how cultural performance effects this change. As we begin this section, our exploration focuses on local river Maori introduced in the opening paragraph, and how during the 1995 occupation they used performance and ceremonial protocol as basic modalities to convert a typical Victorian New Zealand city park and locally favorite picnic place into a *marae*, a sanctified space. Throughout New Zealand, marae meeting places are traditionally sacred to Maori as residences of the ancestors and also serve as memorials to the dead. The momentum for the specific conversion of park into marae in February 1995 originated from Maori culturally driven political actions directed at white New Zealanders, i.e., European descendants known as *pakeha*. What is of interest to us in these circumstances is how the notion of place-making, and all the aspects of its creation were effectively vitalized through cultural performance. The appropriation of park grounds along with the implementation of ceremonial protocol on site mark the major modes of Maori occupiers in taking the first necessary sociopolitical actions toward redressing the injustices behind contentious land rights issues and toward regaining **sovereignty**, the right to independent authority, and power. Thus, Maori occupants of the park known to town residents as Moutoa Gardens literally *performed* the transition from municipal grounds with access to all into a restricted ceremonial space where entry for the public was only granted through strict observance of ancient Maori protocol.

As we analyze all the requisite steps and conditions leading to this transformation, keep in mind the definitions and rationale of cultural performance as mentioned in previous chapters. Above all, be attentive to the multiple ways cultural performance engenders solidarity among participants, binding them together in their purpose and reinforcing their common allegiance to certain values, beliefs, and codes of conduct. By the end of this section, you should be better acquainted with the culturally political and aesthetically powerful use of traditions and customs embedded in cultural performance to subvert the established political order and underscore the ascendancy of cultural identity. Watch how this is achieved through heavily politicized performance-engendered processes. In order to understand the cultural and political dimensions of such a conversion of place (from park to ceremonial stage space), and its bearing on the sociopolitical order, we must carefully examine extant cultural practices associated with the traditional repertoire of marae protocol and ceremony. These practices have been upheld by generations of Maori as *tangata whenua*, who are recognized throughout New Zealand as "First People of the Land." Now let us look more closely at how these customary elements were variously exploited for their performative capabilities, and used in 1995 as political acts of resistance while simultaneously promulgating age-old Maori traditions and beliefs.

Picnics to Stage Space

By February 1995, I had been living in Wanganui, and teaching at the Wanganui Polytechnic Institute in the Quay School of the Arts as an art historian and folklorist for over half-a-year. During that time I was also engaged in fieldwork with Whanganui River communities—particularly Maori weavers. Many of these women were *kuia* (powerful elderly women), who first introduced me to the intricacies of Maori culture. Consequently, because of these friendships and due to my role at the polytechnic, I spent a lot of time on different *marae* up and down the Whanganui River. The park, Moutua Gardens, was close to the polytechnic and I was thrilled that this was the first time my new "field site" was only blocks away, offering me the only chance I have ever had to bicycle to do fieldwork! The proximity of the occupied park to the polytechnic also allowed me to bring students there at all times of the day. On the first day when I was welcomed by Maori friends, Niko Tangaroa, one of the leaders of the occupation, responded to my request to introduce students to members of the local *iwi* (tribal group) now occupying the park, by describing what was occurring as "history being made right here," and he welcomed students "to witness this historic event as it unfolded." Much of this chapter also describes the transformation of a secular space into a ceremonial one. During my nine-year residency in Wanganui, I became very familiar with Maori customs and *marae* protocol. Even then in 1995, at that early stage of my life in New Zealand, I had a good understanding of the principles of *marae* ceremonies and their significance.

The occupants (or usurpers depending on one's perspective) of Moutoa Gardens, which was the setting for this act of resistance, were Maori families from clans belonging to the confederation (*iwi*) of native tribes known as *Te Atihaunui-a-Pāpārangi*, the local iwi, which is culturally, spiritually, and geographically allied with the Whanganui River. Maori express their close ties to the river through the saying, "*Ko au te awa. Ko te awa ko au*" (I am the river. The river is me). Wanganui residents felt they had historical rights to this parcel of land as well. They had picnicked and walked their dogs in this park for over a century. When Maori began to occupy the park and set up tents on the morning of February 28, 1995, town citizens were irate and sent letters to the local paper expressing their anger over being excluded from their place of entitlement—a common ground, which had been sanctioned by generations of use. There was also fear. Bystanders observing from a distance were uneasy. Among them, a Canadian expatriate was reminded of other violent protests of First Nation's People in Canada, and was quite apprehensive about the alienating factors in the community and the eventual outcome.

Moutoa Gardens encompassed almost two grassy acres of parkland, which was studded with monuments, war memorials, statuary, and fountains surrounded by trees planted during Queen Victoria's reign. Sidewalks and streets bordered the park on all sides with the Wanganui courthouse stationed at one of the far edges. The presence of certain public monuments and statuary presided over by a symbolically powerful building representing the Crown, which was primarily associated with arrests and trials, ostensibly promoted and perpetuated the imperial colonial mindset of domination and governance extant from earlier times. Among the various monuments were the ubiquitous war memorials commemorating soldiers from the Maori Battalion, who died in the First World War at Gallipoli, and another significant monument to a nineteenth-century battle at Moutoa upriver (for which the park was named) during the Second Taranaki War between local Maori and warriors from the north. In 1995, one of the first casualties of the Maori occupation of the park was the destruction of the statue of John Ballance, who started a newspaper in Wanganui, founded the Liberal Party, became Prime Minister toward the end of the nineteenth century, supported land reform at the expense of Maori claims, and promoted legislation to give women the vote in 1893. In the early days of occupation, Maori beheaded the statue of Ballance and substituted a pumpkin for its head. By the time the encampment ended after seventy-nine days, the entire statue was totally destroyed.

For Maori, Moutoa Gardens was a place of oppression. Every feature, whether it was a tree, fountain, or war memorial to fallen Maori warriors and soldiers was a visible reminder of hardship and centuries-old grievances. Therefore, at the beginning of the occupation each proclamation, gesture, and performance was an attempt to challenge or erase the persistent vestiges of a contested history within a contested place. Maori occupiers' first provocative declaration to rename the Gardens, *Pākaitore*, was an act of reclaiming the past. The original Pākaitore had actually been a market place and sanctuary for river Maori (outside the jurisdiction of the police), and was once located near Moutoa Gardens on the banks of the Whanganui River. Over the decades, the land had eroded and washed away in subsequent floods. Thus, in the minds of many Maori, the occupied park was an incarnation of this historical refuge. Like its predecessor it was also intended to be a place of safety.

What Is a *Marae*?

Before we describe how Maori transformed Pākaitore into a ritual arena, let us examine components of a traditional Maori *marae* setting and ceremony. First of all, each Maori community has a *marae*. Every *marae* has sacred and secular zones inspired by Maori cosmology. Its essence resides in the powerfully spiritual combination of meetinghouse (*whare*—also regarded as a metaphorical body of the resident ancestor) and the sanctified space in front of it. The term *marae* can also refer to the whole precinct including the secular structures, i.e., the dining hall, ablution block, and toilets. The entire *marae* area is usually surrounded on all sides by a fence demarcating ceremonial stage space, which sets it apart from the ordinary world. There is often a graveyard (*urupu*) in proximity acknowledging the continual ancestral presence in life as being lived in the present moment. The only entrance into *marae* ceremonial space is through a gateway (*tomokanga*). The meetinghouse and "space of encounter" in front of the gate where guests are welcomed are sacred and represent the place where ancestral presence becomes manifest through ritual enactments. Ceremonies enacted in the courtyard (*Te Maraenui-atea-o-Tumatauenga* [the great marae of the God of War]) follow a prescribed protocol for hosts (*tangata whenua*) and guests (*manuhiri*). Once guests have been formally and ritually welcomed through chants, speeches, oratorical challenges, polyphonic songs, and war dances (*haka*), the *tapu* (in this context interpreted as alien elements associated with strangers) is lifted from them as outsiders and they are then considered "kin" and part of the "family" (*whanau*) of the *marae*. At that point, the crowd adjourns inside the meetinghouse, which is presided over by the god of peace, *Rongo*, the locus of peaceful interaction.

At Pākaitore in 1995, performing historical and cultural acts of reclamation not only created the cultural political and performance landscape (transfiguring the former park) where Maori cultural identity could be spatially and ideologically realized, but also shaped the space according to Maori cosmology and belief system, that is, honoring zones of celebratory action and acknowledging divine attendance. Every time the actor-participants engaged in ceremonial activities, they created a mobile "field of action" through their movements and speeches. Once tents for dining, food storage, and eating as well as an ablution block and toilets had been erected and a large generator installed in the former park, then Maori began to layout the internal boundaries of sacred space, always cognizant of the relationship of the inner territory to the outer park boundaries. Another initiatory action was to surround the entire park with a fence of fern tree trunks planted in the earth. Over a short amount of time, many supposedly "dead" trees branched into fern fronds that gracefully framed the gateway and beautified the area. The verdant branches represented regeneration and new life. Revering their symbolic value and mythological association with *Tane Mahuta*, the god of the forest, Maori use fern trees to construct *marae* fences throughout New Zealand. There was only one official gateway for non-residents to access the marae. This allowed Maori to monitor and control entrance to Pākaitore. When outsiders came through the gate for the first time they were subject to the rules and protocol of a *marae* ceremony.

What are some of the main elements of *marae* cultural performance, and what is the ritual sequence? The following is a very skeletal outline of *marae* ceremony listing various ceremonial components.

- *Karanga*—a very high-pitched call of welcome almost like crying or keening, initiated by a woman (*kai karanga*) from the host group, *tangata whenua*, and answered by a woman accompanying the visiting group, *manuhiri*. The mourning sounds of these calls activate the spirits of the ancestors and invite the dead to join the living. Thus, the auditory power of the *karanga* exceeds physical barriers as it sonically crescendos and stretches out from the body to extend the sensory territory of the *marae* beyond its visible limits (Bernice Johnson Reagon quoted in Conquergood, 2013: 52).
- Challenge of a warrior from tangata whenua to the strangers, *manuhiri*, in the form of a war dance (*haka*).
- During the ceremony, *manuhiri* advance forward to the center of *marae* in front of the meetinghouse.
- Pause for a moment to remember the dead.
- Once the procession is standing in front of the meetinghouse, tangata whenua sit on the right followed by *manuhiri* sitting on the left.
- Ceremonial speeches from each faction (hosts and guests) occur, after which *manuhiri* present a tribute or monetary gift (*koha*) to *marae* hosts.
- Tangata whenua conclude speeches and invite *manuhiri* to come forward to *hongi*.
- *Hongi*—guests and hosts line up parallel to each other to shake hands and to press noses and foreheads together, thus engaging all senses in close contact: seeing, touch, smell, hearing, and, as Maori say, the whole experience symbolizes the 'taste' of human contact.

Cultural Performance and Space

Now let us see how these different traditional ceremonial elements apply to cultural performances enacted at Pākaitore. This allows us to measure the extent and power of Maori ritual choreography vis-à-vis culturally political identity formation. With regard to physical setting, the first line that is drawn in space to separate the inside realm (the culturally invented marae) from the outside was to inscribe the sacred area with the aforementioned fern tree fence around its perimeter, thus neutralizing the omnipresent effects of contiguous urban roads and sidewalks by creating a zone of opposition in spatial terms (inside and outside). According to Gaston Bachelard in his interpretation of the French philosopher, Jean Hyppolite, this division, a remnant of the primal "myth of inside and outside" or the classical dyad of "self and other," signifies the perpetuation of a degree of alienation between spheres, and is seen as leading to "hostility between the two" (Bachelard, 1994: 212). We acknowledge that division is customarily necessary in order to differentiate separate realms of performative action (the sacred and the profane). However, at Pākaitore, the concept of opposition plays out in a sociopolitical context as metaphorically engendering, and, in some cases, actually fueling, aggressive feelings of Maori (on the inside) toward the people of Wanganui (on the outside) and vice versa.

In his essay chapter, "Walking in the City," Michel de Certeau proposes a similar idea of opposition or resistance by those subjugated individuals living in urban space regulated by governmental agencies (city council, urban planners, police, etc.), (De Certeau, 1984: 93). He juxtaposes the creative strategies of ordinary citizens against the dominant urban uniformity bounded by established rules and ordinances, and suggests these tactics are both "defensive and opportunistic." The Maori takeover of a city park in proximity with the Wanganui City Hall and Police Department fits this description of opportunistic spatial anarchy in the face of the city as an institution seemingly in control of every corner of its domain until a crack appears, and suddenly everything changes.

Transcending the dichotomy of oppositional space with all its force and tension, let us return to the layout of Pākaitore and the arrangement of the different spaces within. In reference to apportionment of space, the single gateway, another distinctive spatial marker, served as a liminal space, a passageway between civic and sacred domains—a space suspended between two points but neither here nor there. This concept was part of Victor Turner's lexicon of ceremonial space. It can also be applied to a ritual state of consciousness, "betwixt and between," arising from certain transformative rites as discussed in earlier chapters (Turner, 1974: 47). The Pākaitore gate symbolized a transition from the mundane world (*noa*) to the sacred (*tapu*), from light into dark, and from the temporal to cosmic timelessness. Liminality also defined the space in front of the meetinghouse, the *atea*, where actions are suspended in time and space for the duration of the ceremony. The concept of the liminal could even encompass Pākaitore in its entirety (i.e., spatial and cultural segregation, ritual, etc.) in recognition that it existed in a time/space zone of "time away from time" and "place aside from space" on the edge of Wanganui's commercial district.

At Pākaitore, place and space are not opposing concepts but are nested inside one another. According to Edward Casey, "place is never fixed," what is unchanging is the quality of space characterized by "stability and permanence" (Casey, 2001: 719). He equates place to something short term and mutable "that reflects the vicissitudes of becoming, whether in history or in mind or social practice" (Casey, 719). The latter description certainly embodies the place-making dynamics of Pākaitore, which were always in the stage of realization and change, of continuity and flux, "constantly destabilized by the course of events" (Casey, 720). Trevor Marchand also writing about the impermanence and fluctuating identity of place reiterates the idea of the dynamics of place-making "subject to update and revision in fluid response to new stimuli and available information" (Marchand, 2015: 63). Place is the "active" percolating ingredient of space, a product of change and locus of specific identity within the surrounding landscape or urban context as exemplified at Pākaitore. The essential performance ingredients of place-making at Pākaitore or any marae are the discursive power of speech-making (e.g., recitations of ancestral lineage, *whakapapa*, which designate ancestral descent and a place in time as distinct from all other eras, phases, etc.) combined with specifically concentrated movement across the sacred terrain toward the meetinghouse (Rodman, 2003: 207). These performances and actions culturally energize and define the spatial field as realized through its experiential corporal-sensual properties (e.g., sun and wind on one's skin, weariness from standing, elation from listening to songs, etc.), such as the kinetic challenge in the war dance (the haka) or the slow advance of visitors toward the atea in front of the meetinghouse

(Low and Lawrence-Zúñiga, 2003: 7). In this way, a felt or sensed spatial field extends out from the body and its changing positions as it moves sequentially from spot to spot within ceremonial space. The body, then, is wrapped in sensation, and by means of senses and feelings transcends the physical limits of fences and gates to experience an entire spectrum of ritual being and awareness. The recent orientation of the field of performance studies from perceiving bodies in spaces of performance to an emphasis on "how bodies might become or produce performance spaces" (Schechner, 2006: 49) is demonstrated in this example of Maori enacting the legitimacy and authority of the Pākaitore marae with their bodies through movement, song, and chants. Furthermore, Parker-Starbuck and Mock, in their work on researching the body within the interplay between theatre scholarship and performance studies, stress the complementary positions of both the body "in" performance and the body will be pursued in the final section "*The Sensory Body*" (Parker-Starbuck and Mock, 2011: 210).

In previous chapters we also discussed the notion of "markings" or framing events, which are distinguished by beginnings and endings and isolate performance activities from the everyday (i.e., reiterating the notion of "time away from time"). One such marker is at the beginning of a marae ceremony, which starts with a *karanga*. This call disrupts the silence with a prolonged wail, thus sonically activating the stage space of the marae. It resembles expressive weeping often made real by shedding heart-felt tears and beating one's chest. The intensified sound of mourning rekindles the emotions of loss in all those present as well as awakens the "slumbering" ancestors, inviting them to be present as witnesses to what is about to unfold. Similar to Steven Feld's observation that New Guinea Kaluli funerary weeping sounds are "tuneful" and compelling (Feld, 1982: 87), the *karanga* also provokes "wept song," echoed among individual hosts and guests in response to the overwhelmingly emotive call. At Pākaitore, the ceremonial mourning sounds had different intensities and consequences. On the one hand, there was the weeping over the protracted historical loss of Maori land rights and centuries of political and racial discrimination. On the other, there was the deep grief over the death of loved ones and those lost in battle whose names were registered and recorded on the nearby war memorials. As the result of the transition of parkland into sacred space, within the invented ceremonial context of Pākaitore, these monuments became a collective graveyard reliquary, a Maori urupu, replicating the pairing of meetinghouse and cemetery on a traditional marae. Therefore, the wept songs or the sounds of the *karanga*, the attenuated call of extreme melancholy, merged the living and the dead in sonic union, underscoring and sustaining Maori belief in the omnipresence of life and death.

The belief in invoking ancestral presence resonates with Kristin Valentine's category of "implied cultural audience" in her model delineating the different roles emergent in cultural performances as explained in Chapter 2 in regard to Penitente Holy Week rites (Valentine and Matsumoto, 2001: 70). In terms of cultural performance, ancestors are very much a part of the audience as they are actively there "in spirit." Acknowledging and appealing to ancestral authority at Pākaitore had another motive as well because it was essential to legitimizing the current land claims and restoration of Maori rights to sovereignty.

The Final Act

After seventy-nine days of occupation, the police moved in and forcibly removed and evicted Maori occupants from Pākaitore/Moutoa Gardens. Since the 1995 encampment, the anniversary of Pākaitore's revival and subsequent demise is celebrated annually, thus becoming part of a ritual cycle of cultural performance. In the interval since Pākaitore was dismantled and Moutoa Gardens was restored once again to a preserve for dog walking and picnics, there have been other similar movements in different parts of the world illegally occupying public land.

For a moment, let's consider some of the implications of the temporary cultural-political existence of Pākaitore. One of the most profound effects of its subversive creation and brief existence on the banks of the Whanganui River was how the "performance of place" disrupted the "master discourse" of colonialism along with the staid "boundaries of domestication and hegemony" (Bhabha, 1994: 32). Colonialism refers to the residual effects of the British Crown's actions, which abrogated Maori rights to their land. The "boundaries of domestication" represent the layers of civic authority and governance binding Maori to a set of rules, which they do not respect. Maori cultural invention (the creation of a marae under non-traditional circumstances), and cultural intervention demonstrated the potency of decentering the established civic dominion in order to visibly insert a pocket of rebellion in the heart of a somnambulant and predominantly culturally unaware or insensitive community. Cultural performance was a key factor in Maori acting out prevailing historical grievances and revitalizing cultural identity through culturally motivated or aesthetically saturated political actions. Tents may have come down and fence posts been uprooted, but the seeds for the rebirth of a national Maori political party, which became prominent a few years later, were sown on those parklands *cum marae*. Dwight Conquergood sums up the power of performative political actions when he alludes to their associative strengths as transgressive and ripe with "contestation, breakthroughs, and change,"

> Instead of construing performance as transcendence, a higher plane that one breaks into, I prefer to think of it as transgression, that force which crashes and breaks through sediment meanings and normative traditions and plunges us back into the vortices of political struggle…. (Conquergood, 2013: 58)

Representation of a Cultural Re-enactment

The next section deviates from the focus of attention on enacted performance for its own sake to the *representation* of cultural performance as depicted in a material object, an embroidery. With the exception of the nine years spent in New Zealand, my field site in the States is in the San Luis Valley of south central Colorado, specifically the village of San Luis. My research interests center on a genre of **revitalized** Spanish Colonial embroidery called *colcha* embroidery. Colcha, in its modified contemporary version as a stitched pictorial narrative (visual storytelling) linked to a historical artistic practice, is a way to explore issues of colonial legacy and ancestral rights. For the artist, the mode of creation relies on reflexivity as a form of meditative feedback flowing between art and life's experiences.

My ethnographic examination of ethnicity and sense of place inclusive of an art historical descriptive analysis takes "culture" as the investigative subject and foregrounds the study of colcha embroidery as critical to the interplay of aesthetic and sociocultural interaction in San Luis.

In the second part of this chapter, we are going to use an embroidered pictorial narrative to discuss the Hispano ritual of *Las Posadas* as a cultural **reenactment**. Just as topography is concerned with landscape details and geological surfaces and interstices within the span of space and time, artistic visual narration as a story told in thread can be regarded as much a "matrix of related stories" anchored in place (Pearson, 2006: 17) as a weave of body, imagination, and environment. Our discussion turns from analyzing the dynamic interplay of performance components in action to interpreting the iconography (symbols and meaning) of a visualization of an ethnic folk performance. However, we are not entirely abandoning a performance-centered approach because we are not only analyzing cultural performance as the *subject* of a pictorial composition but we are also paying attention to the actual 'making' of an artwork and examining this process for its performance-related attributes. This entails scrutinizing all the kinesthetic and sensory processes of creation (i.e., embroidery needles punching the cloth, hands moving in-and-out as well as the tactility of yarn patterns accumulating on its surface and the sequence of creative decision on the part of the artist to make all this happen). In addition to interpreting symbols in an artwork, if we regard the creative process as performance, then our appreciation of the art object is further enriched. By disentangling different stages of creation, we can apprehend just how it might feel to conceive a tangible and lasting piece of art, and how this understanding broadens our perception of the object and its subject matter. This allows us to "co-experience" or reimagine the process of the creation of the object, and to begin to formulate a series of open-ended questions. In our minds, this then helps to illuminate the ins-and-outs of the artistic process as it unfolds into performance. Finally, during this serial method of interrogating the artwork (i.e., "what," "how," "why"), we can also regard object, textile, or canvas as a type of "stage space" where making, looking, interaction, and perception add to and amplify the dimensions and modalities of experience. Geographer Nigel Thrift's rather whimsical idea that "things act back"

(Pearson, 2006: 16) suggests that the creative object and the viewer are engaged in an evolving sequence of continual questioning and reciprocal action with "no end in sight."

Las Posadas

Artist Josephine Lobato's *Las Posadas* recreates an ethnically unique pageant performed in the San Luis Valley of southern Colorado during Advent. Its climax occurs on Christmas Eve (refer to image on chapter page). In her embroidery, Mrs. Lobato artistically "maps" the emplacement of a specific ritual action onto the San Luis Valley cultural landscape. The compositional format is basically a map-inspired construction of images of a cultural performance connecting the dramatic enactment of Las Posadas (the inn) in one place to other religious—theatrical sites in the local mission church circuit surrounding the town of San Luis. The central image at the heart of the composition is the Sangre de Cristo Church of San Luis, which is encircled by the satellite churches from nearby villages. Their presence indicates a religious sense of place (primarily Catholic), and the various nodes of relationship vis-à-vis the dominant role of the San Luis parish in relation to all the other village churches.

Every night Las Posadas is staged in a different village—hence the inclusion of miniaturized versions of the separate village mission churches ringing the main scene. In her embroidery, Lobato has chosen to represent the culminating event of Las Posadas as it is staged in the town of San Luis on the twenty-fourth of December, Christmas Eve. The medallion-framing device is enlarged to become the central backdrop and primary focus of this drama based on the New Testament account of Joseph and his pregnant wife, Mary, arriving in Bethlehem and seeking a place to stay for the night. Throughout this ritual cycle, each village staging corresponds to the original site of the Nativity in Bethlehem. Consequently, Las Posadas reenacts this legendary, however disappointing and exhausting, search, as community players representing Joseph with Mary mounted on a donkey go from darkened house to house accompanied by village residents and musicians, who sing traditional Spanish songs on behalf of the tired couple, importuning each householder to provide a room for the night.

The village chorus also sings the part of the residents of the darkened houses. People in the houses represent unsympathetic innkeepers, who repeatedly refuse the couple. The procession keeps moving from house to house until they reach the church, which is warmly lit with Christmas lanterns or *candelarias* and a fire in the wood stove. The symbolism of dark versus light is an ancient theme from fire rituals long associated with Winter Solstice ceremonies predating Christianity, but incorporated here into Catholic pageantry to evoke the notion of inhospitality (dark) converted into generosity, welcome, and renewal (light). When everyone finally reaches the warm church, they gather for a brief mass of thanksgiving and then either adjourn to the community hall for food and more singing or stay in the church where cookies and hot chocolate are served. This is the main script for each performance at the different villages around San Luis during the Advent season. The repetition of practice and ritual at every site throughout December binds this cultural performance to place, which, in terms of each iteration of reliving the ceremony, repeatedly "gathers experience" (Casey, 1996: 42), thus, intensifying the power and performance of locale.

Lobato depicts the celebration of Las Posadas in San Luis as a visual story in which festive wishes of goodwill for the Christmas season are exchanged and treasured. This practice fits Edward Casey's designation of "place proper" as the site of hospitality and generosity (Casey, 1996: 41). In the Valley, however, instead of the material exchanges of gifts to which Casey refers, the people of the San Luis parish reciprocate benevolent feelings for each other—an intangible exchange based on communal fellowship, amplified by collectively experiencing the magic of this traditional Spanish celebration night after night.

During Christmas season, Las Posadas is frequently enacted in Hispano communities throughout the Southwest. As a traditional festivity, however, it had vanished from the San Luis area until it was "re-invented" by Father Patricio Valdez, the charismatic priest in this area throughout the 1990s. Recreating this unique winter ritual was part of Father Pat's deliberate spiritual and cultural revitalization of San Luis, where his goal was to reactivate a sense of community and true brotherhood in this impoverished and marginalized region of Colorado. Contrary to Anthony Gidden's idea of the "evacuation of tradition" in the face of modernity (cited in Tilley, 2006: 11), Father Pat reinstated the Hispanic custom of Las Posadas within a larger cultural program in order to integrate the vitality of festivity and celebration and transform it into a deepening spiritual awareness of tradition and place. In harmony with Father Pat's vision, Josie Lobato pictorially narrates a Christmas story acknowledging a shared Spanish cultural heritage within the parameters of a renewed legacy of religious observance and citizenship. On another note, perhaps the local understanding of the theme of outsiders trying to find refuge in an inimical landscape (i.e., "no room at the inn") also plays into the collective cultural memories of San Luis descendants of pioneering Spanish settlers, who left their homeland centuries ago to relocate in unfriendly territory on a remote frontier zone in the "New World." This theme continues to resonate with the recent predicament of migrant workers far from their homes in Mexico laboring in the San Luis Valley today.

The celestial skyscape in Las Posadas is also part of the array of features of earth and sky denoting a sense of place. Near the upper border of the scene, the brilliance of the planets Venus and Jupiter, juxtaposed against the brooding dark blues and deep grays of the night sky, gives the impression of a cold frozen landscape—especially with the snow on the ground and in the hills. Temperatures on December nights in the Valley range as low as twenty to thirty degrees below zero. There were many times when I accompanied Josie on these below-freezing treks around villages during Las Posadas. My memories of that bone-chilling cold certainly underscore her creative ability to realistically capture the crystalline quality of extremely frigid air as well as the luminescence of the snow lit up by candles and starlight. To be able to master the art of embroidery in this way is an extraordinary display of virtuosity. By using layers of white yarn intermixed with strong accents of cool colors to depict the visual effects of subzero temperatures foregrounded through setting, posture, and attire, she represents a spectrum of bodily sensations with which we can empathize. These sensations encompass the textural earthly elements of snow drifts plus the sonic landscape of song in addition to intimations of sounds of boots and hooves on squeaky snow-packed ground and the numbing cold (indicated by figures wrapped in layers of clothing)—all integrated into the visual spectacle of earthly and cosmic delight. Overall, Josie Lobato captures the kinesthetic, i.e., the suggestion of movement through space, as the procession slowly and frigidly progresses from house to house. Visual communication of this type of integral knowledge of the local world as it is lived is one of the imaginative factors of place, which signifies how art and ritual are grounded in locale.

As an artist-narrator, cultural commentator, and creator of her own pictorial landscape-infused biography, Josephine Lobato would personally understand anthropologist Clifford Geertz's observation that "no one lives in the world in general" (Geertz, 1996: 262). Artistic creation—whether an artwork or performance—renders the material world of experience of body and mind comprehensible so that one may know what it means to live in a particular place and time. Josephine Lobato's artistic choice of a topographic template, studded with geosymbols (hills, town sites, and planets), indicating the legacy and meaning of place through the loci of religious observance offers a structure, a schema, upon which to position visual and emotional experiences of landscape. Space and time coming together in place add a pulse to both form and line so that the heartbeat of landscape is attuned to human presence and sensation. As an artistic genre with its own history and origin in the Spanish colonial era, Josephine Lobato's use of colcha embroidery (a skill revived from colonial times) also becomes an agent of place where the sacred and genealogical environment of San Luis's religious observances and aesthetically inspired cultural performances extend to the realm of lived experience with all its variables and contradictions. Josephine Lobato's creative work portraying a traditional cultural performance demonstrates that art engages both the mind and body in the translation of the spirit of place predicated on deeply and aesthetically knowing the land and living its history.

So far, in this chapter we have regarded cultural performance as a vehicle for cultural politics, reparation for past injustices, and cultural revival. In the next section, Callie Oppedisano writes about the spectacularly dramatic staging of the Mormon musical, *Utah! America's Most Spectacular Outdoor Musical Drama* during the late 1990s. Entertainment was more or less a byproduct of cultural performances mentioned earlier. *Utah!*, however, was primarily entertainment (or was billed as such) with a very specific "hidden" agenda of celebrating brave Mormon settlers and their vision of Eden, aesthetically reconstructing a tragic history of settlement, religious obedience, and conflict, affirming the Mormon faith, and proselytizing among audience members.

The performance of *Utah!* occurred in the only location in the world to which it could be adapted. This was a uniquely sublime site in a natural amphitheater, the Tuachan Center for the Arts, within an immense sandstone slot canyon in a remote desert region far from Salt Lake City. Locale and Mormon history are the essential ingredients of Oppedisano's analysis of theatre as a sense of place transformed by artistry and spectacular effects from floods to fires—all staged to enthrall the audience. The cast of characters is extensive and includes historical figures, polygamists, murderers, charismatic religious figures, and an actual roaring river. The play was intended to fortify one's commitment to Mormonism if a member of the Church, or consider conversion, if not. This goal aligns with Brigham Young's apocryphal quote about building a theatre as central to civilizing and converting native people, i.e., the potential of theatre as an ideal site for proselytizing. There is resonance here with the ambitions of Wanganui Maori to "convert" people to their political views through performance as staged on the Pākaitore marae. Maori also sought to acculturate pakeha outsiders to their point of view via marae ceremonies. Even the recreation of Las Posadas was motivated by the desire to rekindle spirituality in the San Luis community and renew everyone's faith in Catholicism.

The presence of ancestors in performance is another theme that reverberates throughout the chapter and becomes a focus in Oppedisano's discussion of the Mormon practice to "Redeem the Dead," understood as baptism rites for the dead. Ancestral presence tied to a certain place of performance was ceremonially manifest at the Pākaitore marae as well as at the center of the prayers and ritual actions of the Penitente Brotherhood during Holy Week, enacted each year in their highland chapels in the San Luis Valley. Pākaitore marae ceremonies and the seasonal Advent celebration of Las Posadas are cultural performances, which were ethnically and regionally anchored in the cultural landscapes of their different locales.

Terms and Ideas for Study

- Sovereignty
- Marae
- Arts revitalization

- Cultural Reenactment
- Cultural performance as transgression rather than transcendence

Questions for Discussions

- Expand on the relationship between cultural performance and the sense of place.
- How can cultural performance become a platform for cultural politics as well as revitalize culture?
- Mention the different ways cultural performance creates cultural identity.

Creative Project

Josephine Lobato chose a map as the compositional format for *Las Posadas*. One way to learn to know a space is to chart it. Choose a place such as a coffeehouse, a playground, a market, a graveyard, a gas station, a church, etc.. Create a map of the setting showing a diagram of how people occupy that space (movements, traffic patterns, objects, obstacles, etc.). Depict areas of noise, where there are certain smells, breezes, etc.. How would you indicate silence? Add any other elements which distinguish that space.

Case Study

"This is the Place, in this Wide Open Space":
Utah! America's Most Spectacular Outdoor Musical Drama
by Callie Oppedisano

Can you hear the hammers pounding?
And the desert bloomin' like the rose as it grows and it grows?
This is the place, in this wide open space,
Brigham Young said it: This is the place
'Cause God sent us here, This is the place!
Lyrics by Doug Stewart
Utah! America's Most Spectacular Outdoor Musical Drama
Paxton and Stewart, 1995: 16

The desert radiates heat and desolation as you drive farther and farther from St. George proper and make your way into the breathtakingly beautiful Southwest wilderness. Red sand and stone stretch for miles caressed by meandering rivers of black rock, a reminder of the landscape's prehistoric volcanic past. Desert cacti and brush grow low in green, gray, and brown tones, and the open blue sky is dotted with clouds that are startlingly white. A long road stretches before you, a short fence on either side so as to protect the endangered desert tortoise from becoming roadkill. All is enveloped in silence and isolation. The long black pavement twists and turns, giving an evolving perspective of the jutting and rolling horizon, but eventually draws you to its destination: the entrance of an imposing sandstone canyon formed by two 1,500-foot-high sandstone walls. You have finally arrived at Tuachan Amphitheatre, a 23 million dollar facility, which seats 1,920 people and occupies 42,000 square feet of an eighty-acre performing arts facility. "This is the place"—the place

Image 6 *The Road to Tuachan* (Photographer Unknown. Tuachan Center for the Arts, Instagram.)

where Mormonism was performed from 1995 to 1997 in *Utah! America's Most Spectacular Outdoor Musical Drama* (henceforth, *Utah!*) to an audience of over 120,000 people during its run.

This enormous semi-environmental theatre is tucked into an even more massive red slot canyon. Admittedly, the entrance is incongruently out of place with modern architectural angles and a long stepped fountain lining the lengthy staircase to the box office and gift shop pavilion, but the gates to the amphitheater bring theatregoers back into the desert. The seats are placed on naturally sloped land facing a stage covered in reddish concrete that runs imperceptibly into the similarly colored sand and stone behind it. So, too, artificial boulders mimic the textured surface of the stone walls on either side, providing a location for costume changes and scene storage that does not distract from the sense of place. In addition, the canyon itself is a stage, a performance space with undetermined depth and remarkable height.

In this brilliant environmental location, Tuacahn Amphitheatre was conceived in conjunction with the writing of an original musical by playwright, screenwriter, and St. George resident Doug Stewart. With help from writer Robert Paxton and well-known Mormon musical duo Sam Cardon and Kurt Bestor, Stewart brought *Utah!* to Tuacahn's massive stage. Aptly named, the musical entertained its audiences with pyrotechnics, live animals, and a recreation of a flash flood that brought over 60,000 gallons of water from the depths of the canyon rushing over the stage. These special effects were meant to supplement the historical account of the first nineteenth-century Southern Utah Mormon pioneers who confronted this formidable desert. The story was told (and sung) six nights a week in three consecutive summer seasons to thousands of people—the majority of them members of the Church of Jesus Christ of Latter Day Saints (hereafter Mormon or LDS Church).[2]

---

[2] The officials of the Church of Jesus Christ of Latter Day Saints have asked that the Church be referred to by its full title and not by the shortened titles "Latter Day Saints," "LDS Church," or "Mormon Church." Despite this, the abbreviated names of the Church continue to be used by the majority of Church members in academic scholarship and in popular culture. I will also use abbreviated titles of the Church throughout this case study. In addition, I will refer to members of the Church as "Mormons," "members," or "Saints" (terms Mormons typically use when describing themselves or their ancestors).

All performance is influenced and informed by space and landscape, but *Utah!* is defined by it (as evidenced by the title alone). Like the locales Mike Pearson describes in *In Comes I: Performance, Memory, and Landscape*, the location of the Tuacahn amphitheater serves as a mnemonic "for reflection upon the theory and practice of performance, upon links between topography and experience, history and identity, and as a means to elaborate the social, cultural, and environmental conditions within which [the] performance is enacted" (Pearson, 2007: xiii). The site of the Tuacahn amphitheater and its conjunctive performance of *Utah!* highlight the cultural identity of Southern Utah and its people by reenacting and manufacturing the history of both in a contemporary performance that parallels the historical struggle to claim and maintain spiritual ownership of a revered land.

Taking place in a land deemed sacred by the Mormon people, in a performance space the LDS Church Prophet and Church President blessed as a place of worship, it was hoped that Tuacahn would become a site of religious experience. Church members would faithfully work to fulfill three-quarters of the Latter-Day Saints Mission: To Perfect the Saints, Proclaim the Gospel, Redeem the Dead, and Care for the Poor and Needy. It was primarily through Redeeming the Dead that the *Utah!* experience would fulfill the LDS mission, because through that fulfillment, it was hoped that the Saints would be Perfected and the Gospel Proclaimed.

To be sure, a performative identification with past bodies is an alternative interpretation of the Mormon requirement to Redeem the Dead, a phrase usually understood as an instruction to perform baptisms for the dead (a ceremony in which living people are baptized in the name of those that have gone before). However, in her study of Mormon hand-cart trek re-enactments, Megan Sanborn Jones explains that because "identifying with the past is not just an educational enterprise, but a doctrinal imperative," Redeeming the Dead has important implications for theatre and performance. The LDS people often communicate physically with the past through frequent reenactments and rememberings of LDS Church history as a way to inspire contemporary Saints to live their faith more fully, and the process results in "complex formations of identity and ideology" (Jones, "Reliving" 2006: 113–114). This performance experience parallels that outlined by Joseph Roach in "History, Memory, Necrophilia," where he insists that there is an "urgent, yet often disguised passion: the desire to communicate physically with the past, a desire that roots itself in the ambivalent love of the dead"(Roach, 1998: 23). Yet how much more effective the identification, the physical communication with the past, in performance if that performance emerges from the landscape, from the same environment that changed lives and history? By placing audiences firmly in the location of the past, the producers of *Utah!* hoped to bring the dead more fully to life on stage in a way that would inspire present believers to live their faith more perfectly. Furthermore, presenting history in this way was considered an act of evangelization as it was hoped that this historical recreation in *Utah!* would inspire spiritual conversion in the non-believers who joined the audience to experience traditional musical theatre and in the process were engulfed in ceremonious religiosity.

The Long Road to Tuachan

When Brigham Young arrived with his party at the Salt Lake Valley in July of 1847, he famously said "This is the place."[3] It wasn't just a "stopping place." It was the Mormon Zion, the Promised Land, the place where Mormons believed they would "make the desert blossom like a rose."[4] And this "place" was not bounded by the surrounding mountain range that constrains the Salt Lake Valley. The Mormon State of Deseret (submitted for statehood into the United States of America in 1847) included nearly all of the present-day states of Utah, Nevada, and Arizona, half of California and parts of Oregon, Idaho, Wyoming, Colorado, and New Mexico. Right in the middle of the proposed state of Deseret is present-day St. George, Utah (in the Southwest corner of the state). Known in Young's time as the Dixie Mission, contemporary state boundaries have pushed St. George from a position of central importance to one of

---

[3] The oft-repeated declaration of "This is The Place," attributed to Young as the Mormon pioneers entered the Salt Lake Valley was a shortened version of his actual words, "This is the right place. Drive On" (Berrett, 1944: 378).
[4] The Mormons saw the Salt Lake Valley as the fulfillment of the prophesy in Isaiah 35:1 "The wilderness and the solitary place shall be glad for them; and the desert shall rejoice, and blossom as the rose." (KJV)

transitional importance. It is less than a mile from the Arizona border and is the topographical gateway to Southern Utah's popular tourist destinations, Zion National Park and Bryce Canyon National Park. Most importantly, St. George is also an entry-point into cultural Mormondom and is a geographic landmark of faith for the LDS people.

With something more than a sense of Manifest Destiny, the Mormon people believe that the formation of the United States was integral to God's plan for the salvation of the world.[5] So, too, was the settling of the Dixie Mission, named so because, like the American South, the settlers there were asked to grow enough cotton to supply the entire territory. From an environmental and religious perspective, the warm climate of Southern Utah was part of God's providential plan to help his people prosper. The significance of Southern Utah to this history of the LDS Church long-impressed itself on Doug Stewart, the most well-known Mormon playwright of all time. Living in St. George following his drawn-out success with *Saturday's Warrior* (the 1974 play that defined a generation of Mormons and that has been seen by over three million people), Stewart wanted to produce an outdoor performance that highlighted the Southern Utah landscape and its importance to Mormon culture and American history in a performance like the LDS Church-sponsored pageant at Hill Cumorah, New York, "only better" (Stewart, 2008: 14).[6]

---

[5] The United States Constitution is deemed a sacred document, due to the fact that, as a result of its ratification, Mormons are "able to meet today in peace as members of the restored Church of Christ" (Benson, 1987).

[6] The Hill Cumorah Pageant plays to over 30,000 people over the course of six days every summer. Staged with the help of over 700 volunteer LDS members, the production plays free to the public and is a dazzling display of spectacle. Considering the impressive financial resources that the LDS Church must utilize to achieve the spectacle at Hill Cumorah, Stewart's intentions for *Utah!* were, at the very least, ambitious. An incredible amount of money would go into the creation of the production and the theatre in which it was housed. This was in addition to the cost of the land, a secluded piece of property near Snow Canyon State Park with a narrowing canyon that provided necessary afternoon shade. Discovered by Stewart in 1993 as he was roaming the desert hills, the land was purchased and donated by Church member, businessman, and philanthropist Hyrum W. Smith, who also donated 15 million dollars to the construction of the 23 million dollar facility that would not only house the amphitheater, rehearsal space, and scene shop, but also a performing arts school and indoor theatre.

Utah! America's Most Spectacular Outdoor Musical Drama

When completed, *Utah!* would be markedly different from LDS Church-sponsored pageants, such as the one at Hill Cumorah, that are largely celebratory in nature. In spite, or because of, the importance of the Dixie Mission in the nineteenth century and its geographical isolation, there is likely no other location in Church history peppered with more controversy. The area was a stronghold of nineteenth-century Mormon polygamy. Furthermore, the Mountain Meadows Massacre occurred just miles from the Tuacahn site. Arguably one of the most tragic events in the LDS Church, the massacre occurred on September 11, 1857 when a group of Mormon men besieged the 150-member Fancher Party wagon train while they rested on Mormon pioneer Jacob Hamblin's land in Mountain Meadows. After the party had been surrounded and denied water for three days, they were promised safety and forced to give up their weapons. They were then brutally murdered, with only a handful of the littlest children saved. In addition, the Native American population in Southern Utah was also woefully maltreated and their lands seized. All of these are subjects rife with fodder for rich drama, and *Utah!* would shy away from none. Stewart and Paxton needed to look no further than Jacob Hamblin, himself, for a subject. A controversial Southern

Image 7   *The Santa Clara River Overflows in Utah*! (Photographer Unknown. Courtesy of Tuacahn Center for the Arts, Ivins, Utah.)

Utah Mormon pioneer and polygamist best known for his nebulous ties to the Mountain Meadows Massacre, he is also considered a Church hero sent by Brigham Young to make peace with (and convert) the local Native American population. His life was undoubtedly filled with extraordinary events conducive to action-packed spectacle. Furthermore—and importantly—audiences would drive by his historical home, an LDS Church-run museum, on the way to the theatre.

As the play opens, Hamblin is called by Young to help settle the Dixie Mission 500 miles from Salt Lake City. The call involves leaving his family and overseeing the hostile Native Americans in the area as well as helping to build a dam on the Santa Clara River to provide water for crop irrigation. He accepts the calling and the hardships, and, in time, he succeeds in making peace with some of the local tribes, enabling his family's relocation to the newly built fort nearby. These achievements are short-lived, however, for one of Jacob's violent Mormon brethren (Isaac) stirs up trouble with the still-hostile Native Americans and leads the Mountain Meadows Massacre. In addition, Jacob is asked to take a second wife, which causes more heartbreak for his beloved (and neglected) wife, Rachel. Jacob attempts to work through these difficulties when forty days of rain cause the dam to break and the Santa Clara River to overflow, washing away the newly created settlement and nearly killing Rachel. Thankfully, however, his wife survives, and her faithfulness in the Lord's plan inspires Jacob and the rest of the pioneers to look forward to the future success of Southern Utah and their Mormon descendants.

This action-packed plot (stuffed into two acts with roughly twenty scene changes and a cast of eighty-five characters) is supplemented with subplots and scenes involving minor characters, such as the fictional, humorously over-the-top pioneers Chester and Minerva, and the historical Mormons Brigham Young and George A. Smith, the namesake of St. George. In addition, Jesus Christ makes a brief appearance in a vision scene in which Tutsegavits, the peaceful Native American chief, confirms the Mormon belief that Christ journeyed to the Americas following his death. The performance is enhanced with music and dance numbers and elaborate special effects, many of which are reminiscent of Buffalo Bill's Wild West Show: Covered wagons are drawn from deep in the canyon down onto the stage, there are gunfights on horseback between "Cowboys

Image 8 *The Flood Scene in Utah!* (Photographer unknown. Courtesy of Tuacahn Center for the Arts, Ivins, Utah.)

and Indians," and a fort is set on fire. During the flood, 60,000 gallons of water burst forth from the depths of the canyon, forming an artificial river that rushes onto the stage in an amazing, sometimes frightening, spectacle, "washing away" the set. Other special effects include Christ's graceful descent from the sky utilizing an elaborate fly system, and the appearance of the St. George LDS Temple as it majestically rises from the canyon floor. Finally, the show concludes in a celebratory fireworks display, lighting up the canyon theatre.

"Canyon of the Gods"

Written in conjunction with the building of the Tuacahn amphitheater in that magnificent Southern Utah red-rock canyon, *Utah!* could not be staged in any other location without significant alteration to production (where else in the world could such a flood be recreated?) and a total transformation of the performance experience that began long before showtime and was tied securely to its "historical" landscape. There is no questions that attending a production of *Utah!* required a pilgrimage. For most locals, it was more of a retreat, a drive away from reminders of modernity and into a landscape of historical reflection as they went by the always-present but sometimes-forgotten reminders of their past: the preserved homes of the early settlers, including the Jacob Hamblin museum, in the outlying towns before heading into the desert wilderness cut through by the Santa Clara River and toward ancient Native American ruins and a current Native American reservation. For others, the journey to Tuacahn started in Salt Lake City, the very place where Jacob Hamblin received his "call" to go to the Dixie mission, and they would follow his path over brush-covered mountains and through desert valleys as they drove the four-and-a-half hours down I-15. Still others would arrive in tour buses from Las Vegas, with Tuacahn just one stop in history during their Southern Utah excursion. For all, however, one element of the pilgrimage was the same. The isolation of the theatre was paramount and contributed to the manufactured holiness of the performance. So, too, the journey to that isolated place was meant to contribute to the fulfillment of the production's goals. The Hamblin House served as yet another location at which to identify with the past. Passersby could revel in "place," soaking in the space between the walls his hands built and in which Hamblin lived. Moreover, the Mormon missionaries stationed at the home unwittingly became complicit performers in the impromptu production pre-show by their eager transmission of the Gospel message of the LDS Church to visitors who might stop by on the way to the theatre.

In a similar way, the marketing of *Utah!* fed into the anticipation of the performance. Hamblin's story is tied to his relationships with the Native Americans he befriended, and the desire for a performance experience that imitated the historical one was evident in the 1996 naming of "Tuacahn," a Mayan word with the meaning "Canyon of the Gods." Never mind the unnecessary insertion of an incongruent Native language (one wonders why a Paiute word wouldn't have sufficed), the naming of the canyon is significant in that it hints at the desire to create a story out of the performance experience. Prior to the arrival of Mormon settlers, Native American tribes held Southern Utah lands sacred, a holiness that Mormons would believe misguided given the polytheistic religion of the American Indian, and one that they would try to correct through

Image 9 *Christ's Descent in Utah*! (Photographer Unknown. Courtesy of Tuacahn Center for the Arts, Ivins, Utah.)

evangelization, as demonstrated by Hamblin's efforts to convert the Natives in the play.

In the same way that early Mormon settlers claimed the Southern Utah lands, deeming them sacred in their own right as occupying a special place and purpose in Zion, Tuacahn was "reclaimed" by its Mormon founders. Stewart's artistic and religious vision had reached the very highest levels of the LDS Church.[7] When *Utah!* opened, the extent to which Tuacahn was intended to surpass its function as a theatre and to serve as a place of religious work, even worship, was revealed. Before *Utah!* played to eager audiences, the theatre and the production were dedicated in a ceremony featuring the world-renowned Mormon Tabernacle Choir and LDS Church President and Prophet Gordon B. Hinckley. Hinckley arrived on stage in a horse-drawn carriage, the same carriage that would transport the character of Brigham Young in the play, an act of significance not lost on spectators, marking the sacred lineage of Church Prophets. Hinckley then dedicated the amphitheater and associated the Church with Tuacahn, comparing the red cliffs of the canyon walls to a Tabernacle, notable because the St. George Tabernacle is constructed of red sandstone bricks from the surrounding cliffs, cut and laid by early Mormon settlers—a literal deconstruction and reconstruction of landscape to assert physical and spiritual ownership of land. Hinckley then prayed, "May the fame of this place spread across the earth" and asked that the play "convey to the world, to millions of people, some true sense of what Utah, and particularly Southern Utah, means in terms of struggle and fortitude" (Hinckley quoted in Cline).

Hinckley's words were significant, as was his symbolic arrival in Brigham Young's wagon. Just as Brigham Young caught sight of the Salt Lake Valley and declared, "This is the Place," marking the geographical location that would define generations of faithful (and cultural) Mormons following the erection of a prosperous city out of desolation, President Hinckley gave his blessing to the ground, the rock, and the sky of the Tuacahn amphitheater. It was an act that established the importance of

---

[7] David Pace observed in his article, "Tuacahn's Tale" that "Utah's latest cultural oasis has a roster that reads like a *Who's Who* of the Church of Jesus Christ of Latter Day Saints." In addition to the noteworthy Mormons that attached their names to the project (including LDS Church Apostle M. Russell Ballard, Brigham Young University's then-Provost, Bruce Hafen, Mormon Congressmen Orin Hatch, Robert Bennett, Jim Hansen, and Bill Orton, in addition to then-Governor Michael Leavitt. David Pace, "Tuacahn's Tale: Behind the Scenes at Southern Utah's New Arts Complex," unidentified magazine clipping, *Utah!* Papers at Tuacahn Amphitheatre and Center for the Arts, Ivins, Utah, 28. The LDS Church was never officially tied to Tuacahn, though it did donate an unspecified amount of money to the Heritage Arts Foundation, the nonprofit organization created by Stewart to oversee the building and maintenance of the theatre.

another isolated desert location as a place from which Mormons could confidently proclaim their faith because the land contributed to and solidified their identity and God-ordained purpose. The slot-canyon, formed in pre-history and then inhabited by pagans, was given by God to his people who then used their faith, their grit, and determination to harness the imposing surroundings, to manipulate its use to spread the Gospel.

"Dust"

The events of the play are true to Southern Utah's gritty history and to Hamblin's life, albeit colored by red-dirt-stained glasses. Moreover, this representation of history on Tuacahn's stage fed into the incessant practice in Mormon culture of reliving the lives of those that have gone before in their effort to "Redeem the Dead." In the case of *Utah!* at Tuacahn, audiences didn't physically re-live the historical Southern Utah events (though most of the actors were Mormon students from Brigham Young University that were doing just that), but because of the natural landscape stage and special effects, the audiences were able to "touch" history during their performance experience.

In her book, *Dust: The Archive and Cultural History*, Carolyn Steedman refers to the "dust of history," describing it as an unconventional archive, "that which will not go away" (Steedman, 2002: 165). Tuacahn's surrounding landscape—those imposing rocks, that ever-present sand, and the unassuming desert brush—comprise such an archive, housing the "dust of history." Sitting in the audience, oppressed by lingering summer heat, straining to see through the dirt kicked up by wagon wheels and horses, and surrounded by towering walls of red stone, the landscape united past and present, breathing history into the contemporary performance. In interrogating such an archive, Steedman argues for a creative examination of history and memory, rejecting any definitive validity to historical works because history, like landscape, never tells a story for which there is an end (Steedman, 2002: 67). *Utah!* could be considered one such creative interrogation, a play concerned less with historical facts and more with certain truths as lived, imagined, and remembered.

One such example of recreated memory in the play is the representation of the Mountain Meadows Massacre. The event is unquestionably abominable, but the LDS Church insists that it must be understood in terms of the hysteria of the Mormon pioneers at the time. They believed that they were under siege by the United States Government in what was known as the Utah War and would be exterminated.[8] The Mountain Meadows Massacre was represented in the play in a way that highlighted this sympathetic Mormon understanding of the events. When the Fancher Party comes through Southern Utah, stopping, at Hamblin's request, on his land at Mountain Meadows, the overwhelming fear, intensified by isolation, of the Southern Utah Mormons is evident. It is an isolation reflected by the theatre's own remoteness. The harsh reality of the desolate landsape, making life fragile and survival precarious, is glaringly obvious. Stewart and Paxton's characters struggle with what Una Chaudhuri describes in *Staging Place* as their "victimage of location," a principal "that defines place as the protagonist's fundamental problem" (Chaudhuri, 1995: xii). Unable to flee, the landscape influences their actions and psychology. In this way, despite its belonging to a mixed genre of the American Musical and religious pageantry, *Utah!* becomes a work of "high naturalism," in which, as Raymond Williams argues, the lives of the characters have soaked into their environment" and in which "the environment has soaked into their lives" (Williams, 1977; cited in

---

[8] Just four months prior to the massacre, President James Buchanan had sent an army consisting of approximately 2,500 men to quell what he perceived as a Mormon rebellion against the United States. In response to this action, then-governor Brigham Young declared martial law. Such events contributed to the paranoia of the Mormon settlers living in Utah, as many of them had survived or been witness to the massacre at Haun's Mill, Missouri, where approximately eighteen Mormons had been killed by the Missouri Militia carrying out Governor Lilburn Boggs's Extermination Order against the members of the LDS Church (which eventually forced the members to leave Missouri). Rumors soon spread that Missourians traveling with the Fancher Party had either taken part in the Haun's Mill Massacre or had been part of the mob that killed Mormon Church founder Joseph Smith at the Carthage Jail. These rumors escalated, and by the time they reached Southern Utah, a group of Mormon leaders held a meeting to decide what to do. History suggests that some hesitant participants insisted that a horseman ride to Brigham Young for council, who sent word too late for the Mormons to let the Fancher Party through in peace. The more eager men of the group planned and organized the massacre to make it look like an attack by the local Native Americans. In addition to dressing up like Native Americans themselves, the Mormons enlisted the help of some of the local tribesmen. Following the massacre, the men took a vow of silence. Only one of them, John D. Lee, was charged and executed, and this occurred over twenty years after the event. Historians still continue to debate the massacre, why it occurred, and who was responsible. Historian Will Bagley argues that Brigham Young ordered the massacre (Bagley, 2002). Church historians disagree (Walker et al., 2008).

Chaudhuri, 1995: 6). Isaac's character is a reflection of the cruel desert, his hot-headed, delirious fury unleashed on hundreds of innocent lives as he leads other Mormon men and Native Americans in taking part in the most violent act in Mormon history.

In this theatrical interrogation of history, Isaac is driven by the pagan influences of his surrounding environment, unable to conquer himself or his surroundings with his own spiritualism, a fact that was troubling for a people looking to the faith of their fathers. The difficulty with the play's representation of the Mountain Meadows Massacre was with the writing of history into an ever-present archive of landscape. The site of the tragedy is mere miles from the amphitheater. Audiences had passed Jacob Hamblin's home on their way to the show, and many knew that if they had continued their journey a little farther, down a small stretch of lonely road, they would have arrived at the large gray stone marking the place where the bodies were laid, where, over the years, bones have resurfaced from time to time due to their hasty shallow burial.

Too many in the audience were from Southern Utah and were direct descendants of the perpetrators. An outcry arose from those who objected to Isaac's character, a fictional compilation of the historical leaders that planned and helped execute the attack. In the process of identifying with the struggle of their ancestors in order to both "Redeem the Dead" and find inspiration for their own lives of faith, it seems that some present-day Mormons were unable to imagine the fear-induced fury associated with the violence, vehemently asserting that the crime was committed sorrowfully by men valiantly suffering the Mormon requirement of obedience when they were asked by their superiors to slaughter the innocents. The geographic location of Tuacahn was, simply, too close to a home that was no longer hostile or threatening.

"Heaven's Banner" of Obedience

In Martin Lee's article, "Relocating Locations: Cultural Geography, the Specificity of Place and the City Habitus," he asserts the powerful performativity of landscape and culture, noting:

> The culture of a location…is the cumulative product of the collective and sedimented history of that location, and like any history cannot be readily

or easily dissolved but manifests a certain durability, marking its presence onto the contemporary social and physical landscape of the location in question. (Lee, 1977: 126–127)

The culture of Southern Utah Mormonism is still infused with a strong sense of obligatory "obedience," a characteristic that led to the massacre at Mountain Meadows, and there is no question that it is still infused with a sense of independence resulting from isolation. Despite the advances in communication and travel, Southern Utah has maintained its own spirit of separation, not only from secular America but also from the wider, advancing culture of the LDS Church.

In Jon Krakauer's 2003 book *Under the Banner of Heaven* he connects the Mountain Meadows Massacre to the modern-day practice of polygamy of the Fundamentalist Church of Jesus Christ of Latter Day Saints (FLDS Church), inferring that both past event and current religious phenomenon are somehow connected to their physical and cultural location. A break-off of the LDS Church, the FLDS Church is a religious sect, some argue a "cult," that was born in the early twentieth century after the Mormon Church halted polygamy and threatened to excommunicate members that continued to practice it.[9] Headquartered in a settlement some desolate miles from St. George that spans the Utah and Arizona border in the towns of Hildale (UT) and Colorado City (AZ), the group has remained mostly unmolested by law enforcement despite illegally practicing polygamy.[10] Notwithstanding, Southern Utah Mormons are uncomfortable with their presence, and there is little interaction between the two groups.

The issue of polygamy in *Utah!* best exemplifies the friction between the past and present of a location's culture. The historic Jacob Hamblin did practice plural marriage with four women, by which he fathered

---

[9] Currently, most contemporary Mormons recognize polygamy as divinely inspired but are uncomfortable discussing it and admit that the practice was not ideal.

[10] The Prophet of the FLDS Church is Warren Jeffs, who continues to lead his people as an incarcerated felon. He is serving a life sentence plus twenty years as a result of being convicted in 2011 of two counts of child sexual assault (as a result of consummating spiritual marriage with minors).

twenty-four children.[11] Armed with this unavoidable fact, Stewart and Paxton composed *Utah's* script in a way that reflects the modern assumption that historic polygamist families struggled under the weight of their task. Conflict in the play is created between Rachel and Jacob when he receives his call from Brigham Young to enter into plural marriage. Jacob is hesitant to accept the call, but this hesitancy does not override his obedience to the Church. The narrator in the play, George Smith, explains his final decision to take another wife in a lengthy monologue addressed to the audience, lightheartedly commenting on the downsides of marriage—to men—and ending with the following:

> Now you're probably wondering why I told Jacob to take a second wife, then. A wedding ring ought to take a man out of circulation, you're saying. And you're absolutely right. Except when the Lord commands otherwise, just like he did with Abraham and Isaac, just like he did with us. And when His purposes were fulfilled and He commanded a halt to the practice, we obeyed that, too. All in all, our folks handled the strains of plural marriage as well as you could expect of a god-fearing people. As long as you don't expect perfect domestic tranquility. (Paxton and Stewart, 1995: 73)

While this statement was likely meant to explain the once-commanded, now-forbidden practice of plural marriage to non-members and to reaffirm the current understanding of Mormon history to members, it also served to highlight the existence of the nearby FLDS Church. The majority of people in those communities are direct descendants of early Southern Utah pioneers who disobeyed Church orders to halt the practice. In addition, these local polygamists did attend the production, visually standing out from the crowd with their distinctive dress and hair styles that, while not meant to recreate the styles of the past, are representative of it.[12] So, like the nineteenth-century costumes of the cast

---

[11] Hamblin's practice of the Mormon principle of plural marriage eventually cost him his life. He died at the age of sixty-seven after contracting malaria in Arizona while hiding from federal agents sent to prosecute Utah polygamists.

[12] Residents from these towns frequent St. George regularly for shopping and entertainment. I personally witnessed a FLDS polygamist and one of his wives sitting in the audience when I attended the revised production of the musical in 1997.

members on stage, the male FLDS members wore long sleeved, but-
toned, and collared shirts tucked into long, belted pants (this, despite the
heat), and the female FLDS members wore long-sleeved, high-necked
patterned cotton dresses adorned with lace and ribbon, and their long
hair was swept up and back into braids of all sorts. One can only imagine
the extent to which these polygamists were better able to identify with the
performative past relived in *Utah!* Not only were they seeing their literal
and spiritual ancestors on stage, but they have more fully continued the
traditions of those ancestors through dress, belief, and sexual practice.
In addition, their pilgrimage to the amphitheater, likely embarked upon
for the same reasons as their LDS counterparts, undoubtedly added to
the performance experience for the rest of the audience. The FLDS theatregoers contributed their distinctive understanding of Southern Utah
history to the collective memory of past events, reminding those in
attendance that the future of St. George lauded in the play includes the
wider, disenfranchised Southern Utah culture, where the literal borderlands of habitation are occupied by descendants of the first Mormon
polygamist settlers.

"Come, Come Ye Saints"

Inclusive of all the descendants of Dixie Mission Mormons, the ending
of *Utah!* is unquestionably a celebratory assertion of the success of
Southern Utah pioneers. Despite nearly insurmountable obstacles, har-
nessing the Santa Clara River was achieved, a fact no more evident than
in the spectacular use of that water in *Utah!* The experience of watching 60,000 gallons of water tumult from the back of the canyon over
sand and rocks and onto the stage was breathtaking theatricality. Just
moments later, the "washed out" set is restored in the play, a reminder
of the successful persistence and fortitude of the Dixie Saints President
Hinckley spoke of in his dedication. And as the play ends, one more
icon of triumph appears: the distinctive St. George LDS temple rises
from the ground, shining luminous in the spotlight, just as the actual
temple would brightly beacon to the audience as they made their way
back into town.

     As the temple rises, so do the voices of the cast as they join together
in a swelling, affected rendition of William Clayton's "Come, Come Ye

Saints," arguably *the* most popular LDS hymn of all time. The title of the hymn is an invitation, but the lyrics transition to affirmation:

> *We'll find the place which God for us prepared,*
> *Far away, in the West,*
> *Where none shall come to hurt or make afraid;*
> *There the saints, will be blessed.*
> *We'll make the air, with music ring,*
> *Shout praises to our God and King;*
> *Above the rest these words we'll tell -*
> *All is well! All is well!*

With this final performative ode to contemporary Mormonism, a Church now over 15 million members strong, the dark desert sky erupted in fireworks, lighting up the closed canyon.

There was no question that audiences were meant to share in this final testimony of achievement. In spite of the tragedy of the massacre at Mountain Meadows and the scandal of polygamy, the performance experience at Tuacahn led spectators on a journey into the wilderness to prove that it had, in fact, been conquered, with the Tuachan amphitheater the supreme example. Any Mormon theatre artist will quote Brigham Young: "If I were placed on a cannibal island and given the task of civilizing its people, I should straightaway build a theatre for the purpose" (Young quoted in Hansen, 1976: 42).[13] With the desert slot canyon the actualization of the "cannibal island" metaphor, the creators of Tuachan had attempted to finish what Hamblin started: civilizing the vast Southern Utah wilderness. Through fiction and fancy, guiding the collective memory of the audience into a geographical archive, *Utah!* was a play as much about the present culture of Southern Utah Mormonism as it was a play about its past. And though the production may not have prompted mass baptisms of the tour groups that arrived and left the theatre on plush air-conditioned buses down that long paved road, it did succeed in helping members fulfill their mission to Redeem their Dead in the sacred isolation of Zion.

---

[13] It should be noted that there seems to be no direct source for this statement. Rather, Brigham Young's daughter, Jeannette Young Maston, reported that her father said these words in 1861.

Image 10   *Utah!'s Celebratory Conclusion* (Photographer unknown. Courtesy of Tuacahn Center for the Arts, Ivins, Utah.)

Perhaps it was this same isolation that contributed to *Utah!*'s demise. Though the first year 75,000 people attended, over the next two years numbers continued to decline. Stewart and Paxton had created the most spectacular mega-Mormon Broadway-style musical audiences are ever likely to see, but the message they wanted to send out to the world was mixed in among plot complications, dance numbers, religious pageantry, and stereotyped comic characters, making a production comprised of uneasy genres, and one that tour buses became less-inclined to book. Unable to be supported by the local faithful audience (who didn't feel the need to Redeem the Dead in this way every summer), Tuacahn switched gears in 1999, mounting *Joseph and the Amazing Technicolor Dreamcoat* and *Seven Brides for Seven Brothers* (adapted so that a flood could be used instead of an avalanche to keep the stolen daughters from their families) that played on alternate days.[14] Stewart's original vision for Tuacahn was lost, but not completely. The venue remains, for many, a sacred space, and is often used as a place of religious contemplation and worship, the most notable of which is a live Nativity every Christmas season, in which the Southern Utah desert stands in for Bethlehem, another location many believe was ordained for a higher purpose.

References

Bagley, Will. *Blood of the Prophets: Brigham Young and the Massacre at Mountain Meadows*. Norman, OK: University of Oklahoma Press, 2002.

Benson, Ezra Taft. "Our Divine Constitution." *Ensign*. November 1987, 4, The Church of Jesus Christ of Latter Day Saints.

Berrett, William Edwin. *The Restored Church: A Brief History of the Growth and Doctrines of the Church of Jesus Christ of Latter-day Saints*, 4th edition. Salt Lake City, UT: Deseret Book Company, 1944.

Chaudhuri, Una. *Staging Place: The Geography of Modern Drama*. Ann Arbor, MI: University of Michigan Press, 1995.

Clayton, William. "Come, Come Ye Saints." *Music: English Folk Song*. https://www.lds.org/music/library/hymns/come-come-ye-saints?lang=eng

Cline, Damon. "May the Fame of this Place Spread Across the Earth." *The St. George Spectrum*. Undated newspaper clipping, *Utah!* Papers at the Tuacahn Amphitheatre and Center for the Arts, Ivins, UT.

Hansen, Harold I. *A History and Influence of the Mormon Theatre from 1839–1869*. Provo, UT: Brigham Young University Publications, 1976.

[14] Tuacahn now houses a performing arts charter high school and produces Broadway Summer stock annually from June to September.

Jones, Megan Sanborn. "(Re)living the Pioneer Past: Mormon Youth Handcart Trek Re-Enactments." *Theatre Topics* 16.2, 2006: 113–30.

Krakauer, Jon. *Under the Banner of Life*. New York: Doubleday, 2003.

Lee, Martin. "Relocating Locations: Cultural Geography, the Specificity of Place and the City Habitus." In *Cultural Methodologies*, edited by Jim McGuigan. London: Sage, 1997.

Pace, David. "Tuacahn's Tale: Behind the Scenes at Southern Utah's New Arts Complex." Unidentified magazine clipping. *Utah!* Papers at Tuacahn Amphitheatre and Center for the Arts, Ivins, UT.

Paxton, Robert C and Doug Stewart. *Utah! America's Most Spectacular Outdoor Musical Drama*. Unpublished Revised Production Draft. 14 August 1995.

Pearson, Mike. *In Comes I: Performance, Memory, and Landscape*. Exeter: The University of Exeter Press, 2007.

Roach, Joseph. "History, Memory, Necrophilia." In *The Ends of Performance*, edited by Peggy Phelan and Jill Lane. New York, NY: New York University Press, 1998.

Steedman, Carolyn. *Dust: The Archive and Cultural History*. New Brunswick, NJ: Rutgers University Press, 2002.

Stewart, Doug. Interview by Callie Oppedisano. Lindon, UT. 17 May 2008.

Walker, Ronald W., Richard E. Turley, and Glen M. Leonard. *Massacre at Mountain Meadows*. New York, NY: Oxford University Press, 2008.

Williams, Raymond. "Social Environment and Theatrical Environment: The Case of English Naturalism." In *English Drama: Forms and Development*, edited by Marie Axton and Raymond Williams, 203–23. Cambridge: Cambridge University Press, 1977.

Part III

The Sensory Body

5

The Somatic Experience

Image 11 *Salad Plate* © Kevin Landis

In a sleek, austere room in a luxurious neighborhood of Chicago, four diners sit in front of a pristine white table, silent so as to not disrupt the aura that hangs in the air. Midway through a meal of twenty-one courses, a waiter brings out what appear to be pillows filled with air and sets them in front of his expectant guests. Another server swoops in and sets a plate of perfectly crafted and arranged food on the pillow and instructs the guests to eat the contents of the plate as the aromatic air in the pillows slowly seeps out and engulfs the table. The diners are overcome with the essence of nutmeg-scented fog that swirls around them and floods their senses and their taste buds dance with the tastes of pancetta, beans, and butter.[1]

In the village of Bray, England, at a restaurant called the Fat Duck, a waitress glides over to a table of diners and announces that she will be serving them a lime-flavored amuse-bouche (mouth "amusing" appetizer). She reaches into her pocket and grabs a spoon and proceeds to squirt foam into a perfectly formed orb. She quickly drops the scoop of foam into a large metal bowl that she has rolled over to the table on an elaborate trolley. The contraption is filled with liquid nitrogen and when the foamy substance hits the bowl, it instantly freezes. She fishes out the morsel and plops it directly in the mouth of the surprised diner. It dissolves in his mouth, effervescent and scrumptious. Lime fog billows out of his nose.

At a restaurant in Dubai, servers sporting expensive night vision goggles serve diners delicious courses from a 5-star chef in a dining room that is pitch-black. Patrons giggle as they eat things that they are not permitted to see, delectable treats that must be experienced without the benefit of sight. In this new way of eating, the diners are forced to assess how the loss of one sense affects the others.

A similar experience/performance occurs in Tokyo and in Berlin and Buenos Aires. In many major cities around the world, food, and the aesthetics of consuming food, has been elevated to the level of spectacle and could be described as a neo-avant-garde form of performance. Consider other real examples of unusual dining experience. Dinners hanging above a city on a crane. Dinners in the middle of a cornfield. Underwater dining experiences. These examples, of course, are wildly extravagant forms of dining and entertainment that cost large sums of

---

[1] Description of Grant Achatz's Alinea Restaurant.

money and express culture in curious ways. But they illuminate how a shared corporeal (bodily) experience can frame an important aspect of cultural performance. While at first blush these sorts of dining experiences may not seem to reach the sacral heights that we expect of ritual, you are encouraged to look closer and see the cultural needs for somatic experience and the myriad ways in which they are expressed. You may have never eaten at such an extravagant restaurant, but by this point in the book, you are primed to assess what these unusual dining conventions say about the societies that create them.

We have begun this chapter with a description of something lavish, something elitist, and something highly sensory, in an effort to convey the exciting and yet slippery area of personal somatic experience that confronts the student and anthropologist studying performance and culture. We continue to go back to our central question: Can we fully understand and *then* describe a cultural performance without having had the physical response to that performance? Is all performance understanding necessarily bound up in personal and physical response? Paul Stoller in his *The Taste of Ethnographic Things* writes of this conundrum, "Anthropologists engaged in the study of shamanism ... may observe or experience something so extraordinary that they can find no reasonable explanation for it. How do we represent these data? Should we include them in our discourse?" (Stoller, 1989: 39). From an anthropological standpoint, Stoller aptly grapples with the question, even wondering if he should use the data in his description. As performers and ethnographers, we believe that the answer is an emphatic yes, but the question and its implications require more digging.

In the coming pages, we will look at the physical as it applies to theatre and other arts and attempt to understand why body response is important in our development of a cultural performance comprehension. We will use several artists who highly favor the body and its senses in their creations in an effort to illuminate the necessity of considered somatic analysis. While you may not feel in your own body the sensations that our examples effect in their audiences, it is critical to know that one must consider the power of the somatic. Indeed, this final section completes our zeroing in on our analysis of cultural performance—from a broader look at aesthetics to a consideration of perception of space/place and geography, and finally, here, to the purely bodily. How does cultural performance physically and biologically "play" in and through our bodies and create unique corporeal experience?

First, what is meant by **somatic performance**? Simply taken, we are here referring to performative events that are developed with the body and its response as a central factor of creation. We have already encouraged you to immediately ask, "isn't all performance inextricably linked to body response?" It's a valid question and the answer is yes. But here we will see several examples that prioritize the body above and beyond the mind or the narrative structure of the event. In other words, it is good to consider if a certain performance is more interested in physical response or the structural telling of a story. Remember too, that a physical response can be a story unto itself.

If we turn to ancient Greek theatre, always a good touchstone for cultural performance in the western world, we can easily see how creators forefront the body in their performances. We are reminded of Aristotle's notion that a **catharsis** (the critical aspect of performance in Greek tragedy) happens not on the stage and in the characters but in the audience, both as a whole group and as individual beings experiencing other individual beings being acted upon. A catharsis is a purgation of emotions, and while the spectators may not physically purge, great dramas act as a way for the body to release emotion, tension, and cultural and personal anxiety. For example, seeing a horrible event on the stage, combined with the intricately woven plot and lead-up to a climax, might make many in the audience weep, and this outpouring of emotion allows the audience member to feel cleansed. There is a compelling story in theatre history that in the original production of *The Oresteia* at the Theatre of Dionysus, there were reports that the sight of the furies on stage was so frightening that it caused one pregnant woman in the audience to miscarry.[2] This evidences early and astonishing levels of audience involvement! True or not (and it's probably not), it is clear that individual and collective biological response helps create and grow community through shared experience.

---

[2] Multiple contemporary sources refer to women miscarrying at the sight of the furies. There is some debate as to whether women were even allowed in Greek theatres.

One can look at the highly physicalized kabuki theatre of Japan, with its powerful stage stomping and elaborate and sometimes terrifying makeup, to see a deep consideration of the power of the body both in the actor's experience of the role, and the way the audience is affected by the performance. Think of the performances in your life—from stage plays, to sporting events to rock concerts to monster truck rallies—and you see a deep reverence and prioritizing of the physical and its intersection with the cerebral to create a full performance experience. Already, in all of the case studies in this book, we can apply the body and its response to the efficacy of the cultural performance: the adrenaline in the hyena feeding ritual, the sensory relationship to architecture, the crisp air in the San Louis Valley, the low rumble of the cars in the Maori procession to "occupy" a city park. We will add a few more examples and discern why the body plays such a critical role in cultural performance.

We ask you to think of examples in your life in which physical response to the creation of a performance became a central focus in your experience of the performance. We start with a deeper dive into the specific use of food in performative situations from an anthropological point of view and then will look at the nature of touch and sound as it relates to the development of a somatic and shared experience. Finally, we assess how several theatrical performance practitioners in the twentieth century refocused training around the body (as separate from the mind) and a specific intentionality of relating it to the cultures in which the training was developed. The chapter concludes with a superb essay by Sean Williams about communal experience and body response to singing performance in Indonesia and Ireland.

Taste and Nostalgia

Let us return briefly to the discussions that began this chapter. Several scenarios revolving around eating and fine dining were presented. You may have found yourself wondering what this has to do with performance but, hopefully, after reading so many perspectives on cultural performance you have come to the understanding that performance can be far more than a "show." It encapsulates all of the ways that we experience cultural life, in the moment. You may be thinking that dining culture cannot be seen in the same light as many sacred rituals because it is hardly as essential as the religious festivals and services that have been assessed thus far. Resist that notion. We have now broadened our understandings such that we can assess myriad collective experience through the lens of cultural performance. What is at play in the examples that are presented above? We can look at the somatic from the perspective of the audience member or from that of the performer. Eating is a terrific entry point to this sort of exploration and it should be noted immediately that the connection between eating and cultural creation is as old as time. In fact, dining is important to cultural understanding.

We often, even unfairly, identify cultures based on what they eat: the French are defined by baguettes and brie, Americans by burgers and fries, Italians by pasta, Ethiopians by injera, the Chinese by dumplings and duck, the Thai by spicy stir fries. While we know that cultures are far from these limited defining characteristics, it is beyond question that the experience of food is an important element of cultural makeup. If the old saying, "you are what you eat" is at all true, the *way* we eat can say quite a lot about how we show, or even perform, our cultural identity.[3]

The relationship between food, culture, performance, ritual, and theatre are tight and inextricable. An easy example in American culture is the Thanksgiving dinner. As we noted with our discussion of tradition and ritual, the meal exists as a performance of culture in which traditional steps are taken each year. The **memory** or **nostalgia** of previous meals and the anticipation of future meals are wrapped up in the experience. The actual smell of the turkey cooking may unleash intense memory that connects you to your family, your community, your nation. As David Sutton aptly asks in his book on dining and anthropology, "Why food and memory? Because whole worlds of experience and interpretation are contained therein" (Sutton, 2001: 15). Whole worlds! That is a bold but

---

[3] As always, it is important to remember that all of the concepts introduced here can be further explored in full-length studies on the specific topics. Food studies in relation to anthropology and theatre are illuminated in numerous superb books and articles. We encourage you to read further on all of these topics.

accurate understanding of the power of the sensory. A communal meal, like Thanksgiving dinner, connects us through steps of repeated performative actions. There are many examples, and ethnographers have taken great pains to explore them, describe them, and illuminate what they reveal about a community. What are the powerful sensory/performative stimuli in your life?

Again, individual experience as it is encompassed in the communal is key. Just as food and the broad subjectivity of taste is personal and *in the moment,* so too is the ephemeral art of the theatre. So many theatrical performances of our past are deeply connected to and rooted in the sharing of food. From the Theatre of Dionysus, celebrating a god of revelry and wine, to dinner theatre, where an audience might take in a play while noshing on roast chicken, the inherent connection is evident. And that connection is almost ritualistic. So much so, according to the famous American company Bread and Puppet Theatre, that there actually may be no point in differentiating performance and eating. As you can see in the name of the group, food (bread) and performance (puppet) are placed together to form a cultural identity. The company, founded by Peter Schumann, created political puppet theatre on a large farm in Northern Vermont. Schumann saw food consumption and theatre consumption as centrally important to the creation of culture and community and providing a space where both could be highlighted was of great concern to him.

Descriptions of the performances at the Bread and Puppet Theatre outline how the need of food in union with theatre actually caused some difficulty for the company. John Bell has written, "Schumann baked and distributed his trademark sourdough rye bread in ever increasing amounts, finally building a ten-foot-long oven right next to his bread house on the *Circus* grounds in the early '80s" (Bell, 1999: 69). Bell goes on to remember that the food trucks and picnickers eventually began to clog up the roads on the way to the farm and actually encroached on the performance space. In this example, we see the preparation of food in the performance venue to be at least as important as the event itself. This is not unusual, and one need only look at the massive industries that grow out of professional sports as further evidence of our cultural need to combine entertainment with consumption. The "tailgate party" before college sports games often is more memorable than the game itself.

Performance creators are certainly not ignorant of the human need for these connections, and there are many examples in theatre history of an interlocking connection between physical experience of food and story-telling. In *Consuming Passions: Eating and the Stage at the Fin de Siècle*, theatre scholar Laurence Senelick writes about a performance of David Belasco's *The Governor's Lady* in 1912. In that performance, the audience was wowed when the legendary director allowed the smell of buckwheat pancakes to spill into the theatre at the moment that the actors entered Child's Restaurant, a well-known American eatery at the time. You can imagine the response. Complete delight. But why? There is something deeply gratifying about the body response to the senses of food, especially when those responses are shared. Belasco's choice became the thing of theatre lore. Senelick writes, "By taking the public inside as observers, without the obligation to be customers, Belasco was doubling their pleasure, offering them a position of privilege and investing the overlooked quotidian with semiotic significance" (Senelick, 2005: 48). The "over-looked quotidian" is an excellent description from a theatrical standpoint. The quotidian (the everyday) is in fact the thing that made the experience so memorable. Food as a performative element, indeed food as a central element of many rituals, makes sense because it is universally understood and necessary for survival. The somatic also provides a sense of immediacy; a sense that the experience is of the moment. It is the same impulse of the theatre.[4]

There was a famous theatre director in France named André Antoine who used real sides of beef on stage in his 1888 play *Les Boucheres*. The audience was completely enthralled and Antoine himself recounted that the real beef created a "sensational effect" (Henderson, 1971: 52–53). It may seem a quaint response, but the story well illustrates the very real power that the immediacy of the somatic brings to a performative event. It gathers the viewers together powerfully as a community partaking in a shared experience. When we open ourselves up to the world of food in performance, we begin to see that there

---

[4] For a longer assessment of the performance of theatre and its relation to food and the avant-garde see: Landis, Kevin "Culinary Pataphysics: Food, Theatre and the Historical Avant-Garde," *Gastronomica: The Journal of Food and Culture*, Vol. 14, No. 2, Summer 2014, 46–55.

are connections in almost every culture. The hyena feeding that began this book, of course, highlighted a meal. Feed the hyenas dinner lest they make you *their* dinner. One might also identify religious ceremonies and their focus on food in the milieu of performance; from the taking of the Eucharistic host and wine to the offerings to the gods in Balinese Hindu ceremonies to the often extreme imbibing at Brazil's Carnival.

Here we have looked at food as one way that performance and ritual can connect to a specific audience at a specific time, inviting a community into a communion with the performers and indeed with each other. Food, and the immediate associations that the various tastes create, can and does have powerful dramatic effect. We see clearly with these examples that any ethnographic study of performance needs to look deeply at the sensory components of the performance. In theatre, too often we refer to what we see and what we hear while taking in a play. As ethnographers and performers, we have to be careful not to only favor the ocular and text-based approaches to understanding an event. With food, we see that the somatic experience of a performance is tied to smell, taste and thus, by extension, cultural memory.

Sonic Intentions

Sound and hearing should not be ignored or taken for granted either in an understanding of somatic performance. It is often noted that in Shakespeare's time people would say that they were going to "hear a play." Today it is de-rigueur to say we are going to "see a play." In theatre, there has been a shift to a favoring of sight, of spectacle in the reception of the performance event. But, if we play out our food example a bit more, we may note that many restaurants spend a great deal of time considering what the diner will hear while eating her dinner. The Fat Duck Restaurant, mentioned above, is well known for its popular dish *Sounds of the Sea*. As the diner consumes a fish dish he is given an iPod, stuffed in a shell, that has sounds recorded from a nearby seashore. At the restaurant Koks, in Tórshavn on the Faroe Islands, the chef has hired a local composer to create a soundscape that goes along with the entire meal. The food is elaborate and painstakingly related to the local culture and its flora and fauna—little comes from the mainland. So too, all of the sound is "foraged" from the hillsides and villages of the maritime community. As diners sit at tables overlooking a foggy bay, food arrives that looks like the moss-covered hillsides just outside, and the sounds of a fog horn or a seagull can be heard from the speakers that surround the table.

These restaurant-based examples show many of our identified elements of cultural performance, from the specific analysis of aesthetics (skill, audience, performer/creator) to the use of geography and architecture to, finally, and most obviously here, the detailed consideration of taste, sound, and smell. The dinner has allowed for a very complete sensory experience. But to do that, the sonic environment needed to be highlighted and it is well for us to remember how important that is. In your anthropological and performance careers, you must gauge how the use of sound affects the impact of the art you are creating or critiquing. If the quality of voice has not been thought through in a performance of *Romeo and Juliet*, what is the impact on an audience who has come to "hear a play"? Likewise, if you describe a cultural performance to a friend, perhaps your hike to the Tiger's Nest Monastery, you are missing a great deal if you forget to convey the sounds of the flags flapping in the wind or the rattle of the prayer wheels that the pilgrims spin.

This is certainly not lost on cultural ethnographers and musicians, especially those with acute and attuned sense of sonic environments. While this study is not specifically focused on music traditions in cultural performance, a couple of examples of sonic intentionality related to community and culture are helpful. The twentieth-century avant-garde musician John Cage, in particular, identified the importance of listening in the assessment of one's surroundings. He wrote: "Wherever we are, what we hear is mostly noise. When we ignore it, it disturbs us. When we listen to it, we find it fascinating. The sound of a truck at fifty miles per hour. Static between the stations. Rain. We want to capture and control these sounds, to use them not as sound effects but as musical instruments." (Cage, 1961: 3). Famously, Cage created the piece *4'33"* a work of music that instructed the musicians to *not* play their instruments for four minutes and thirty-three seconds. By doing this, Cage was not meaning to create a piece of silence, rather by encouraging the listeners to hear the sounds of their surroundings, to become more attuned to sounds that are often ignored. Thus, **nonintentional** or aleatoric (sounds left to chance) music could be realized.

What, you might ask, does this have to do with the somatics of performance? The composition described above highlights the need to ponder the specificity of the unique experience. Cage's *4'33"* forces site-specificity, requiring bodily awareness and connection with participants that is, necessarily, *in the moment*. The work highlights a modern appetite for improvisation, the founding principles of jazz, a form dedicated to culture, dance, environment, and embodiment. Jazz demonstrated a need for improvisation and deeply influenced American music in the last century. Further, like many music traditions, it helped bond a group of people in an engagement with artistic and cultural creation: in this case, the African American community. Identifying trends, the computer music pioneer George Lewis has written, "I would identify improvised music as a social location inhabited by a considerable number of present-day musicians" (Lewis, 1996: 110). Here, the juxtaposition of "social" and "location" is noteworthy as it identifies forms of expression that are more fully connected to bodily presence and co-presence rather than a focus on a predetermined musical narrative. While jazz and Cage's groundbreaking work were clearly important, they are reflective of a twentieth-century zeitgeist; musicians and other artists were grappling with many of the same considerations. Cage was certainly influenced by the principles of the *dada* movement of the early twentieth century, a trend that encouraged haphazard arrangements and art forms that had to be reacted to in the moment. Other artists from across disciplines have found similar ways to access corporeal specificity in relation to art analysis.

Take, for example, the Deep Listening Institute in the United States. Founded by Pauline Oliveros, a noted musician and professor, **Deep Listening** has become a field of study in many arts programs. Like Cage before, Oliveros espoused the need for people to be more attuned to the sounds that surround them and insisted that there is a great difference between **hearing** and **listening**. She wrote, "I have learned that hearing can be measured and that listening still remains mysterious and is particular to individual perceptions and interpretations" (Buzzaetém, 2012: ii). Again, when we look at different ways to analyze art and cultural performance, it is noteworthy that so many artists and ethnographers, from varying fields, go back to central themes and considerations. Oliveros rightly noticed that the way an "audience member" listens is varied, nuanced, and unique. Thus personal sonic response has to be deeply felt.

Theatrical Co-Presences

To further illuminate the unique personal experiences as related to the assessment of a cultural performance, think about the following description. Several years ago, this author visited a farm on the beautiful island of Sardinia to partake in an acting workshop with Rena Mirecka, the former lead actress in a company headed by Jerzy Grotowski, one of the most famous western theatre practitioners of the twentieth century. The goal was to gain a greater understanding of Mr. Grotowski's work and, perhaps, to become a better actor. As you will read, the experience was something quite apart from any traditional acting workshop. The following are excerpts from my journals from the experience, and reflections after I arrived home:

> I was the first to arrive and was met by Mirecka and her assistant, Martín at the door. Mirecka, in white flowing vestments, carried a smudge stick and began cleansing my aura, passing the smoldering bundle of white sage around my body before grabbing me in a tight embrace. After a moment, I was free to go to the inner part of the work room where an altar was set in the center with candles, a rose, a Buddhist bell and rattle. There were mats for the five participants of the workshop in a tight circle around the altar. After the smudge ceremony was finished we joined hands and greeted the "maestro" in the sky and asked for his blessing and help. The ceremony that first day lasted four hours and included prayers, meditation, stretching, salutations to the sun and moon, improvisational singing with accompanying instruments and reverent and solemn breaks for tea and polish pancakes (again, food consumption!).

> Mirecka was clearly in a heightened state during sessions in the studio, and through her utter force of convictions, brought us into that world over the course of our time there. Mirecka's face was often intensely twisted in a

complex and impassioned emotional trance. She did not speak, but rather sang or intoned her prayers and instructions. Lessons from exercises were summed up in deeply enigmatic statements repeated in Italian, English and Polish "Go! Go! Go! Go through the gate. Go... gooo... The Way is long." The participants held candles high in the air while listening to Mirecka offer salutations to the great powers of the north and south.

Certainly you noticed that the experience was described as an acting workshop and yet the accompanying journal entry paints a picture of something akin to a religious ceremony, with the smells of sage smudge sticks, embraces, ceremonial food offerings, and the ringing of chimes and bells. And while, in actuality, Mirecka would perhaps acknowledge that what she does is no longer theatre in any traditional sense, here it is important to see that the somatic experience has primacy. As a theatre scholar and practitioner, I can describe the experience, and while it may evoke some feelings for you, it is impossible to experience what I felt in the Sardinian foothills.

Let us take a step back, for Ms. Mirecka is perhaps an endpoint in this brief consideration of somatics as it relates to cultural performance. Her teacher, Grotowski, was himself a central figure in western theatrical history and actor teaching methods. In the mid-twentieth century, Grotowski found himself dissatisfied with theatrical training that insisted on textual awareness and mind-centric acting. He believed that theatre, in total, had religious and spiritual connotations and that essential performance must be connected to community communion, spirituality, and bodily awareness. He wrote "The theatre, when it was still a part of religion, was already theatre: it liberated the spiritual energy of the congregation or tribe by incorporating myth and profaning or rather transcending it" (Grotowski, 2002: 22). Theatre, as he understood it, had always been linked to religion. In fact, he referred to his performers as the "holy actor," a conduit between the audience and the spiritual world of the performance. To create an actor who could completely embody that critical role in the spiritual community communion, Grotowski developed an array of actor training methods that emphasized the power and complexity of the human body. His *plastiques* training, forced the actor to deeply consider every joint and every muscle in his body as critical and worthy of investigations. Many hours might be spent observing the joints in the index finger and the various ways in which the actor might articulate them. In these ways, some of the training techniques of Grotowski and his followers can barely be distinguished from exercise and physical labor.

As briefly described in the first chapter, eventually Grotowski came to understand that the somatic experience of his methods, in and of themselves, became the performance and, thus, any traditional audience/performer relationship seemed somehow wrong. With his advent of paratheatre, Grotowski fully illustrated the necessity for everyone in the performance space to have the physical sensations of performance. There need not be distinction between audience and actor; they were all the same. No longer could someone stand back and observe the performance; one must embody the performance. He wrote, "The core of the theatre is an encounter. The man who makes an act of self-revelation is, so to speak, one who establishes contact with himself. That is to say, an extreme confrontation, sincere, disciplined, precise and total— not merely a confrontation with its thoughts, but one involving his whole being from his instincts and his unconscious right up to his most lucid state" (Grotowski, 2002: 56–57). The whole body experience is essential to a performance.

You might think that this concept of paratheatre is a bit strange, especially if you are used to a traditional form of theatre that you might find on Broadway or the West End. But bodily connection was not unique to the theories of Grotowski and, as we will see shortly, these sorts of methodologies actually have profound impact on the performances you see in traditional performance venues—creating a link between cultural performance and traditional theatre.

When we look at performance as a somatic engagement, we necessarily need to credit the French theatre pioneer Antonin Artaud. While his book *The Theatre and its Double* should be required reading for any theatre scholar, actor, or anthropologist, it is important to note here that he believed that an "audience" must feel accosted by a performance, that it should find itself in a swirl of danger and sensory overload. In his writings, he aggressively described theatre as a painful enterprise both for the actor and for the audience member, a place where "… violent physical images crush and hypnotize the sensibility of the spectator seized by the theatre as by a whirlwind of higher forces" (Artaud, 1958: 83).

If that weren't enough to stomach, he also wrote, "A violent and concentrated action is a kind of lyricism: it summons up supernatural images, a bloodstream of images, a bleeding spurt of images in the poet's head and in the spectator's as well" (Artaud, 1958: 82). It is intense and corporeal language from a theatre director, but you would not be alone if you thought that there was something in his description that sounds almost ritualistic. Artaud was, in fact, artistically obsessed with shamanic cultural performance.[5]

While Grotowski and Artaud indeed need (and have) entire books for analysis, they should be familiar names to you since they well exhibit a twentieth-century need to reconnect the theatre with the somatic experience that was so often tied to ritual and religion. There is a common tension in theatre and cultural performance between story and experience and we have seen several examples of artists and cultural performers negotiating the two needs. Late in my workshop with Rena Mirecka, in an interview in a room near her studio, she turned to me and said, "Sometimes, it's possible ... to give information if a person can listen in between the words. If they can feel the vibration of the language."[6] While the context of the comment is not important here, the juxtaposition of the words "information" and "vibration" is necessary to understand. Mirecka said that my understanding of the information that I was gaining in the workshop came directly from vibrations in language. That is, comprehension comes from a deep listening and assessment of the physical feeling that I hear.

This may seem a bit bizarre, as we are now saying that we should feel sounds! But, indeed, it is not, and the sensory overlap is something that many cultural performers understand innately. There are many artists in western theatrical and dance traditions who speak similarly; to vibrations, to the interconnectedness of the sensory to performance. The

---

[5] It is good to pause here and note that Grotowski and Artaud, like many other artists, sometimes are accused of **cultural appropriation**, since they seemed to have a desire to explore or recreate the performances of cultures outside their own, sometimes inaccurately. Cultural appropriation in art certainly falls under the heading of "ethics" and is important to consider and discuss the pitfalls and nuances in your classes and studios.

[6] Quotes from Rena Mirecka from interview with the author in Santa Maria de Palma, Sardinia, 19 June 2008.

early twentieth-century expressionist dancer Mary Wigman was said to often refer to the *vibrato* in her body, a sense of vibratory movement that possessed her as she danced (Ruprecht, 2015: 32). At nearly the same time, a whole field of artistic analysis and practice developed called **synesthesia**, in which colors were said to blend with sound and sounds had almost physical qualities that plucked the strings of the heart and created inner vibrations. In his manifesto on the topic, *On Stage Composition*, Wassily Kandinsky wrote, "This final goal (knowledge) is attained by the human soul through finer vibrations of the same" (Knopf, 2015: 156). This is a remarkable statement from a remarkable artist and this, in effect, highlights all of the points in this chapter. When studying cultural performance, we have to continually be aware of that *thing* that live performance implies: the bodily co-presence of spectators or listeners and performers or creators. This is a central consideration, especially in a digital age when we can often see a performance online or on our smart phones. The question that inevitably comes is this: is something lost when the corporeal presence is removed from the place of cultural performance? Is the somatic response in the audience necessary in our analysis of performance? You no doubt have some thoughts on that and the questions at the end of the chapter will allow you to further explore these ideas.

We return to the ideas that began this book. How does the performance illuminate the culture that creates it? How do we, as anthropologists and performers, understand the goals of performance vis-à-vis the community? Finally, the cultural performance hopes for a total experience, where audience and performer commune in a shared space. The British theatre group Punch Drunk has recently recognized the theatrical power of allowing audience members to become a part of the performance, by donning masks and letting them wander around the performance spaces. Juxtapose that sort of performance with what the legendary Japanese director Tadasha Suzuki has said about body and communal relationships: "In my opinion, a cultured society is one in which the perceptive and expressive abilities of its people are cultivated through the use of their innate animal energy" (Suzuki, 2015: 63). Suzuki became renowned for his unique training system that focused on the actor's body as a center of energy. Through the use of foot stamping and exhausting exercises, his style made actors, and indeed everyone viewing the work, keenly aware of the body as the focal point of the expression of culture. There is an undeniable relationship between the power of the body (even animalistic), somatic awareness, and the creation of performances that tie cultures and communities to each other, to strengthen bonds and feel a sense of shared experience. It should not be lost on the reader, that the title of Mr. Suzuki's collection of theatre writings is *Culture is the Body.*

The following case study by the ethnomusicologist Sean Williams outlines Indonesian *tembang Sunda* singing in comparison to the Irish music tradition of *sean-nós*. Williams' work is an evocative encapsulation of many of the themes that we have introduced in this chapter, from the importance of presence in the assessment of a cultural performance, to considerations of bodily engagement in culture making, and the acknowledgment of shared social needs from around the world. It is worth noting that Williams has also edited a popular book called *The Ethnomusicologists' Cookbook* (2006) that includes recipes from many cultures, articles about the specific societies represented, and recommended listening. With that book, the relationships between food, sound, art, and cultural creation come to life, clearly demonstrating the need for anthropologists to fully embrace the body while writing about culture. As you will see, Williams writes in a personal style, demonstrating her need to bring personal experience to bear in an analysis of the art of another culture.

Terms and Ideas for Study

- Food as performance
- Somatic performance
- Catharsis
- Memory
- Nostalgia
- Sound

- Nonintentional music
- Deep listening
- Hearing vs. listening
- Cultural appropriation
- Synesthesia

Questions for Discussions

• Is the somatic response in the audience critical in analysis of performance?
• What is the difference between witnessing a performance in person versus on your smart phone?
• Describe a dining experience in which you shared with others an experience that could be analyzed through the language of culture and performance.

Creative Project

Create a performance that may be sensorially experienced in different ways. Perhaps part of the class watches the performance from a remote location via Facebook while others in the class witness it in person. Maybe some of the audience members are given different sensory stimuli—headphones to listen to sounds concurrent with the performance or even things to taste and smell. Perhaps some are only allowed to hear the performance.

Be creative when assessing and creating different audience's somatic response to your work. Discuss with the class how individual response affected the telling of the story or experience of the work.

Case Study

The Singing Body as a Fieldwork Site

by Sean Williams

The performance traditions of *sean-nós* (Ireland) and *tembang Sunda* (Indonesia) each encompass a local form of sung poetry dating back several hundred years. Each vocal tradition exemplifies local ideas and ideals of connection to the natural world, emotional grounding (and often heartache), and modeling best practices of behavior and creativity. As a student of ethnomusicology, I conducted fieldwork at home and abroad in both traditions, studying with internationally acknowledged masters of each genre. Joe Heaney (1919–1984), the great Irish *sean-nós* singer and storyteller, lived in the United States during the final years of his life and was a visiting artist when I was a graduate student at the University of Washington. Euis Komariah (1949–2011), the finest exponent of *tembang Sunda* in West Java, made dozens of recordings, taught many students, and represented Sundanese aristocratic traditions to people all over the world through recording and tours; I studied with her in person for two years and from a distance for more than twenty years. This case study has as its focus the surprising and effective connections between these two very different traditions, and the ways in which ethnographic fieldwork and kinesthetic performance practices can connect the body of the fieldworker with the field, and connect the singer with the community. In being *both* an ethnographer and a performer, I tried to locate what my teachers were doing through the medium of my own body and my own attentive presence.

In the case of both Ireland and Indonesia, the process of musical participation through ethnographic fieldwork, followed by the practice of performing and teaching both of these genres in the United States and elsewhere, has led me into a feedback loop of communication across communities and language barriers. One of the many connections between the two traditions—beyond remarkable similarities in lyric content, performance style, audience reactions, and pedagogy—has been the centrality of physical performance practices within a community of like-minded people, most of whom perform the same songs and have known the songs their entire lives. Performance for a disengaged, paying public is an anomaly in these two musical contexts, where there is no sense of "onstage." It is much more common to sing in the physical company of others who already understand the songs, their contexts, and their histories as well as their best-loved exponents. An outsider to the tradition, as I was (twice!), must approach such a setting with the expectation of singing in front of knowledgeable insiders again and again, from the very first day to the last, as part of what it means to do ethnographic fieldwork.

Parts of this study include my own background as a vernacular (non-classically trained) singer, windows into "the field" of rural Ireland and urban Indonesia, and the ways in which two very different traditions bear similarities in spite of their separation. As part of this examination of cultural performance, I want to clarify the point that knowing the notes, rhythms, and languages of sung poetry is a fraction of *knowing* at its deepest levels. If I sang a Sundanese or Irish song with only the right language, the right timing, and perfect pronunciation, the local result would be chaotic laughter because everything about my performance would be wrong. Cultural performance goes below the surface of notes and rhythms into the very body of human communication.

Singing—as one of the earliest activities humans experience in their lives—is a very powerful form of communication, and it is widely perceived as an essential tool in the socialization (and emotional development) of infants and young children. Infants begin to produce recognizably musical intervals (called *vocal contagion*) after about six months of age, and they react strongly to a parent's singing voice quite early on (McDonald and Ramsey, 1978: 26).[7] By the time a child is a young teenager, the overwhelming power of social group pressure can lead to the silencing of the singing voice except through school choirs or musical theater. Few adults sing after high school. But of those adults who sing—whether in church choirs or at adult music camps or even in the Virtual Choir (an online choir comprising thousands of people from all over the world[8])—there is great connectedness across lines of race, class, and gender.

In a chilling but very effective comparison, Thomas Turino explored the effects of group singing on people in both Nazi Germany of the 1940s and the American Civil Rights Movement of the 1960s (Turino, 2008: 189–224). In each case, very different people who sang together came

---

[7] I can attest that this is true. When my daughter was seven months old, rather than waking me up at sunrise with her customary wails of despair, hunger, or boredom, she woke me up with the sound of her singing voice. Considering that most of our interactions had been conducted with song, it was no surprise. It was, however, a joyful relief to me, and one I've never forgotten.

[8] I am a member of the Virtual Choir, started by composer Eric Whitacre, together with thousands of others from all over the world. Each one of us records a video track of our part or parts (soprano, alto, tenor, and bass) and posts it online, at which point it is joined with the recordings of thousands of others. See http://ericwhitacre.com/the-virtual-choir/about/ for the resulting videos; I am in about half of them. See also a subset of the Virtual Choir (the Virtual Choir Friends) performing an arrangement of Vienna Teng's incisive "Hymn of Acxiom" (about data mining online); there are 58 of us: www.youtube.com/watch?v=QKkv4Z1aXaU/.

to be of like mind. "Songs have the capacity to condense huge realms of meaning in an economical form through layered indexical meanings as well as the juxtaposition of varied ideas as indexical clusters without the requirements of rational ordering or argument" (Turino, 2008: 218). In other words, you don't need to know everything that a song refers to (whether through its lyrics, its melody, or its other musical or contextual features) to automatically create relationships between all those points referenced by the song. It is often the community itself that depends on the connections provided by all of those people breathing and singing together.

The two genres I studied are solo traditions, rather than traditions involving large groups of people, but they are done within a community of insiders. When doing ethnographic fieldwork with a shared repertoire, in which all members of a community of singers know the song or are at least closely familiar with the genre, it quickly becomes clear that part of your own work as an ethnographer is to know not just the songs, but everything about the songs' context and history that you can find out. Being "in tune" with the other singers and prepared to offer a song at a moment's notice is a part of both of these traditions, but it is often the non-musical elements that can reveal the most about the song as well as the singer; much of the skill lies in reading between the lines of the melody.

You Are Always in the Field

As a pretty good singer with no formal training in any of the western classical traditions, I was raised on gory murder ballads (thanks to my Kentucky-born mother), African-American rhythm and blues (thanks to the rainbow neighborhood of my Berkeley childhood), and the Beatles (thanks to the era of the 1960s). Everyone I knew (in my family, neighborhood, and school) sang along with the radio and with LP recordings. Singing was the norm, not the exception. In high school, I was part of an all-girl bluegrass band, and I joined the advanced small choir called the Madrigal Singers; as part of that small group over several years, I learned to read music, perform publically, sight read easily, and connect with other singers in non-spoken-word ways. At folk festivals, I found myself spending hours at the loud and proud gatherings of Sacred Harp "sings" (a type of American folk choir harmony singing tradition using printed sacred texts, strung together in book form as a figurative "harp"). To this day, that experience of unaccompanied group singing has been among my most profound, and it taught me that cultural performance goes beyond knowing just the notes and rhythms. Being able to quickly learn to alter my voice so that I blended with others was an important skill that stood me in good stead in both Ireland and Indonesia and their solo singing traditions because I was adapting my voice to a very different sound.

After I went to graduate school and had significant contact with singers from around the world, everything changed in my mind. I learned immediately that of the thousands of musical contexts opening up for me opera and the western vocal tradition of solo classical singing would simply not be among them. The rest of the world was, however, fair game because of not being limited to one acceptable standard of performance practice. Instead, I could learn to sing in a tonal language, or sing outside the boundaries of the 12-tone chromatic scale, or even learn five different ways of using vibrato in a melody without having a (figurative) door slammed in my face because of how I sounded when I began trying to learn a new genre.

Part of learning to sing in front of others is an act of transcendence: You leave your physical and emotional comfort zone, and allow something from deep inside your body—your breath—to come out in tune, at the right time, in the right language, and with exactly the right tone color, or so you hope. As soon as you do this, you are open to being judged (and found wanting) by others, and your private identity becomes subsumed by your public one. Singers—so often judged simultaneously on their voices *and* their bodies—contend with so much potential for humiliation that the joy can be overwhelmed by shame at times. The good news, even perhaps the best news, of this experience is that learning to sing with and in front of others is excellent training for doing fieldwork, because your body and your singing voice are your field. As you prepare yourself for "life in the field" (whether it's at college, in another country, or on a stage), you learn about shifting roles, dealing with potential adversity, and the transcendence of understanding information in ways that reading and writing cannot approach.

As part of my graduate work at the University of Washington, the Ethnomusicology Division there brought in musicians from all over the world to give us graduate students practice in learning musical traditions from people for whom English was not necessarily their first language. I had the lucky opportunity to work with the famous Irish *sean-nós* singer Joe Heaney of Carna, Connemara. He lived in Seattle for the last several years of his life, and as the only one of his students with the ability to speak and understand the Irish language, I learned many of his oldest and most treasured songs *as Gaeilge* ("in Gaelic"). I worked with him several times each week, over the summers when he was in town, and up until his untimely death in 1984 from emphysema. My work with him turned into my master's thesis. Decades later, I co-wrote a book about him titled *Bright Star of the West: Joe Heaney, Irish Song-Man* (2011) with an Irish friend and scholar/singer, Lillis Ó Laoire of the National University of Ireland at Galway.

As I proceeded on to the Ph.D., I chose the Indonesian vocal tradition of *tembang Sunda* in West Java to explore for my dissertation research. I received a Fulbright-Hays Doctoral Dissertation award, which enabled me to live in the city of Bandung (pronounced "bahn-doong"), West Java for two years. I studied with Euis (rhymes with "Joyce") Komariah, but also worked with a number of other local singers in the region as I explored the finer points of how to sing in that style, what the songs meant, and what the historical and cultural context of the tradition was all about. My first book, *The Sound of the Ancestral Ship: Highland Music of West Java* (2001) was the result of the research of those two years and several more fieldwork visits afterward. I have taught singing traditions both within and outside of the university setting, where I make my living as a college professor of ethnomusicology.

Yes, the sounds of *sean-nós* and *tembang Sunda* are different from one another. The place where these two very different traditions connected, however, was in my field-working body. When I arrived at the home of Euis Komariah in 1987 in West Java, I had some skills in speaking Bahasa Indonesia (Indonesian), and I had already lived in East Java for several months. I introduced myself, said that I was in Bandung to study *tembang Sunda*, and that I hoped she would teach me. There was a flurry of conversation in Sundanese, the local language, which I did not yet understand. Then she turned to me, smiled invitingly, and said (back in Indonesian), "Sing for me." I was flummoxed! I didn't know any Indonesian songs yet (which, in hindsight, shows a shocking lack of preparedness on my part). I started talking about my Irish heritage (er, mainly Swiss and Welsh, but never mind), and how what I was going to sing was a "song of my ancestors." I then gave them a precise translation, and sang this song, "The Nobleman's Wedding," which I had learned from Joe Heaney in 1982:

I once was invited to a nobleman's wedding
All that were there were to sing just one song
The first one to sing was the bride's former lover
The song that he sang was "Of Days That Were Gone."

"How can you sit at another man's table?
How can you drink of another man's wine?
How can you go to the arms of another
You being so long a sweetheart of mine?"

This lady was sitting at the head of the table
Hearing these words, she remembered them well
Hearing those words, she no longer could stand it
It was down at the head of the table she fell.

Sighing and sobbing she arose from the table
Sighing and sobbing she went up to bed
And early next morning when her husband awakened
He went to embrace her, and found she was dead

"Oh, Molly, lovely Molly, oh cruel-hearted Molly
Your love and my love did never agree
When first I separated yourself and your Johnny
It was then I separated the bark from the tree."

By the time I was nearly done singing the song, complete with all of
its ornameand twists and turns, there was a crowd of two dozen people
in the room, and I could hear people shrieking in high-pitched voices

outside to "Hurry up! There's a white girl singing!!!" even as I finished up. There was another flurry of discussion as I sat there, clueless, thinking about how poorly I must have sung. The fact that some of them appeared to be *frowning* made the waiting even worse. Euis Komariah then turned to me and calmly said, "We have that same type of song ... the subject matter, the ornaments, the breathing. When can you move in?" In 2010, Euis Komariah and I were remembering that day, and she said, "I knew that you could learn to do this because of the way you held your body when you sang. You sat up straight, but you were calm and focused and you were in a different place ... the place of your ancestors. You were paying attention to them and they were singing with you." As I learned during those two years of intensive fieldwork that followed as well as the years afterward, the two genres of *sean-nós* singing and *tembang Sunda* had much in common. Euis Komariah was right. I was in "the field" in Indonesia, but I brought "the field" of Ireland with me in my singing body.

Developing Community through Singing in Connemara and West Java

There is a type of village within a village in both the rural communities of Connemara, in the west of Ireland, and the huge city of Bandung, in the west of Java. Within the larger community, many people do not sing. In addition, some people never even think about the songs or the act of singing, except to engage in pop song sing-alongs in the car or with friends. The first "village" in question, then, is the group of people not only aware of but also familiar with the songs or the genre of singing *sean-nós* in Connemara and *tembang Sunda* in Bandung. In each place, the numbers would include about a thousand people; the "village" is about the same size even though the context is quite different. Within that group of a thousand people, certain singers are known for their exceptional skills. These singers might have a very large repertoire of songs (numbering in the hundreds), or be known for the lineage of teachers they learned from, or have a particularly fine vocal timbre (tone color), or they bear a special skill in regard to vocal ornamentation/breath/intonation. These people constitute the village within the village. They are fine, established singers, and everyone knows it and looks to those people at the moment when a song is called for. As important musical events revolve around the presence of musical authority figures, the physical presence of their singing bodies is a reminder to all that they are the keepers of sung history, and that the sung spiritual and emotional histories they share cannot, and will never be, transmitted through the written word.

In each case, the people who sing these songs speak a minority language: Irish/Gaeilge and Sundanese/Basa Sunda. These languages constitute a further insularity of singers; in Ireland, the Irish speakers are separate from the English speakers, while in Indonesia, the Sundanese speakers are separate from the (majority) Javanese speakers as well as the (nationwide) Indonesian speakers. Because the oldest and best songs are couched in the most elevated level of these minority languages, being a singer of *sean-nós* or of *tembang Sunda* carries implications of political activism (resistance against the hegemony of the nation's majority), and simultaneous representation of, and separation from, the non-singers of one's community.

Community members in both Connemara and West Java participate in music making long after they have passed away. Such is the reverence for a particular singer's gifts that in the case that someone performs a song that "belonged" (more or less) to a now-deceased singer, the singer appears in many people's memories and is perceived as sitting among the participants, one way or another. The participants might acknowledge the deceased person by saying his or her name out loud in Connemara— "Now, Joe Heaney was a fine singer of that song"—or in West Java simply by looking at one another, eyes glazed over with tears, and say, "I remember." There is room for the deceased singers in any gathering, and that means the sense of community extends beyond the small room in which an event is taking place.

Our English word "spirit" comes from the Latin word, *spiritus* ("breath"). We have many words that connect to the word spirit, and we use them without even thinking about them. To inspire is to breathe in; to expire is to breathe out. To perspire is to breathe through (the skin), while to transpire is to breathe through (to the outside). To respire is to breathe again, and to suspire is to sigh. Whales and dolphins have spiracles, also known as breathing holes. But my favorite word in all of these is *conspire*: to breathe together. And in the spirit (!) of breathing together, singers tend to begin breathing at the same rate as they sing, and their heart rates stabilize and they sing together; further research points to a profound connection between joint action and joint perspectives (Vickhoff, 2013: 13). In other words, as people move together, sing together, and participate by being present at a singing event, they synchronize. Watching singers at a singing session in Connemara or a singing session in West Java, you can see their faces soften, their gaze lower, and their breathing—their spirit—gaining focus and stability. Even when people are not singing, but listening, their bodies synchronize with one another, and the sense of *singing* characterizes all of them.

Sean-nós Singing in Connemara, Ireland

The term "*sean-nós*" (pronounced "shan-nōs") means "old style" in the Irish language. Irish, often called Gaelic, was the original language of Ireland before Ireland was colonized by the English between the sixteenth and twentieth centuries. In the twenty-first century, the majority of Irish people speak English, but there are small districts all up and down the west coast of Ireland where the majority speak Irish as their first language. It is in these districts, called *Gaeltachtaí* ("Irish-speaking districts"), where you will find an extraordinary wealth of older songs. These *sean-nós* songs in Irish, many of which are several hundred years old, tend to focus on topics of love and loss rather than on telling a story. Songs that tell stories—ballads—are usually found in the English language, and are sung all over the island. Not everyone sings (in either Irish or English), though Ireland is famous for its songs. If you can imagine an island of about five million people, then picture a subset (7%) of that population who speaks Irish regularly, that gives you a context of a potential audience. Of the Irish speakers, only a small fraction of them know, like, and sing the old songs in Irish. Those people are the enthusiasts of *sean-nós*; they are the ones who can remember all twelve verses of a song about a fishing accident from the eighteenth century, for example.

The region of Connemara—to the west of Ireland—includes the largest *Gaeltacht* (Irish-speaking district), though everyone speaks English there as well. Connemara *sean-nós* singing features songs that are often in free rhythm, that include a lot of vocal ornamentation (such as melismas, in which many notes occur on one syllable), and that speak to aspects of the community or individual's emotional life. For example, a song might be in praise of the beauty of a woman and compare her to an aspect of nature. Another song might mention watching a wedding procession go by and not being a participant because one's sweetheart is marrying another person. Or a song might be about the despair of Jesus' mother with the implication that all mothers risk losing their sons. Most of the people in these communities are Catholic, and some of them weave an older, more folk-based version of Catholicism into their lives as well.

Although there are both performances and competitions of *sean-nós* singing, the norm is *not* to perform. Perusing YouTube clips labeled "Corn Uí Riada" will give you evidence of some of the award-winning singers and the type of songs they would offer in a small gathering. Instead of a stage performance with a microphone, people sit in a circle or around a table or even at the bar in a pub. One person sings, followed by a different person, followed by a different person. Everyone knows the songs, and many people sing what is called their "party piece" or song that they bring out every time there is a singing session. The *fear a' tí* or *bean a' tí* ("man of the house" or "woman of the house"), if there is one, takes the initiative in inviting specific individuals to sing. You might hear something like, "Come on, Séamus, give us your 'Anach Cuain' tonight." The *fear a' tí*—sort of a Master of Ceremonies—knows that Séamus does the song "Anach Cuain" well, and calls the song from the singer. Séamus, of course, will refuse at first to be polite, but will ultimately give in, with pleasure. The entire community benefits as a result of paying attention to the ritual of invitation, acceptance of that invitation, and the return gift of the song by a member of that community.

In my lessons with Joe Heaney, he focused again and again on the importance of the melodic ornaments. He asserted that no one could actually teach anyone else how to do them, or where to put them, but it became clear that they were occurring at quite specific places within the poetic rhythm of the songs (on unstressed syllables, generally). This type of implicit knowledge was perceived to be a type of secret code for insiders, and included turns, grace notes, melismas (many notes per syllable), and other ornaments that shaped the overall performance practice for the singers in the region. Because the Connemara style of doing *sean-nós* leans so heavily on melismas as a defining feature, people in the area (represented by Joe Heaney and others) differentiate that sound from the singing of the Irish southwest and north, which are characterized by other features. I was (and still am) challenged to do melismas as rapidly as the experienced singers, but I do understand what I'm aiming for.

One of the strongest and oldest physical aspects of *sean-nós* singing is the occasional moment when one singer sits across from another and grasps his or her hand during the song. The one doing the singing either has his or her eyes closed, or is looking straight ahead or down, unfocused. The person across, also and always a singer, picks up the hand of the singer and slowly begins winding the singer's hand in a counterclockwise fashion, which the singer Joe Heaney once described as "turning back the clock." It takes about three seconds to complete a single rotation, and at the ends of phrases the singers may tighten their grip and pause before winding again. Only once did I ever experience it in Ireland; a woman I knew walked up to me as I was singing in a pub (at a festival in honor of Joe Heaney, actually). She grabbed my hand and began winding it. It caused a powerful shock to run through my body, and at the risk of sounding rather eccentric, I must write that it felt as if there were a sudden connection to all those who had ever known, sung, or listened to that song. For at least one moment, I belonged.

Tembang Sunda Singing in West Java, Indonesia

The term *tembang Sunda* refers to the sung poetry of the Sundanese people of West Java. It is closely connected to the hereditary elite members of the society in that the ones who sing and listen to it speak at the most advanced levels of a multi-level language, pay attention to issues of class and refined behavior, and tend to be associated with the wealthier members of society, whether they themselves are wealthy or not. These people are Muslims, and strong elements of Hinduism and Buddhism (which were present in West Java long before Islam arrived in the fourteenth century) remain part of their cultural practices. When *tembang Sunda* singers have a singing session, they gather at someone's house in the inner living room (the better homes of the region have a greeting area at the front door and an inner living room where family and close friends meet). People sit in a circle on the floor, with their backs to the wall.

Three accompanists on a pair of large and small zithers and a bamboo flute sit with them in a small group, and the evening follows a fixed progression through different types of song within the genre.

Just as is the case in the west of Ireland, in the west of Java there is a host who invites different honored singers to contribute a song. The presence of the host allows the evening to proceed smoothly, specific people to be celebrated, and an orderly series of known songs to bind the group together. At a performance or competition (usually sponsored by a family hosting a wedding, a wealthy politician, or a branch of the government), just a couple of singers face forward—to the audience, none of whom are actually paying attention—and use a microphone. Song topics, regardless of the event, include the mythic past when the entire region was primarily Hindu-Buddhist, issues of heartache and lost love, and the natural world as a metaphor or stand-in for love or the spirit world. The oldest and most revered songs are, like *sean-nós* songs, performed in free rhythm, use many melismas (again, many notes per syllable), and speak to aspects of the community or individual's emotional life.

One of the physical and sonic elements that separates *tembang Sunda* from *sean-nós* is the extensive use of vocal pressure and multiple types of vibrato. By vocal pressure, I mean using one's diaphragm in an almost percussive manner to create variations in loudness and softness on a single note. For an example of *tembang Sunda*, and especially of the different kinds of pressure and vibrato types, check out the YouTube clip of Neneng Dinar singing the two songs, "Bentang Kuring" and "Ukur Cimata."[9] As you listen to this award-winning singer, note the much more dramatic sound of the first song and the lighter-weight, fixed-rhythm verses of the second. Forms of vibrato in this genre range from no vibrato at all to a light shimmer (*vibra*), a rapid flutter on a single pitch that masks the actual pitch (*sorolok*), an emphasized and slow vibrato (*reureueus*), a short, choppy vibrato (*cacag*), and others.

As someone who has never been comfortable singing with a steady (or any) vibrato, learning to perform these ornaments was my biggest challenge. I could easily hear and notate the differences, but calling them out

---

[9] www.youtube.com/watch?v=nr8X01JsaY8.

of my body required that I recall all the times I was told that—because of my lack of vibrato—I was simply "not a good singer." Now I had to go straight to the place of humiliation in my past and somehow transform it. What enabled me to get past it was the recognition, with the help of my teacher, that in her home, I was no longer an American, but a Sundanese person with a Sundanese body, mind, spirit, and singing voice. I disconnected from my upbringing and simply became her student, and the vibrato appeared. However, the ornamentation in these songs ranges far beyond using multiple kinds of vibrato. Rather like in *sean-nós, tembang Sunda* ornaments include turns, grace notes, mordents, slides, and the aforementioned melismas. The key to the best performances of *tembang Sunda* lies in the judicious use of ornaments to celebrate not just the meaning of the lyrics, but to connect the singer to his or her community, all of whom know the songs intimately and can value and assess the skill that it takes to correctly execute each element of each song.

These two genres of *sean-nós* and *tembang Sunda* are performed thousands of miles apart from one another. They are 100% disconnected; there is zero evidence for any sort of transmission between them. Catholics sing one genre, and Muslims sing another. *Sean-nós* uses a particular set of western modes (ionian, aeolian, dorian, and mixolydian) while *tembang Sunda* uses a different set of Indonesian modes (pelog, sorog, and saléndro). One genre is sung mainly in Irish (but sometimes in English), and the other is sung mainly in Sundanese (with loan words from Sanskrit and Indonesian). Yet when my teacher, Euis Komariah, pointed out that the song I sang had similar features in lyric content, melismatic ornaments, and breathing, she was not at all far from the truth. She was talking about approach, how I focused, and how I held my body.

The Researcher's Body

Few of us receive any training or suggestions on what happens to our own bodies as part of the fieldwork process. However, many people understand that the way to make an interviewer like you—the interviewee—is to adopt the interviewer's body language. Subconsciously, interviewers sense that you are just like them, and (usually without realizing it at all) you stand a better chance of landing the position. In an ethnographic fieldwork experience, if you are observing a singer—how he or she sits, moves, breathes, focuses attention, and produces sound—your chances of producing the right affect increase dramatically. For one thing, you won't stand out in the crowd quite as much (though my red hair, blue eyes, and white skin, not to mention my height and weight, have always made me stand out in a crowd of 5'2" tall Indonesians with darker skin and black hair and eyes). But more importantly, working in a genre in which differences stand out dramatically, removing the remarkable from one's body language and performance style allows people to focus on your *sound*. Using local body language to create local sounds comes across as respectful, and can help to transcend most perceived flaws in one's singing voice.

Neither of these two genres tells a story. Narrative elements—first I did this, then I did that, then this happened and *you won't believe what happened next!*—are irrelevant in these songs. Instead, the singer engages the informed audience members' bodies in a shared physical experience of shared emotion and shared history. They know the songs, and their bodies tense and release at all the same places as in the body of the singer. By using the system of diaphragmatic pressure in performing *tembang Sunda* songs, the singer creates that same pressure to the point that one can see people's abdomens tightening, faces frowning, and bodies slightly leaning forward. People make short sounds with their mouths closed, subtly shake their heads, and quietly offer supportive words. In a *sean-nós* gathering, people make short sounds with their mouths closed, subtly shake their heads, and quietly offer supportive words.

If you know what's happening, your own body does all these things. The cathartic reaction of the audience mirrors the building and release of tension, but it is the *knowledge* of each tradition that allows for catharsis to occur in the first place. That knowledge sometimes extends beyond the insider circles, though. Those physical and emotional reactions have become so characteristic in each place that (local) outsiders to each genre like to perform short parodies of audience members' bodies, often to great laughter and recognition. We are who we are because we *feel*.

References

McDonald, Dorothy T. and Jonny H. Ramsey. "Awakening the Artist: Music for Young Children." *Young Children* 33, 1978: 26–32.

Turino, Thomas. *Music as Social Life: The Politics of Participation*. Chicago, IL: The University of Chicago Press. 2008.

Vickhoff, Björn. "Music Structure Determines Heart Rate Variability of Singers." *Frontiers in Psychology* 4, 2013: 1–16.

Williams, Sean. *The Sound of the Ancestral Ship: Highland Music of West Java*. New York, NY: Oxford University Press, 2001.

——— and Lillis Ó Laoire. *Bright Star of the West: Joe Heaney, Irish Song-Man*. New York, NY: Oxford University Press, 2011.

6

Bodies in Nature

Image 12 *Cattle* © Pauline Foss

The Western Apache of Arizona speak of a strange nocturnal and rather mysterious dance performed by deer before mating season in the San Carlos Mountains of Arizona. Anthropologist Keith Basso once witnessed a group of spectral deer performing this ghostly dance in a clearing near a stream:

> Four or five does come within 500 yards of the stream. The bucks go down to the stream and drink, and afterwards the does drink. At some signal, the bucks stand up on their hind legs. The does don't, but the bucks do it again and again. At last the does rear up too, and they all do it. They keep falling back because they can't keep their balance. The animals accompany their actions by a low noise – "u-u-u-u-wheeze; e-e-e-e." After this performance but before the actual mating, the males battle antlers-to-antlers, pairing off against each other in competition for the does. (quoted in Schechner and Appel, 1990: 95)

Throughout this book we have explored multiple meanings and definitions of cultural performance. In the opening passage quoted above, the word "performance" is used in regard to animals engaged in enigmatic ritualized movements as a preamble to mating. How many of us are accustomed to consider animal behavior as performance located way beyond the realm of human contact and human scrutiny? Kevin Landis mentions the hyena feeding in Harar in his first chapter as a cultural performance. The questions he raises about performance will be addressed again in this chapter with its theme, "Bodies in Nature." As a complement to the previous chapter about sensations and embodiment, we will examine a range of actors (human and nonhuman) within performance-oriented occasions. These are situated in different natural environments where nature moves to center stage as first the focus of seasonal or calendrical festivals, and finally culminating with a discussion of its role as inspiration for a staged performance about environment and nature-related themes in the PearlDamour production of *How to Build a Forest*.

Before looking closely at the combination of nature and performance, let us briefly return to Basso's description of deer awkwardly yet beautifully moving in a kind of synchronized dance. Although an awareness of this secretive *ritual* practice of deer during mating season is part of the Western Apache repertoire of cultural knowledge and storytelling, does this make it a *cultural performance*? Do animals, or more particularly different species, share something akin to culture? These questions may not have definitive answers, but in this chapter, in order to understand their significance for our study of cultural performance, we will pursue the findings of scholarly research on animal performance as well as the notion of **agency**, i.e., actively producing, influencing, and participating in a particular outcome without being passive. Agency denotes process. It is dynamic and directly engaged.

Winter Festival

Perhaps the most common creative cultural expression of the relationship of nature and performance is found in the ritual cycles celebrating the changing seasons such as festivals and rites associated with the solstices and equinoxes; for example, midsummer's eve and winter solstice celebrations. These are ancient rites annually re-enacting the dominant themes of human existence, life and death, or mortality and renewal as expressed through ritual performance. From time *in memoriam* actors and celebrants utilized magic and drama to attempt to control mysterious, supernatural forces like the waning light, the inevitable darkness, powers of the sun, moon, and constellations. Ritual is usually associated with effect or causing something to exist, for example, in Richard Schechner's phrase, "a showing of a doing," where he is emphasizing the efficacy and goal of ritual (Grimes, 2003: 35) realized through performance. The motivation impelling ritual is to "order the world" according to the cosmology or belief system shared by those enacting the ritual performance.

Typical **winter festivals** include feats of virtuoso ice carving, winter sports, and often a cast of characters from Greek and Roman mythology linked to fire rituals like Vulcan and his merry revelers from the underworld with its fires of hell. Then there are invented traditions, which are created to respond to particular sociocultural circumstances and embrace innovative ritualistic actions that deviate from long-lived replicative traditions. This is achieved in order to incorporate various contemporary elements in a ceremonial context as well as to promote social cohesion and bring a semblance of homogeneity and continuity to an otherwise disparate social order. However, one such invented celebratory tradition, *Frozen Dead Guy Days* (FDGD) in Nederland, Colorado, is more characteristic of Roger Abraham's description of **folk performance** as "the management of social misalignment" (Tuleja, 1997: 6). Conceived as an invented tradition, FDGD contains many of the standard ritualistic components found in winter festival repertory—ice carving, plunging into a glacial stream, etc., plus some features unique to this particular location and these cultural circumstances. At the heart and center of this annual late winter celebration lies the frozen corpse of Grandpa Bredo Morstoel, brought to Nederland by his grandson, Trygve Bauge. Thus, the FDGD festival repertoire incorporates a few thematic twists: Grandpa's Blue Ball, Ice Queen and Grandpa Look-a-like Contest, Cryogenic Parade, Coffin Races, the Afterlife Auction, and a more localized variant of consumption and valor, the Rocky Mountain Oyster Eating Contest (i.e., bull testicles eaten raw).

Frozen Dead Guy Days, however, is the "flip side" of the customary mortuary rites celebrated during winter festivals honoring the "death" of the cold winter embodied in some mythological figure, and reveling in the resurrection of spring. Instead of commemorating and celebrating life, Nederland celebrants focus on death and the presence of the cryonically[1] preserved corpse of "Grandpa" Bredo Morstoel lying-in-state in a Tuff Shed[2] in a suburban mountain neighborhood above the town. Grandpa Morstoel is the famous original "frozen dead guy" around which the festival coheres. The following is an account of Nederland's winter festival as a cultural performance not only dependent on its location as a natural high-altitude setting in the front range of the Rocky Mountains,

---

[1] Cryonic preservation uses cryogen, a refrigerant that produces extremely low temperatures, to deep-freeze bodies of those who have died of incurable diseases in the hope that a cure is found in the future. Its appeal matched Trygve Bauge's interest in futurist causes and technology as well as his profound commitment to a radical version of individualism and freedom of choice.

[2] Tuff Shed is a trade name for a metal utility shed. These modular buildings come in all sizes and are generally used for agricultural and industrial purposes. Tuff Shed capitalized on all the publicity surrounding FDGD, and became a visible sponsor with its logo on all the signs installed during the festival.

but it also foregrounds the classic ceremonial theme of death and resurrection inspired by the natural trajectory of mortality.

Nederland sits 8,000 feet above sea level, yet its etymological roots suggest the "nether world"—the underworld, i.e., the realm of spirits and ghosts. As if in acknowledgement of this, in 1993 Trygve Bauge and his mother, Aud Morstoel, both Norwegian citizens then living in Nederland, acted on their futurist beliefs and brought the body of their father and grandfather, respectively, back to town and installed it in a shed behind their house.

Bredo Morstoel died in Norway in 1989 at the age of eighty-nine. He had died in his sleep, but according to one account, Grandpa Bredo's pillows were arranged in the form of a "T," which Trygve interpreted as a sign that his grandfather wanted to honor Trygve's original plan to cryonically preserve his body (Lawlor, 2001: 5). The first stage of preservation occurred in Norway while the final stage was completed in a California cryonics facility. After four years of liquid nitrogen treatment, Grandpa Morstoel's corpse reached its current resting place in Nederland.

The following year, in 1994, when Trygve Bauge was clandestinely deported to Norway due to immigration infractions, the town was chagrined to learn about Grandpa's final resting place within city limits. Eight years later, however, Nederland transformed residual civic distress into an internationally acclaimed festival by creatively responding to the presence of the corpse and retroactively legitimizing its frozen presence. The creation of FDGD demonstrates how a community can imaginatively appropriate a negative stereotype to successfully confound their critics as well as garner economic benefits.

Frozen Dead Guy Days actually inverts common festival tropes (i.e., nonliteral use of words as metaphors, irony, etc.) and symbolism. As a "counter-festival" (i.e., one that privileges technology [cryonics] over the usual ancient celebratory themes of planting and harvests), the FDGD festival merely intensifies the carnivalesque, which is already manifest through the ramifications and subversive disorder of Trygve Bauge's actions. Bauge is a steadfast supporter of Libertarian politics. Thus, anomalies in Nederland's situation (i.e., a cryonically preserved corpse, people willing to maintain it at the requisite temperature, and the omnipresent former resident, Norwegian expatriate and anarchist, Bauge, himself, trying to control everything from afar) smoothly transform into carnival's "Reversible World" of upside down behavior and lawless aesthetics. Elements such as nostalgia or patriotism and nationalism are redeployed by Nederland residents and festival organizers as parodic displays of Libertarian antics and futurism vis-à-vis cryonic technology. The belief in rebirth and resurrection, which typically underlies so many end-of-winter festivities, changes into an interest in a future awakening realized through technological advances in medical research (and, in the case of Morstoel's corpse, suspended between the present and the future, gives new meaning to "liminality").

In the interval since the festival's inception in 2002, end-of-the-winter revels have attracted global attention as well as refreshed and fused Nederland's community spirit out of a frequently discordant past. Victor Turner describes the aftermath of cultural performance as forging and cementing sociocultural cohesion through an intensification of a social centripetal force thus firmly binding a group or society together as a consequence of communal festivities. As described in Chapter 2, Kristin Valentine also places this dynamic of societal fusion as a post-performance effect at the center of her model of cultural analysis. The overt byproduct of a cultural performance can result in permanent transformation of those involved or, as in the case of Nederland, a transitory change affecting community solidarity for a certain time span, which needs to be revitalized every year. Regarding Frozen Dead Guy Days, we have a festival cycle oscillating with an economic one. This annual celebration not only generates substantial tourist income but also creates an entertaining showcase for a renegade local history privileging a legacy of non-conformity related to miners, hippies, and reclusive anarchists. Identifying death, decay, and regeneration as salient themes of the enacted "grotesque" within the Nederland festival arena enables us to examine carnival folk culture as applied to FDGD and critique the relationship of the "bodily element" to various enactments and events. Throughout birthday celebrations, champagne feasts in his honor, and tours to view his Tuff Shed mausoleum, how is Grandpa Morstoel's corpse perceived by family and onlookers? Is he a being in limbo awaiting revival with his soul intact, an entity in touch through psychic communication, or Nederland's guardian spirit?

Frozen Dead Guy Days is now an entrenched expressive tradition, which rapidly grew from an amalgamation of happenstance, community spirit, and the Nederland Area Chamber of Commerce's vision to create an economically viable yet distinctive and unique winter festival. Nationalism (pride and loyalty to country) is often a player in festival choreography. Norway not the United States fulfills this role in FDGD. Visible references to Norway abound, including the Norwegian flag, Viking impersonators, and the Polar Plunge (a venerable Scandinavian activity). On the eve of the festival in 2005, Trygve Bauge frequently rang from Norway urging Nederland planners and organizers to invite the King and Queen of Norway, who were visiting the White House around the same time as FDGD that year. Norwegian elements associated with the festival obviously refer to Bredo Morstoel and his family's nationality; however, the alpine setting of Nederland with a ski resort just down the road also evokes imagined connections to Scandinavian life style and winter sports. Grandpa Morstoel was reputed to be a good skier and had skied right up to his death.

Although national identity is often a standard component of festival scripts, FDGD subverts this by including references to Trygve's interest in anarchy and Libertarian politics in addition to his more profound belief in a world without national borders or boundaries of any kind. Signs with an image of the Statue of Liberty accompanied by "Libertarian" are posted on Grandpa's Tuff Shed mausoleum and around the shell of a house that was once Trygve and Aud's home. Festival visitors who go on tours to view Grandpa's "coffin" meet Bo Shaffer, who is the tour leader and periodically supplies dry ice to the corpse in order to keep it frozen. Because Bo has frequent contact with Grandpa, he was concerned that he might be upsetting him and consulted a psychic. According to Bo, "we know Bredo isn't upset. He's happy to be doing other things—he doesn't want his old decrepit body back. One psychic said that Bredo doesn't even know he is dead" (Lawlor, 2001: 5).

Bo and Trygve share a common political interest in Libertarianism. Bo always participates in the annual FDGD parade, flinging dry ice from his truck bed festooned with bumper stickers, which read: "I'm Pro-Choice on EVERYTHING!" and "Enough is Enough! Vote Libertarian!" or "Prohibition Doesn't Work!" What is missing is another bumper sticker imperative, "Question Authority!" which is one of the universals of festival performative behavior. Anarchy, that is, unconstrained and unexpected behavior, is a common festival trope along with marginal or fringelike elements manifest in the transgression of boundaries both spatial and social. The difference between Bauge's ongoing political activities tending toward anarchism and festival performance is mainly in degrees of time and distance.

Aesthetics and style, rather than tradition or authenticity, are more applicable to the tenor of Frozen Dead Guy Days. Style's inclusiveness accommodates all the idiosyncratic displays of expressive social behavior aimed at the story and the reality of "Grandpa in the Tuff Shed." Of course, the real *leitmotif* (dominant theme) is death, which mostly elicits the ribald rather than the reverent. Yet, it is the promotion of activities and their enactments with regard to style, which unifies all the disparate elements of FDGD within a zone of iconoclastic behavior where innovation and creativity are hyperbolized without mercy. In a sense, parody is one of the most important elements of style employed in this festival context as a playful and ironic "play" on the somberness surrounding death tempered by the hilarity created through the imitation of funeral rites and all the accouterments such as hearses, coffins, funeral attire, gravestones, etc. In his contribution to this book, David Donkor describes the use of parody in the first section when he applies it to his interpretation of certain features of Akan storytelling sessions. Frozen Dead Guy Days festivities share a similar sense of parody characterized by the relationship of the distorted imitation of the event (FDGD) to traditional funerary practices and the inversion of audience (spectator) expectations and behavior in terms of attitudes toward death vis-à-vis the Nederland pageant.

Questions remain about publicly treating Grandpa's remains as a spectacle and the intellectual property rights of Trygve Bauge and his family. His grandfather and all the narratives and symbols associated with Bredo Morstoel have become the hallmark of Frozen Dead Guy Days. In 2005, however, there was an acrimonious dispute between the festival organizers and Bauge, who implied that Nederland businesses were profiting unduly from his family. As a result, there is now a renewed emphasis on winter festival elements rather than primarily showcasing Grandpa.

Norway's laws concerning cryonically preserved bodies have become more lenient. There is the possibility that Bauge may repatriate his grandfather back to his homeland in the spirit of a kind of return migration. Until then, Trygve Bauge is closely monitoring events in Nederland and their impact on his family. As he says, "As long as any part of the festival leads to anything that is frozen or dead, it is obviously about my grandfather."[3]

In Chapter 4, in a discussion relating cultural politics to cultural performance, we cited Dwight Conquergood's statement describing performance as transgression rather than transcendence, expressed as "the force which crashes and breaks through... normative traditions." The Nederland festival is a busy arena of ribaldry and jest as well as a stage to promote the stereotypical culture of the "lawlessness of the West." Libertarian politics of independence from governmental control, or a politics of resistance, underscore the belief system guiding Trygve Bauge's actions from preserving his grandfather's corpse to his persistent fight with United States federal immigration officials. Although FDGD is not a Libertarian or overtly political festival *per se*, the celebratory tone of antiestablishment mockery does elicit a plethora of transgressive actions. Advocating civic non-conformity by means of a performative script also exemplifies Conquergood's observation that "performance flourishes in a zone of contest and struggle" (Conquergood, 2013: 27).

In the comedic tradition of carnival, FDGD upends customary funerary rites by spoof and buffoonery. The stage for this is nature itself and much of the FDGD depends on a wintery and snowy atmosphere. In recent years, global warming has wreaked havoc with snowfall and frigid temperatures so that Coffin Races kick up dust instead of snow. Expectations of a snow-clad alpine setting suggestive of a Norwegian landscape or the Swiss Alps are thwarted every season. On the one hand, we could say that nature is not performing according to the script in order to present Nederland as a high altitude "Christmas card" village. On the other hand, the negative environmental impact on winter revels affects

---

[3] Martin, Richard. "Dead Guy Dispute Draws Ire," *Arts Blog, Arts, Film & Events, Boulder, Colorado, Festivals & Events, New West Network Topics, The People's Republic (c94)*, New West, Arts, Film & Events, April 26, 2005, http://newwest.net/main/article/dead_guy_dispute_draws_ire/.

nature's role and its influence on the various acts (e.g., Polar Plunge, Cryogenic Parade, etc.) as well as the state of the central character's corpse (in danger of thawing), and necessitates adaptation and innovation in order to accommodate the effects of recent climatic change. In this way, nature is a primary catalyst for changing tradition (no matter how short lived). Thus in its performed capacity as an agent of transformation, nature "conspires" or collaborates with the community to continue to stage an ever-mutating and evolving "winter" festival.

By including nature as an agent of change in the context of performance, we are not critiquing it as a free-ranging entity on a world stage subject to the human notion of performance. Instead, we are attempting to enlarge the concept of performance in terms of our understanding of nonhuman elements by situating these within cultural contexts that have significant meaning for those involved. These thoughts lead into the next section on animals vis-à-vis an expanded, flexible application of the definition of performance subject to continual readjustment with regard to animal encounters and their unpredictability (see Cull, 2015: 24).

Nonhuman Animal Frolics

In our treatment of animal performance outside the realm of human control, that is "beyond the human," we will refer to some of the interesting findings as described in Chapter 1, emerging from the intersection of the field of Animal Studies with Performance Studies (see Orozco and Parker-Starbuck, 2015: 2–4). Similar to how nature was regarded as an important element of performance above, this part of the chapter requires that we reorient our thinking away from a reductive or "readymade," definition of performance as only human-centered, and try out approaches leading to an expansive understanding of performance as applicable to animal behavior in different situations (Cull, 2015: 24). Of course, our emphasis is on cultural performance, which is a further refinement of performance categories and requires attending to the cultural properties of these experiences. The concept of "**zooësis**" created by scholar and writer, Una Chaudhuri, is particularly helpful in guiding us in our descriptive analysis of animal practices as performance. *Zooësis* relates to the "myriad performance and semiotic elements involved in and around the vast field of *cultural and animal practices*" (as quoted in Orozco and Parker-Starbuck, 2015: 2, emphasis in the original). The term "semiotics," as it is used here, refers to examining the meaning of signs and symbols relative to animal behavior. Chaudhuri writes more explicitly that zooësis "refers to the ways the animal is put into discourse: constructed, represented, understood, and misunderstood" (Chaudhuri, 2017: 5).

Interspecies Performance

In the first chapter we encounter the hyenas of Harar as cast members in a cultural performance underscoring the promotion of Harar socio-cultural identity. In terms of this chapter and the work of scholars such as Chaudhuri, we can also assess the Harar happening as an interspecies performance—a form of collaboration between Yusuf, who supplies the reward of food central to making the performance happen, and the hyenas as willing to share the public limelight night after night. The intricacies of the performed collaboration as described by Kevin Landis entail a finely tuned choreography of "give-and-take" dependent on the relationship between Yusuf, the handler, and the hyenas. Landis' description of one hyena as he "gingerly gnaws the meat off the stick" confounds our expectations of this ferocious animal's mode of accepting food. Instead of "savagely" ripping the meat off the stick as anticipated, we are given an image of "delicate" demeanor. Each night the hyenas of Harar arrive as wild animals temporarily entering a domestic performance space to interact with a handler, who provides food, and then leave as wild animals virtually unchanged by the experience. Spectators/witnesses, however, are left with myriad impressions and musings.

Another example of interspecies performance is the Longhorn Cattle Drive, which occurs annually in downtown Colorado Springs in Colorado as a prelude to the next day's rodeo competition, "Ride for the Brand," sponsored by the Working Ranch Cowboys Association. In this instance, the interspecies collaboration consists of a large herd of Longhorn cattle being driven down a major city street by professional working cowboys mounted on horseback. Thus, the drive is actually a performance of a longstanding working relationship among cattle, cowboys, and horses—one that is enacted daily on ranches, and replicates the historical round-ups and cattle drives of the early American western frontier, which ranged over an unfenced domain. In fact, the unsettling but fascinating juxtaposition of nearly wild cattle with horns that span five or six feet running down a paved urban street bounded on both sides by a combination of high-rise office buildings and store fronts underscores the idea of site-specific performance. Here, civic space is transformed into stage space where this kind of action on the streets is not part of the everyday experience in that locale. Although the cattle drive partially retraces the route that frontier cowboys and cattle took to the railroad yard in the past, the Longhorns today look entirely out of place within the concrete and glass cityscape of downtown Colorado Springs. In a strange sense of reversal, it is as if the afterimage of the historical cattle drives is embodied in this culturally wild herd of cows and calves as they race down the street to end up in a holding pen where they are loaded onto stock trailers, and, ultimately, returned to the ranch—not shipped to the stockyards.

Spontaneous Animals

Others have recently written about unexpected animal appearances onstage where they did not belong, similar to the effect of Longhorns being driven through Colorado Springs' commercial district. Nicholas Ridout famously added to the conversation about animals spontaneously appearing in the midst of a theatrical performance when he wrote about observing a mouse scampering across a stage in London's West End. His thoughts led to ruminations on the place for animals in the theatre, questioning theatre's representational tactics, aesthetic control, and the intentionality of performance (Ridout, 2006: 96–98). In turn, Ridout's observations and questions inspired a few performance studies scholars to pursue aspects of animal studies in order to better understand the field of animal behavior where examples of performed actions abound (mating displays, Basso's nocturnal deer dance, Humpback whale songs, etc.). The notion of deliberate performances in nature, however, has not yet been fully explored. Another "animals in sight but out-of-place" story appears in Ben Brantley's 2009 review of a performance of *The Bacchae* at the Public Theater's open-air stage, New York City's Delacorte Theater in Central Park. Brantley opens his piece by introducing a "wonderful raccoon" as "serene and silent as a rising moon," which appears briefly onstage and then exits accompanied by two more rather nonchalant companions going about their nocturnal business as raccoons (Brantley, 2009: C1).

Both Brantley's and Ridout's accounts concern animals unexpectedly intersecting with the human world in a very public setting. Although programmed every year, this is still partially true of the Longhorns running through the Colorado Springs streets as well. The cattle drive, nonetheless, is more pertinent to our discussion of cultural performance relative to its position within the narrative repertoire of cowboy traditions of the West. The horses, cowboys, and cattle are historically interdependent and necessary components of round-ups and cattle drives. The cultural context of the urban cattle drive is also reinforced by the association of cowboys as a folk group subsumed under the category of **occupational folklore** inclusive of a set of emic (i.e., insider) customs in common such as language, colloquialisms, slang, attire, the nature of the work, jokes, and expressive culture as exemplified by the popular genres of cowboy poetry and song.

In order to reexamine the foundational aspects of performance as applicable to the cattle drive, we need to refer again to Chapter 1 where Peter Brook is cited as indicating that the three basic elements needed for a performance are an empty space (transformed into stage space by the action of someone walking across it); a relationship between performers and spectators; and something happening. During the Longhorn Cattle Drive, the empty city street becomes the performance corridor where the action occurs. The audience of spectators and onlookers thronging the sidewalks and edges of the street join the other interspecies actors (cattle, cowboys, and horses) and react in various ways to the unfolding tumultuous pageant of thronging animals. Peter Brook's theatrical elements described in Chapter 1 result in "something shown," which encompasses all the drama produced by nearly stampeding cows and calves guided by their cowboy escorts on horseback. Moreover, the primary performance of all these human and nonhuman actors in concert fits Richard Schechner's earlier statement on the effect of performance as "a showing of a doing."

By applying performance-based elements to our descriptive analysis of the Longhorn stampede (notwithstanding under human control), we also need to mediate between the time-honored dichotomy of polar opposites, i.e., "nature versus culture" in order to understand the cattle drive and its constituents as being linked in performance. Traditionally, nature versus culture implies one or the other seen as foils to each other. It is more constructive to consider humans and cattle interacting within a longstanding and enduring dyadic tradition (composed of two entities) rather than in constant opposition. Cowboys and cattle are two groups entirely dependent on the existence of each other to constitute a certain venerable culture—partially domesticated and partially wild. Without one or the other, there would be no shared cultural representative of the western history, past and present. Since we regard the Longhorn cattle drive as a cultural performance inclusive of authentic cowboy customs with a focus on how animality (the essence of being a nonhuman animal) manifests in all of this, we can tentatively conclude that it is an amalgamation of culture and nature. As stated earlier, cowboys and cattle are interdependent in this type of performance, but differences are not *dissolved* in it. Rather the cattle drive could be viewed as a variant of Una Chaudhuri's "Theatre of Species" literally taken to the streets. Chaudhuri's concept honors the otherness of animals and cites a performance space of "embodied and productive difference, a means of encountering and considering *the particularities* of the bodies, territories and limitations of specific animals, both human and nonhuman" (Chaudhuri, 2015: 138, emphasis in the original). All in all, the Colorado Springs spectacle effectively demonstrates one of the primary goals of the "Theatre of Species" to "produce an interspecies awareness" (Orozco and Parker-Starbuck, 2015: 11). Can you identify examples of interspecies performance and collaboration, of which you are aware or have witnessed? How do you determine what constitutes interspecies collaboration? What roles do aesthetics and improvisation play? Perhaps in order to better interpret some of the dynamics of nonhuman performance, it would be useful to revisit a few of the concepts associated with cultural performance introduced earlier such as aesthetics and the role of the senses.

Aesthetics

In the first chapter, our working definition of aesthetics ranged from Richard Schechner's inclusion of contextual beauty as one goal of performance to an understanding of the principles and values underlying a piece of art or performance and how they are used to judge the overall effectiveness. In the field of material culture and folklore, ethnoaesthetics or applied aesthetics is also a powerful tool to evaluate cultural expressions such as performance. Ethnoaesthetics was briefly mentioned in Chapter 2 and comprises the internal set of criteria used by members of a cultural group to assess their work in terms of their own intrinsic cultural values. This is not a set of evaluative criteria superimposed from the outside by people judging the effectiveness of an art form relative to outsider standards. Rather, ethnoaesthetics depends on a local understanding of artistry by means of recognizing internal creative dynamics and using reflexivity (a process of referring back to itself) as a form of meditative feedback flowing between art and life. This means that ethnoaesthetics is a term or label for a category but it is also a process. The process of judging and categorizing arises from evaluating the effectiveness of an art or a performance relative to style, rigor, delivery, competency, etc. and noting how it complements the artistic life of the community or group involved in creating it. Applied aesthetics, aesthetics "at work," registers the tenor or degree of artistic engagement while concurrently measuring the impact of cultural factors (e.g., local politics, religious systems, civic authority, etc.) on social and cultural behavior.

Aesthetics also involves the world of sensory impressions (refer to Chapter 5 for a detailed discussion of the senses). Despite moving naturally as a herd under unnatural circumstances, Longhorns perform their animality with a bellowing chorus of chaotic noise vibrating and ricocheting off the hard surfaces of the surrounding cityscape. In competition with the auditory cacophony is the smell. The olfactory ambiance of animal sweat, the stench of fear, droppings redolent of grass-fed diets, and the dry smell of heat rising from sunbaked asphalt contribute to a sensorium of animal presence. Finally, the visual and kinesthetic senses are brought into play by the beauty of the animals and their powerful moving bodies. Much of this description could be applied to Una Chaudhuri's concept of zooësis with regard to what the cattle represent (wild beings now domesticated on parade in an alien environment), and how their presence is absolutely necessary in order to constitute an integral component of the active cowboy culture that symbolizes the West (see Chaudhuri, 2017: 5).

Quality

The notion of **quality** is as difficult to define as aesthetics. **Quality** subsumes aesthetics to become the overarching descriptor of performance. The characteristics that contribute to quality of performance in the cattle drive embrace the dignity and skill of the horsemen, their expertise at handling the herd, and how they sense the need for and handle any intervention between cattle and spectators. Other factors involve the elements of selective breeding in terms of the Longhorns as revealed through animal power plus physical attributes including size, the span of the horns, coloring, and behavior; and, the consummate interspecies awareness of horsemen and cattle interacting together under challenging circumstances. Although the Longhorns belong to a domesticated herd, they possess a degree of wildness. In his study of bullfighting, Garry Marvin identifies the trait of "culturally wild" as one of the principles implicit in breeding Spanish bulls for the bullring. It means that traditionally the bulls have been bred "to conserve and maintain certain valued qualities of wildness" with their wild spirit intact (Marvin, 2015: 43). The Longhorn cows are not ferocious Spanish bulls, but as they trot down the city street with their young calves, they exude an intensity one imagines left over from a lingering frontier spirit accustomed to the open range long ago.

Up until now, we have focused on animals as performers. What about performances that have been especially created for animals? This recalls

David Rothenberg's experimental performances playing his clarinet in aviaries and performing with Humpback whales in order to gauge their capacity for "vocal learning," that is, their ability to learn to make new sounds (Cull, 2015: 26–27). These experiments were inspired by the modern-romanticist idea of a "universal language" of music, which could be communicated across cultures as well as across species. Long before Rothenberg started performing duets with a white-crested laughing thrush in Pittsburgh's National Aviary, eighteenth-century French musicians staged an outdoor concert for two Indian elephants, Hanz and Marguerite, in the Jardin des Plantes in Paris in 1798. The intention behind this performance for elephants was to observe their reactions to different musical stimuli—or at least try to make correlations between animal behavior and sound (Cull, 2015: 27). No doubt, the choice of a garden setting was inspired by an attempt on the part of the organizers to recreate a familiar atmosphere reminiscent of the lush tropical foliage of their Indian birthplace in order to make the elephants feel more "at home."

The theme of nature and staged performance leads into the final section, which accompanies this chapter. The last contribution to this book is in the form of an interview about *How to Build a Forest*, a production created by performance artists Lisa D'Amour and Katie Pearl along with visual installation artist Shawn Hall. The concept for this project of creating a complex forest—a stand of trees imaginatively and materially connected to each other—and dismantling it within the eight-hour timespan of the performance powerfully connects with other ideas throughout this book. The production will be more fully explored by the artists in the following section.

The artists refer to *How to Build a Forest* as a hybrid project comprising a visual art installation, a performance piece with no actors (builders, a ranger, a gatekeeper), a field guide to the production, an audience presence onstage and off, a drama centered on the objects being created on the stage, and various modes of creating awareness about the forces of nature, natural elements in the earth, and industrial exploitation of these resources. The performance piece is inventive, comprehensive, and transcendent in the sense that people are changed by experiencing it. *How to Build a Forest* was conceived in response to the devastation of Hurricane Katrina around New Orleans, and the consequent demolition of an old forest surrounding Lisa D'Amour's family home. The production was created during the BP (British Petroleum) oil spill in Louisiana. *How to Build a Forest* exemplifies the dynamism of nature and multiple ways of humans working with and in nature. The process of creation and maintenance (short term) underscores David Crouch's approach to British garden allotments, where community members work together in their different garden plots, that nature is not entirely prefigured but "is constituted and understood through practice" (Crouch, 2003: 23). *How to Build a Forest* demonstrates how this could work in terms of the relationship of community to nature and conjures up an allusion to a range of wild and cultivated natural garden environments where practice and performance conjoin. In the context of this theatre piece, performance as a process and an event consummated in artful aesthetic arrangement are the focuses, not a backdrop or set piece, for spectacle and theatre. Approaching from a different direction, but certainly applicable, Una Chaudhuri's comments on a theatrical topiary garden in ruins as a setting for the play *Bengal Tiger at the Baghdad Zoo* point to notions of nurturing and stewardship of natural places and help to orient our thinking about *How To Build a Forest*. Chaudhuri writes about the garden as "a space where art is aligned with tending nature, a space for the dialogue of nature and culture" (Chaudhuri, 2015: 142). This is created when *How to Build a Forest* is installed in its stage space.

So far, this chapter has presented nature in the form of festivals, parades, processions, and round-ups. Nature's performance can also be experienced on a more intimate scale, particularly relative to gardening and cultivating as arenas where human efforts, planning, and practice intersect with nature's process of growing and inevitable decline (or devastation). As we anticipate our conversation with Lisa D'Amour, Katie Pearl, and Shawn Hall, we must remind ourselves that both natural gardens and theatrical forests emerge from seeds (real and imagined) nurtured from an act of intimacy where human action engages the non-human world at its most basic level (Morten as cited by Chaudhuri, 2015: 148).

In the interview, the artists convincingly describe the elements that qualify their piece as a cultural performance. Dancer and anthropologist Anya Peterson Royce, who writes about anthropology and the performing arts, bridges the realms of cultural performance and staged performance in these words, "Performing arts, especially music, dance, theatre and all the combinations of those genres, offer us a view of the world in which our ordinary understanding of who and why we are is brought to a heightened consciousness" (Royce, 2004: 1). Usually, cultural performances are more inclusive of group participation, but that does not preclude those moments of "heightened consciousness." Royce also proposes that style should be considered in performance contexts as strongly as tradition. She believes that style allows for greater latitude in the appreciation of personal choice and diachronic change (transformations over time). Style has been mentioned earlier in conjunction with aesthetics and the quality of performance. *How to Build a Forest* is also exemplary of how style and aesthetics underscore the greater message of the piece and really aid in cultivating the audience's total immersion in the project—imaginatively as well as ideologically. Style is one of the preeminent features, but *How to Build a Forest* also establishes a singular tradition in performance and theatre art with the capacity to metamorphose into many changing variations. Let us turn to the artists themselves to hear more about process and performance.

Terms and Ideas for Study

- Agency
- Winter Festival
- Folk performance
- Zooësis
- Occupational folklore
- Quality

Questions for Discussions

- How would you apply your understanding of the concept of tradition and transmission practices in terms of this chapter's topics about cultural performance?
- In reviewing how cultural and political issues are actualized through performance, what characteristics of cultural performance can you identify in the FDGD celebration? What are some of the traditional elements of festival and which are invented?

Creative Project

This exercise provides another opportunity to engage in close observation by creating "double-entry" notes. Looking and listening are two important elements in ethnographic research. Here you can practice your observational skills of "just looking."

- Select an object or event in nature to observe every day for a week (examples can be snow drifts, bird nests, a houseplant, trash, etc.).
- Record your notes in double-entry form: one side describes evidence of specific changes happening; the other side records your impressions.
- At the end of the week examine your notes and write up a brief personal essay reflecting on this process of observing change over time.

Case Study

How to Build a Forest

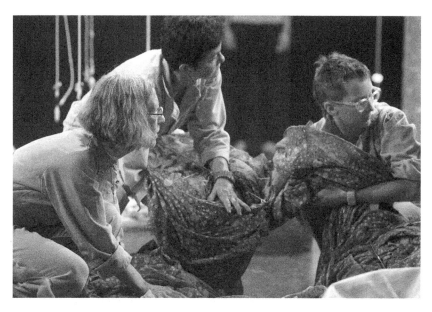

Image 13   *Forest Builders* © Paula Cort

On November 28, 2016, Kevin Landis and Suzanne MacAulay interviewed Lisa D'Amour, Katie Pearl, and Shawn Hall. Katie Pearl and Lisa D'Amour are theatre artists, who have a longstanding collaboration under *PearlDamour*, an interdisciplinary theatre company. Shawn Hall is a visual artist, who joined the team to help create *How To Build a Forest*.

Here is a brief synopsis of the production: *How to Build a Forest* is a hybrid project, part visual art installation, part theatre performance, which unfolds over an extended eight-hour interval. Beginning on an empty stage, theatre artists Katie Pearl and Lisa D'Amour, along with visual artist Shawn Hall and a four-person build team, work obsessively to first construct, then dismantle and remove an elaborate fabricated forest. Over the course of the first six and a half hours, the forest comes together in ways that range from surprisingly intimate (the team quietly sitting around one builder as she raises the smallest, most delicate tree using a string and a pulley), to large-scale spectacular (the entire team lifting the many-branched "big tree" using an elaborate rigging system). For one-half hour, the forest is "complete". Over the course of the final sixty minutes, the forest disappears.

Kevin Landis: Suzanne and I have written a book that... uses practice and theory to describe what cultural performance is in performance studies. And we wanted a last section of the book [to be] an interview with artists who have created in the milieu that we're discussing. And the last chapter is about nonhuman and animal and environmental performance. And so we thought, "well, it would be sort of perfect to talk to you all, especially about *How to Build a Forest,*" so that's what we're doing.

Before we get started, is there anything you want to know sort of generally about the book?

Katie Pearl: I'd like to know a little bit more, especially when you say like the milieu, how you would describe it, or what you mean by that.

Kevin Landis: I'll say a little bit about the book and then Suzanne can say a little bit about the chapter that this will be connected with. The book is geared towards introducing freshmen to some of the concepts of performance studies like cultural performance, ritual making, traditions, those sorts of things. And we go through three major sections.

We go through aesthetics. We go through geography, the way that performance groups around the world use their geography and nature, actual architecture in creating performance. Then the last section is sort of an unusual take on modes of performance, and Suzanne can talk a little bit about that.

Suzanne MacAulay: I'm a folklorist and an ethnographer, so I look at all of this through the eyes of ethnography. And Kevin is coming in from theatre history, theatre studies, and performance studies. So we have this wonderful collaboration from these different fields and a lot of the practical work, which I write about in my sections, all has to do with ethnography as folklore study.

So my chapter that we're appending this wonderful interview on, concerns bodies in nature, and that means humans and nonhumans. So I have a couple of case studies. One is about a frozen dead guy, a festival in Nederland, Colorado, near where I live, and that all has to do with this idea of the winter festival, celebrating life, celebrating death. But it's all inverted because this corpse has been sitting there on dry ice for about twenty years!

But anyway, that's kind of the madcap side of all of this. Then I've been looking at, you know, all that work in animal and performance studies on non-humans in performance, that is, animals. So the overall thing is nature, obviously. For a while there, we thought we would have somebody write about gardening as performance.

So then Kevin mentioned your wonderful piece, your collaborative piece, *How to Build a Forest*, and I became entranced. So let's take it from there, and do ask me questions about the content of the chapter, but I'd rather that we just launched into a discussion so that you're fresh, you know, and not trying to think of an angle.

Shawn Hall:	Sure.
Kevin Landis:	Sound good?
Katie Pearl:	Yeah.

Kevin Landis: Okay, so I guess just to start out, I wonder if one of you could say just a little bit about the impetus for this piece, *How to Build a Forest*. Why did you decide to do this? What was the goal in starting out with this work?

Lisa D'Amour: This is Lisa. Can I start?

Katie Pearl: Sure, yeah.

Lisa D'Amour: So the collaboration that had many different segments to it, but the very, very beginning moment had to do with just a very particular story that happened to my family during Hurricane Katrina, which was there's a house that's co-owned by many aunts and uncles on the north shore, not far from New Orleans. And while my immediate family was actually not there ... They were with me in Minneapolis, which is another story ... many members of my family went to this house to kind of [batten] down the hatches.

And the house was surrounded by several hundred century-old pine trees, and during the night of the [hurricane] about one hundred of them came crashing down. They either snapped in half or they were uprooted, and my cousin said, you know, they were running from porch to porch kind of watching these trees fall. And when they awoke in the morning, my cousin described it that it was like a giant had played Tinker Toys with these trees. And this landscape, which had been, you know, kind of core to my family's, culture was completely destroyed.

No lives were lost. Only one tree fell on the house and the house was fine, you know. So in the scale of Katrina's tragedy, it was minor but it was symbolic for my family of a lot of the greater losses that both my family was experiencing back in New Orleans and many people were experiencing in New Orleans. But, you know, just a general just sort of super traumatic experience, almost like [a threat to] my family's [memories] and imagination, you know.

And so, you know, the trees got cleaned up and, you know, life went on. And as Katie and I were thinking about our next project of the company, we were like well, what do you think we should work on? I said, "Katie, I'm haunted by those trees." And Katie said, "Wouldn't it be incredible if we could just build them back again on stage and make it all better?" And I kind of laughed and said, "Yeah, that would be great, if we could actually make it all better."

But that was just the seed that made us start thinking about like, "wow," you know, those trees can't be rebuilt. It's folly to think they can be rebuilt by human hands. What does that look like when you try and grapple with that question as performance artists? Now the piece evolved out of that story and came to be about much more, both when more collaborators were brought in and as we continued to develop the team, so I'll just stop there.

Katie Pearl: Maybe the next thing we can talk about is how the piece found its identity through finding Shawn as a collaborator, and so maybe Shawn will you tell the story from your angle, like how you entered it and where your thoughts started going?

Shawn Hall: Sure. Yeah, so the seed of the idea obviously had, they had it. And when they brought me in, you know, they knew in order to build this, they needed some kind of visual person on their team, ... So we started talking about it and what was interesting to me, well, certainly it was the challenge, the scope of it. I mean it was clear from the start that I was interested in being a full collaborator and really, really interested in the aspect of it being performance and installation, and not a set in theatres. So that's a discussion we had ongoing for a long time.

What was also really interesting to me was that when they had talked around the idea a little bit, the greater assumption was that this was going to be a piece about recycling or something, that that's how *How to Build a Forest* was going to relate to the environment, like they would use recycled materials et cetera, and that just didn't ring true to me. I mean we hadn't decided but we were just, you know, talking about all of this. That didn't ring true to me in terms of my own practice.

You know, I'm a pain and I don't use recycled junk and, you know, it's just not... And we are all conscious of how we all are in this world, because we're all a part of this. And so what was interesting to me is to try to use materials that were not recyclable and point to that. And so I think that that alone was a lot of our core values, I think led us through our research and to, you know, and to the piece, I guess.

Kevin Landis: Shawn, going off of that, could you describe some of the materials that you did use?

Shawn Hall: Yeah, for me, I wanted it to also to relate to my work, which at this point, in particular, is painting and is very ephemeral. It's very transparent. It's evocative of natural processes. So specifically, we, you know, talked about a lot of different materials and I explored a lot of different materials, but it ended up being mostly fabric and translucent fabric, so that you could kind of see through and has that sort of ephemeral quality. There's lots of steel in it. There's lots of foam, spray foam, and florist foam, and plastics of different sorts.

And of course, all of the materials, all these fabrics, [are] sprayed with flame retardant because of the toxins. Lots of the forest is made from oil. So just choices like that, basically fabric, and that really just changed from … That came out of a practical and aesthetic idea of, you know, up and down and weights and all of that. It's like what are we going to do? How are we going to be able to take this up and down easily?

Katie Pearl: So, to tag on to what Shawn was saying, I missed a couple of things. One of the things that came through pretty clearly for us in our thinking, and I can't remember if this was before we talked … I think we came to Shawn with this idea that it was important to us that we wanted to build something and take it away, that we wanted to create a force and remove it, that we wanted to look at a whole cycle that could really acknowledge how long something takes to come into existence, whether that's a mountain, a city, a theatre project, and how quickly it disappears or can be destroyed or eradicated.

And so that was one of the main challenges that Shawn really had to wrestle with, like how do we create something beautiful and intentional that can be put up and taken down every day? And so we did a lot of explorations with simple pulleys and things of that nature. And the idea about recycling was something Lisa and I quickly discovered that as we started writing [drafts] for *How to Build a Forest*, it got curated into environmental theatre, which was not, you know, as Lisa described.

Our impulse coming into it was really personal. We hadn't actually expanded to think about how it lived in conversation with environmental issues and climate issues. And so when that started happening, people made a lot of assumptions about the piece, including what Shawn was talking about that it would be made of recycled materials. But when it became clear how insincere that would be, that it didn't really come from Shawn's aesthetic, and that it also wasn't possible, we became very interested in where the materials did come from.

And that became a huge part of the drama of the piece and a part of what structure the audiences experience looking through the piece, where the field guide we made that tracked most of the materials in the forest all the way back from where we bought them to where they were distributed, to where they were manufactured, to where they were taken out of the earth, to where they started deep in the earth.

Kevin Landis: So I wonder, before you go too far into the details, if one of you could describe a little bit of what the trajectory of the evening looks like. I know it's about six hours of building and then could you just talk a little bit about what the audience saw in that time period.

Katie Pearl: Sure. Lisa, will you do that?

Lisa D'Amour: Yeah, sure. Yeah, so the piece is designed to be experienced for any amount of time that an audience member would like to experience it. So you can come for an hour, eight hours or twenty minutes. And another thing to note is that whenever we've performed the admission has been free, and that's been pretty important because it allows people to come back on multiple days. So some people will come in the beginning on one day and the end on another.

So when you walk into the space where it's performed, which has mostly been theatres but also in an interdisciplinary gallery theatre space, there's a bare floor. Let me describe the arc of the whole experience quickly and then I can explain kind of how people fit [in it]. But if you did come in at the beginning you would see a bare floor, and then you would see seven builders enter the space and just begin, first kind of sweeping the floor and picking up material to prepare it. And then begin bringing in materials which look nothing like a forest. You might see Ziploc bags. You might see a long strand, a long line of kind of like metal objects on stage. You might see plastic tubing. So you're seeing the component parts of what will all eventually be a forest.

While you're sitting down, you're greeted by what we call a ranger, which is someone that has a lot of information about the experience. The ranger tells the audience member how long the builders have been building, a couple of details about where in Louisiana this story comes from. And the ranger also gives people a field guide which is kind of a guide to the forest, especially where all of the materials that are used to make the forest, where they come from in the earth.

The ranger says whenever you're ready you can go up inside and visit the forest, and when you do so, you have to go and see the gatekeeper. He points them to kind of a little desk inside the forest that you have to go visit when you enter. It's almost like the gateway to a park, or something. So when you're ready to go in and kind of get more of an immersive view of the forest, you go visit the gate-keeper who kind of tells you that the builders are busy, that they're not going to speak to you, that you kind of stay quiet in the forest and don't touch things because the forest is delicate.

The ranger then says, "Before you go into the forest we'd like to check the tag on your shirt and see where your shirt was made." And this is when the assistant checks the tag on the shirt, and the gatekeeper keeps track of all of the countries where peoples' shirts were made before they go in. And at that point you also have to take off your shoes, again, just because of the delicate nature of the material.

Once you're inside, you can do kind of whatever you want. You can sit and watch the forest emerge. Some people write in their journals. Some people take naps. Some people use their field guide to explore all of the different materials. But it's almost like you'll be in one place checking out one bit of the forest, and then if you cross the stage and look at another section for a while and then turn around, the place where you were like ten minutes before has changed because it's constantly evolv-ing around you. And that's very much kind of … It's almost like the slow narrative of the piece, of that watching this forest or this story kind of being built around you.

And then when you're ready to either leave the forest or take a break, or maybe go sit back out in the audience, you've been instructed to leave and go visit what's called the overlook, which is a section that we set up usually behind the audience [seats]. And it kind of gives you a wide view of the forest, and that's where you can find your shoes. So everyone has to go up there to get their shoes. And when you're up at the overlook, you're not only looking at the forest from that perspective, but there's also a place to record your thought, and that is where the sort of giant chart of all the shirts and dresses, or whatever, that have come through the forest is listed there.

So what we're really trying to do is give this feeling that you are a part of a system or you are a part of this ecosystem of materials, you know, that kind of makes up our daily lives, and that these materials that we use come from nature and come from forests.

So within that structure there are many different experiences that someone can have. There's also, at different periods of times, some actual spoken text that happens very, very quietly in the audience. So it almost feels like you're overhearing the subconscious of the forest speaking to you, but it's very fleeting and very quiet. So the experience really isn't like a play at all where actors are saying lines, but any kind of story is happening really quiet. Any kind of conventional spoken dialogue is happening really quietly on the edges.

I guess the last thing I will say is the other kind of interaction with text is the builders have in their pockets, so that we don't interact with the audience in a spoken way, we have little messages in our pockets that look almost like strips of what you would get in a fortune cookie. And they hold phrases that say things like "intimacy is awesome", or "we have no idea what we are doing", or "tree time", these little koans (paradoxical puzzles) that kind of gets to the heart of what the piece is about.

Shawn Hall: Actually, there's one other interaction builders have with the audience about once an hour. Most of the builders go out into the audience to kind of get a look at the forest, see the progress, we sit down next to somebody or next to a group of people and we have a very simple interaction with them that kind of describes what is happening in very literal terms that might explain the materials. And then that sends us into a reverie, a shared reminiscence about what that makes us think of, a time in nature for that.

And then we say we have to go back to work. So they're just like little ... The piece itself is really forest. It's a very anti-theatrical in that way, that it's not a controlled event so that we are creating that people are supposed to sit still and watch. It's a growing inspiration and that is the event, and it invites people to move through it and be with it in all sorts of ways.

Lisa D'Amour: Just in terms of family, I think that's all a really good description. One thing I would say that the gatekeeper does do and that the piece does. It's like basically you can go in and do almost anything within rules. I do feel like this whole piece sets a tone about stewardship, especially the first six hours. So you can't be silly in the forest and do whatever you want to. You can't pick things. You can't walk wherever you want to. There are rules and I think that that's one of strengths of the piece.

And within anything, there are parameters. Yeah, have a lot to do with, you know, especially the first six hours, seven hours experience of the piece.

Katie Pearl:	We talked a lot amongst ourselves, knowing that we would get this question a lot; "Can I help," that audience members would want to be involved. And we went back and forth about that a lot, but ultimately we've landed on the answer is "no, you can't help", for a couple of reasons. Sometimes they say that the builders have to do it on their own, but the more interesting answer … and you guys can help me remember how we articulated this, is that there's a limit to what humans can do, whereas the forest happens just to take care of itself. Is that accurate?
Shawn Hall:	I think that is partially accurate, yes, and also I think that it was important … It's kind of odd to say this but it's not entertainment as well. It's contemplation so, in a sense, when you're allowed to help … And I'm just talking off the top of my head. I don't remember exactly how we framed it but you're not just thinking … You may be. I mean you might be the type of person that could help and think about the implications as well, but it isn't common … There were a few comments throughout the piece about the colorful nature of it, for example, that it inspired reminiscence, you know, which is fine.
	But to sort of dispel that, it wasn't a playground. It was an ecosystem that was fragile in its own way and that's the thing that we were trying to distil. So, in essence, how can you even help if you don't even understand what it is? How can you help? That might be a question.
Kevin Landis:	I wonder if we could build off of this a little bit because this idea of stewardship I think is really interesting to me, to us I think. Because, you know, we are dealing with the idea of, in this book,

starting with human performance and some other basic ideas of performance that we all can recognize as performance, a play, you know, a concert, a speech, or so forth. And then we're also looking at nature as performance. Can I go to Niagara Falls and sit and watch the falls and call that a performance?

But this idea of stewardship makes us consciously aware of the intersection of nature and humanity. I wonder if we could hone in on that a little bit more to talk a bit about what is the responsibility of the viewer. Why is this necessarily different than just inviting the audience out into a forest?

Shawn Hall: Well, to me, one of the ways, and again, I think Katie and Lisa can speak in different ways and better, but when I think about the field guide and our field guide not only talked about where things came from the earth, but it also talked about the species and what they were made up of. It didn't name what the species was. It names what the materials were. How do I say this? I'm not sure. Let me think about it. I kind of got lost in the thought a little bit.

Kevin Landis: No, that's okay. So, I mean it's just getting the intersection of human and nature. Where are those intersections most clear in this work?

Lisa D'Amour: Well, let me see if this gets to your question. I mean this piece, in many ways was designed to be performed in the cities. It was originally, you know, its premiere was in New York City. I think in many ways, it's designed to … I hate to generalize, but get city people to slow down for a second and realize that they are living in nature, even though it doesn't feel that way every day. It feels like they're kind of, you know, well, [only living] an urban life and nature is far away.

And so part of the pace that we worked on as builders ... And if you get a chance to kind of look at the sort of core values on the sheet that I sent you, you'll get a feeling for it. It was all about getting the builders into a rhythm and a kind of focused intention that would create a pace that would encourage everyone else to slow down. And really contemplate that link and start to think about like, oh, we are in nature right now because all of these materials that we're using, that we're eating, that we're wearing, that we're sitting in, they come from nature.

So I think that's the kind of the [perceptual] shift that we're trying to support, gently support, without being didactic, and making a lot of room for how you get there. But there's a lot of encouragement from both the pace of the piece, the particular language that's used in the field guide, and also we worked really hard on what the words that the ranger and the gatekeepers use to guide your experience. Does that kind of get to it?

Kevin Landis:	Yeah, oh absolutely, that's great.
Shawn Hall:	Yeah, I think that it does ... Well, you can also kind of -
Katie Pearl:	I find myself thinking about the whole art of the piece, which includes not just the building and the being inside of this incredibly beautiful intricate forest, but also the demolition of it. And the fact that the whole thing is contained in one cycle, and that we don't ... Maybe we should talk for a second about how the piece changes in that last hour.

So one thing that happens is that for six and a half, seven hours, the primary focus of attention that the leader of all the action has been the materials themselves, the forest itself. The builders are really there to serve and allow those materials to come into their full manifestation. And then in the half an hour that the forest is complete, the builders are present just as like light animators, like helping the forest live.

And then when hour seven starts, for the very first time we intrude into this space with a very mechanized human-derived sound, which is the sound of like a truck backing up, that beeping, a sound that's so recognizable, and [through] that microphone that's [dropped] down right in sort of the focal point of the forest. As we start to take the materials away, one by one, we step up to the microphone and speak various checks into the microphone, sort of demanding that the focus becomes the human.

The way that we interact with the materials totally changes and they kind of go back into just being [that] … They're just lost baggage, so we just strip them of their identify that we've crafted over time. And people who were there for that part describe it as being a really emotional and difficult experience to go through, especially if they've spent quite a bit of time throughout the day in the forest.

But I think that's one of the ways [instead of] them being in a real forest and like time, tree time, which was such a core value for us in terms of understanding how to be in the performance of the whole installation itself. When you're in a real forest, you can't see fifty years in the future and two hundred years in the past, or two hundred years in the future and fifty years in the past. And so it stays abstract, you know, on the sort force of dominance on nature to humans, humans to nature. And within our eight hours, we kind of force ourselves to live fully in both relationships.

Suzanne MacAulay: Yeah, so when we started this conversation I said, "oh gee," we *were* going to have an article about gardening. But I think we do have an article about gardening. It's really interesting you know, the idea of stewardship, the gardener. The audience, let's say at the formal Gardens of Versailles, the people that are walking through, they don't go, you know, interacting with gardeners and the staff or anything like that. It's always being a spectator, but feeling. You know, it's not like it creates distance. So I can see where this might dovetail [with our original intent].

Something else that occurs to me, the idea, the de-installation, the demolishing, reminds me of the times that I've been around Tibetan monks when they've done the Sand Mandala, which is created over time. It's not an eight-hour span, but that visceral feeling when they brush the sand off and then toss it into nearby water or something. Here is the audience, you know, with you so intensely off and on, watching the set grow and being built, and then all of a sudden, down it comes.

Does the design change? Do you do a different kind of forest with each performance, or is it fairly determined? Maybe Shawn can answer that.

Shawn Hall: Well, if you mean by design, the objects, no.

Suzanne MacAulay: Yeah, and like the placement.

Shawn Hall: The layout or the footprint of the piece does change slightly, depending on the stage, but in general, it's the same. It's always a little bit different, just like when we perform it we're very loosely choreographed. We know what our jobs are. So I think it's always different every time within a space.

Katie Pearl: And also Shawn, every time we've done it the forest has evolved a little bit. One challenge of this piece was that we couldn't envision it. Shawn could never see it fully until we were doing it, and also she's part of the build team. And so, like those moments of stepping out into the audience so she [could] look at this forest, are really important to her, just in terms of the process of like what is this thing I made and what do I want to do next time? So we sort of had [installations become] a little more intricate each time.

Lisa D'Amour: I'd also like to say that we've performed this piece in many different sizes of spaces and configurations. So in addition to sometimes slightly changing the design of a big object, like maybe the big tree or adding aspects to support, often there's just a sort of slightly new configuration of the forest that needs to be adapted each time. And because it's the only way to sort of rehearse this assembly was to have the forest completely up, disassembly has really evolved over the course of touring the piece in terms of …

The first time we did our disassembly there was actually no spoken text at all. It was all recorded text. But then we've moved to that being the first time where a microphone invades the space, and each builder has a chance to kind of come up and kind of like … So the text is set but it's almost like they're venting about the loss of their own forest, in a way. That aspect of how we disassemble has really evolved and that's been very interesting to see that evolve over a couple of years, really.

Suzanne MacAulay: I can personally relate to this. I live high in the mountains and I have a giant ridge covered with trees. Those trees are threatened by a clear cutting project that the Forest Service is proposing. We're fighting it all the way but, you know, it's kind of the bookend to Lisa's original story of nature just flattening a personal forest. I consider mine a personal forest too, but you know, this idea of forces beyond our control, you know, just doing that.

Now I've got the $64,000 question. This book is all about cultural performance, more or less. So how do you see this as a cultural performance?

Katie Pearl: Can you just define cultural performance?

Suzanne MacAulay: Oh, I was going to do that too, sure. I'm sorry. Just a basic, you know, working definition is the idea of performance embedded in a cultural ethos, a worldview, let's say. It can be a group, you know, like Boy Scouts, or it can be a community. It can be a nation. An obvious [example] is ethnicity. When you think of Ukrainian Easter Eggs, making the eggs and [creating] the designs are a cultural performance. That's really, you know, the "street definition."

Lisa D'Amour: I have two different answers. I don't [know] if either of them will win the full 64,000. So here are my two thoughts; the first is there's an aspect of this performance that is very rooted in Louisiana culture. The seed of the piece was Katrina, the way that we developed the entire piece in New Orleans during the BP (British Petroleum) oil spill, which very much influences the aesthetic and politics of the piece. And in addition to that, you know, there was a real community that developed around the piece as we made it in New Orleans.

All of the performers, all of the builders who work on the piece, they live in New Orleans or very connected to New Orleans, like Katie, and all of the people that we hired to weld, to screen print. So we're all really kind of anyways all living in the same neighborhood of New Orleans. I would say that Shawn is a New Orleans visual artist, and not only is her sort aesthetic kind of woven throughout the piece, but there was a real desire to create a forest that could evoke an above-ground forest and a deep sea forest, because this piece is so connected to Gulf Coast issues.

And especially because we were making it during this threatening oil spill which, you know at the time… The Gulf seems to be healing itself [now], but that remains to be seen. But we were in a state of complete panic when that was happening because, I mean, it felt worse than Katrina. It couldn't be stopped. It was going on and on and it really infused its way into our thinking about the piece.

And I guess the other thing I'd like to say in brief, and Katie or Shawn could elaborate on this, is we've kind of built [the] forest to create its own culture and community wherever it goes. So when we go to a university, you know, we travel there with our team of seven builders, the stage manager, and a sound artist, but it requires the participation of like at least twenty other performers. Performers is not quite the right word. That's my "fall back" language. Participants, rangers, gatekeepers, people who install the piece, and people who create self-guided tours based on the local environmental issues we want to address.

So it's weird. It needs an ecosystem of people in the local site just in order to make it happen. I don't know if there is such a word. The [performance/installation] kind of evolves every time we do the piece, and that's very intentional on our part, that like we want it to need to involve the intention of many other people as we tour the piece.

Suzanne MacAulay: Wonderful, perfect, very good.

Shawn Hall: There's just one thing just that I would add. I think that it is also a part of a larger community, a small but growing community of environmental artists and educators and activists, I think, through the arts. And I mean I would consider that a culture.

Suzanne MacAulay: Yeah, right. Yes, there are many intersections here and it's a great answer. It's like, you know, looking at tree rings. There are many, many overlaps and they keep circling around each other. You have identified a lot of interesting connections here.

Kevin Landis: I have one other quick question here. Well, maybe it's quick but Lisa, you had mentioned before this sort of care about not being overly didactic. Could you, or any of you actually, speak a little bit about why that's important, especially in the context of a piece that, as you also admitted, is political? It has lots of political overtones with the BP spill and with Katrina, and you know, the materials that you used, the oil-based materials that you used. You know, talk about the negotiation of not being terribly didactic while at the same time, if I could say it like this, having a slant, or maybe that's not the way of putting it?

Shawn Hall: Having a what did you?

Kevin Landis:	A slant, I mean if I could put it-
Shawn Hall:	A slant, okay, I thought you said a splint.
Kevin Landis:	Or that, fine.
Suzanne MacAulay:	That fits with the forest.
Katie Pearl:	I can start that and then other people can fill it in. When you were describing the tree rings, you know, that are overlapping it made me think about this is the way to answer that question. The issues that the piece is in conversation with are so complicated and layered and complex. And one thing that I think we felt really strongly about is that we don't have an answer. We don't have particular argument and it's not just one story. It's not just the story of Lisa's family. It's not just the BP oil spill. It's not just any of those things.

And so I think that were we to try to hone more directly to one narrative line or one argument, that's where I think the didacticism would come up. But it would also allow people to kind of stay on the outside of that story or argument and make a judgment about whether they agree or disagree with it, which is not something that we're interested ... That's not the relationship we wanted to have. And so the porousness that I brought up earlier serves so many purposes, but what it mostly does, is it invites people into a structure and experience, and a durational event that has a very clear aesthetic, clearly articulate aesthetic, clearly articulated point of view, I think.

But it gives people permission to be inside of it and have their own responses and narratives and stories and experiences in the options, and that brings people closer to the issues I think, because there's nothing for them to be on the [outside]. There's nothing for them to say like, "Oh, well they were saying this but that's just their view," you know. It's sort of like tae kwon do or tai chi. Like we just sort of go with [the energy] instead of having some concrete barrier for people to bash up against.

Shawn Hall: That's a great way to put it Katie, I think definitely. Just in the way that all things exist at the same time as well, it's sort of a model for that. We wanted to have a sense of wonder. We wanted to have it feel like somebody could walk in and feel like it was like what we'd call tree time, that just, you know, hushing quiet, you know, sense of other. And at the same time, yeah, it really just presents the facts [of events] you know. It's like with all of the facts of the piece in terms of where it comes from and what we're doing, it just stands on its own. It allows somebody to think for themselves and feel for themselves without us... yeah, great.

Lisa D'Amour: Yeah, and I would also say that if you really engage with the piece and use the field guide and start to really look at the ... If you read the field guide, if you just start seeing oil, oil, oil in terms of where all these materials come from, so I don't think you have to look too far to kind of see our point of view. It's just that we're not really shouting at you. And I think that's a through line in a lot of [build a force] work, which is inviting people in and trying to encourage them to look closer. And also experience a kind of sense of wonder that might soften your assumptions and allow you to start thinking more politically.

Shawn Hall: I think that that's something both of our works share. I would say that's an aspect of my work as well. It never has been didactic. It hits you on the head but it addresses all of those issues and—

Katie Pearl: I think it's interesting. I hadn't considered this before but, you know, it's probably one of the benefits of working with materiality, as opposed to like character. Actually, that sort of strenuous objectivity, like you can't argue with a material. It just is there. Or like as performers and as a build team, for example, in the final hour during disassembly we were very careful not to try … We tried very hard not to be like angry or mean as we were taking things down. You know, we were just doing the job as efficiently as we could.

And the difference between efficiency, which is a human value, like an industrial age capitalist value, is different than values that grow out of the natural world. So just lining that up side by side is enough. Like we don't then need to say, "And this is that."

Lisa D'Amour: Right.

Kevin Landis: Well, this has been terrific. Suzanne and I keep glancing at each other very excited, because so much of this is just right in line with things, the things, that we're writing about. Is there anything that we must know that we haven't asked? There's just so much good in this, I'm so happy. This is perfect for the chapter and perfect for the book.

Lisa D'Amour: We could send you a couple of images. I mean we could talk, the three of us, and then decide and send you a couple of them just to choose from, perhaps.

Kevin Landis: That would be great.

Lisa D'Amour: There's two images that we really kind of like using side by side. One is one of just the completed forest. But then there's a really amazing picture we have of like five women sewing the big tree in the studio. So they also like somehow capture the sort of stewardship and the handmade-ness of the piece. Because I do think that a big part of the experience is being on the outside and kind of seeing these strange objects, and then coming in to the forest and, you know, there's a lot of really, you know, delicate hand embroidery on all of the trees. And suddenly you're getting this close up view of the labor that it took to make this work, so I think it's a big part of the experience.

Shawn Hall: Yeah, and in that same sense, kind of helping to instill or promote observation, you know, just because it takes a certain settling down and settling in to actually observe what's around you. I think that's one thing that this piece does. The more you look the more that you see, just like you do actually in nature.

Lisa D'Amour: Could I add one last tangential thought before I forget, in terms of this sort of performing object thing? I think it could be helpful, which is, you know I'm primarily a writer. And during the process of figuring out what this forest was and how we were going to present it, I probably wrote like one hundred pages of text. I was like maybe there will be a scene in the forest with like three old women sewing and talking about the end of the world. Or maybe there'll be like a little play that happens like during disassembly.

I just wrote and wrote and wrote and I would bring it in when we were kind of rehearsing the installation, and you know, have people go in the forest and do these scenes. Over and over and over it just became clear that like none of it was appropriate to this event. And the way that I see it is that it took a lot for the forest to sort of teach me to get out of the way.

Suzanne MacAulay: Yeah, wonderful.

Lisa D'Amour: Like get out of the way and let the objects speak, and I fought it and fought it and fought it. But you know, in many ways I think that it's what makes the piece so successful that I kind of like let go of the word and let the experience be something different. But it also just reminds me like how long it takes to, you know, escape our small mind and understand like what we had to do in order to steward the environment or understand our relationship to nature.

Kevin Landis: That's great.

Suzanne MacAulay: Yeah, that's perfect Lisa.

End of Interview

Image 14 *How to Build a Forest* © Shawn Hall

Afterword

We began this study with a somewhat cheeky question, "What should we call this book?" There was, though, a certain reality behind our query. *Cultural Performance: Ethnographic Approaches to Performance Studies* frames a conversation that has and must continue to unfold about the nature of human interaction and performance. But, as we acknowledged from the outset, and as we hope you have seen, the area of inquiry is enormous. When one dives into cultural performance it quickly becomes clear that structure can break down and almost anything can fit under that moniker. Within this study we have traveled to Ethiopia, Colorado, the West Village, Ireland, Iceland, Ghana, Bhutan, New Zealand, Indonesia, Greece and a forest that, with enough time, could be constructed in any place on Earth.

While we embrace the broadness of the subject, it is clear that there are common themes that arise. As you read in the interview with the artists who created *How to Build a Forest*, decisions that were made in the development of their work fit within many of the parameters that we have discussed in the book. We saw the need for community engagement, a recalling of tradition and history, and an intentionality around somatics and bodily experience, among many other "terms" and "criteria" that you have explored.

It is important though, when considering ethnography, not to be limited by structures and definition. What constitutes cultural performance? The answer is yours and throughout the book we asked you to apply discoveries embedded in the various case studies to your own lives. To frame the conversation, we offered three lenses: *Aesthetics of Experience, Place and Space* and *The Sensory Body*. Within those categories we discovered many more elements relating to cultural performance.

We have noticed that there is a clear sense of journeying that seems to be a part of many of the traditions that we discussed. Think of some examples: the early exploration of pilgrimage to the Tiger's Nest Monastery, the mobility of *Bluebeard* around the West Village, the Maori motor caravan to the town of Whanganui, the long, lonely road to Tuacahn, Utah, the drive to Peter Schumann's farm in Vermont, the ethnographer's sonic education that took her from Ireland to Indonesia, the tourist descent onto Nederland, Colorado for Frozen Dead Guy Days. We continually see examples of cultural communities using travel, or at least traversing space as a curious component of cultural performance. In fact, as we have looked at the intersections of theatre, performance and ethnography, it has come into focus that there is an intentionality to cultural performance, a deliberate consideration of interactions and connections. We posed questions throughout about technology and its effect on cultural performance. How might your viewing of a work be changed if it were on your smart phone? Watching an episode of a reality show in your living room doesn't quite feel like a cultural performance, even if the themes expressed on the show reflect some of the mores and traditions of your society. Why is this?

We are not suggesting that cultural performance cannot be technologically sophisticated and you can certainly think of examples of communities embracing technological advancements to propel their cultural performances. But here the element of journey or pilgrimage implies something else worthy of some thought. It suggests that our cultural performances require a desire for connection, and to accomplish that, we must congregate with our community members. Thus, another theme that came up quite a bit: presence and co-presence. These terms are by no means new in the field of ethnography or performance studies, and many scholars were cited who used the concepts regularly. We saw that performance is generative and that it actually creates presence, a communion of sorts between the performers, the viewers, the setting and the general atmosphere. In this way, the cultural performance must imply effort at making connection in a specific time and space.

This is slippery ground, to be sure. You might rightly ask: can presence be engaged over the internet? Can you effectively participate in a cultural performance from the other side of the world? Consider the following example: The Virtual Choir or its subgroup, the Virtual Choir Friends, has a membership of one thousand singers from all over the world. Each singer records their individual parts (soprano, alto, tenor and bass).

Then posts their recordings online where their performances merge with all the others to create the vibrant sound of a choir. This represents a unified, evocative performance in a different space and time from the reality of being in the moment. We've discussed all these features (space, time, effect, etc.) throughout the book. Having access to these virtual performances whenever one feels like it, is a vastly different experience from attending a local cultural performance, but suggests myriad possibilities for audience and performer interactions in the future. These possibilities also align with our flexible, more open-ended interpretation of cultural performance. Again, it would be up to each individual viewer to determine the cultural elements at work in each case, and consider what constitutes a community of performers and audience in this 4D world of space and time. It seems that we could at least say that cultural performance relies on the will of the performers and watchers to be aware of their communion and their mutual complicity in creating presence, wherever they happen to be. To ape the old aphorism, if a cultural performance happens in the woods, with no one there to witness it, did it really happen?

And maybe we should leave it there. While we did title the book *Cultural Performance,* we have come to realize that to succinctly define the term would be reductive. As with many artistic genres, movements or broad categorizations, meaning and clarity (if it exists) happens in the dialectic; the discussion and assessment of what you see, hear and feel. That is the job for you, the ethnographer, the theatre maker, the artist, the cultural agent. Enjoy.

Bibliography

Abrahams, Roger D. "An American Vocabulary of Celebrations." In *Time out of Time: Essays on the Festival*, edited by Alessandro Falassi, 173–83. Albuquerque, NM: University of New Mexico Press, 1987.

Arnott, Peter. *Greek Scenic Conventions in the Fifth Century BC*. Westport, CT: Clarendon, 1962.

Artaud, Antonin. *The Theatre and its Double*. Translated by Mary Caroline Richards. New York, New York: Grove Press, 1958.

Bachelard, Gaston. *The Poetics of Space*, 1994 edition. Boston, MA: Beacon Press, 1994.

Barcelo, Diane. Interview with Suzanne MacAulay, Avery Point, CT, 27 June 2013.

Baudriallard, Jean. *Simulacra and Simulation*. Translated by Sheila Faria Glaser. Ann Arbor: the University of Michigan Press, 1994.

Bauman, Richard. *Verbal Art as Performance*. Long Grove, IL: Waveland Press, 1984.

———. "The Place of Festival in the Worldview of the Seventeenth-Century Quakers." In *Time out of Time: Essays on the Festival*, edited by Alessandro Falassi, 93–8. Albuquerque, NM: University of New Mexico Press, 1987.

Baynes-Rock, Marcus. *Among the Bone Eaters: Encounters with Hyenas in Harar*. University Park, PA: The Pennsylvania State University Press, 2015.

Bhabha, Homi K. *The Location of Culture*. New York, NY: Routledge, 1994.

Bell, John. "The End of *Our Domestic Resurrection Circus*: Bread and Puppet Theatre and Counterculture Performance in the 1990s." *The Drama Review* 43.3, 1999: 62–80.

Berger, Harris M. *Stance: Ideas about Emotion, Style, and Meaning for the Study of Expressive Culture*. Middletown, CT: Wesleyan University Press, 2009.

Bonnemaison, Jöel. *Culture and Space: Conceiving a New Cultural Geography*, trans. Josée Pénot-Demetry, edited by Chantal Blanc-Pamard, Maud Lasseur and Christel Thibault. London and New York, NY: I.B. Tauris, 2005.

Bourdieu, Pierre. "What Makes a Social Class? On the Theoretical and Practical Existence of Groups." *Berkeley Journal of Sociology* 32, 1987: 1–17.

Brantley, Ben. "God vs Man in an Open-Air Fight." *New York Times*, August 24, 2009. http://www.nytimes.com/2009/08/25/theater/reviews/25bacchae.html.

Brockett, Oscar G. and Franklin J. Hildy. *History of the Theatre*. New York, NY: Allyn and Bacon, 2003.

Brook, Peter. *The Empty Space*. New York, NY: Touchstone Press, 1968.

Bruner, Edward M. *The Anthropology of Experience*. Urbana and Chicago, IL: University of Illinois Press, 1986.

Bull, Michael and Jon P. Mitchell, eds. *Ritual, Performance and the Senses*. London: Bloomsbury Academic, 2015.

Buzzaetém, Monique and Tom Bickley, eds. *Anthology of Essays on Deep Listening*. Kingston, NY: Deep Listening Publications, 2012.

Cage, John. *Silence: Lectures and Writings*. Hanover: Wesleyan University Press, 1961.

Camp, Pannill. *The First Frame: Theatre Space in Enlightenment France*. Cambridge: Cambridge University Press, 2014.

Carlson, Marvin. *Places of Performance: The Semiotics of Theatre Architecture*. Ithaca, NY: Cornell University Press, 1989.

———. *Performance: A Critical Introduction*, 2nd edition. New York, NY and London: Routledge, 2004.

Casey, Edward S. "How to Get from Space to Place in a Fairly Short Stretch of Time: Phenomenological Prolegomena." In *Senses of Place*, edited by Steven Feld and Keith H. Basso, 13–52. Santa Fe, NM: School of American Research Press, 1996.

———. "On habitus and place." *Annals of the Association of American Geographers* 91.4, 2001: 716–23.

Chaudhuri, Una. *Staging Place: The Geography of Modern Drama*. Ann Arbor, MI: University of Michigan Press, 1997.

———. "Embattled Animals in a Theatre of Species." In *Performing Animality: Animals in Performance Practices*, edited by Lourdes Orozco and Jennifer Parker-Starbuck, 135–49. Basingstoke: Palgrave Macmillan, 2015.

———. *The Stage Lives of Animals: Zooësis and Performance*. London and New York, NY: Routledge, 2017.

Conquergood, Dwight. "Beyond the Text: Toward a Performative Cultural Politics." In *Cultural Struggles: Performance, Ethnography, Praxis*, edited by E. Patrick Johnson, 47–63. Ann Arbor, MI: The University of Michigan Press, 2013.

Crouch, David. "Performances and Constitutions of Natures: A Consideration of the Performance of Lay Geographies." In *Nature Performed: Environment, Culture and Performance*, edited by Bronislaw Szerszynski, Wallace Heim and Claire Waterton, 19–30. Oxford: Blackwell Publishing Ltd., 2003.

Cull, Laura. "From *Homo Performans* to Interspecies Collaboration: Expanding the Concept of Performance to Include Animals." In *Performing Animality: Animals in Performance Practices*, edited by Lourdes Orozco and Jennifer Parker-Starbuck, 19–36. Basingstoke: Palgrave Macmillan, 2015.

De Certeau, Michel. "Walking in the City." In *The Practice of Everyday Life*, trans. Steven Rendall, 91–110. Berkeley, CA: University of California Press, 1984.

Eliason, Eric A. *To See Them Run: Great Plains Coyote Coursing*. Jackson, MS: University Press of Mississippi, 2015.

Emigh, John. *Masked Performance: The Play of Self and Other in Ritual and Theatre*. Philadelphia, PA: University of Pennsylvania Press, 1996.

Feld, Steven. *Sound and Sentiment: Birds, Weeping, Poetics, and Song in Kaluli Expression*. Philadelphia, PA: University of Pennsylvania Press, 1982.

Feld, Steven and Keith H. Basso, eds. *Senses of Place*. Santa Fe, NM: School of American Research Press, 1996.

Fernandez, James. "The Argument of Images and the Experience of Returning to the Whole." In *The Anthropology of Experience*, edited by Victor Turner and Edward M. Bruner, 159–87. Urbana, IL: University of Illinois Press, 1986.

Fischer-Lichte, Erika. *The Transformative Power of Performance: A New Aesthetics*, trans. Saskya Iris Jain. London and New York, NY: Routledge, 2008.

Fuchs, Elinor and Una Chaudhuri, eds. *Land/Scape/Theater*. Ann Arbor, MI: University of Michigan Press, 2002.

Garner, Stanton B. Jr. "Urban Landscapes, Theatrical Encounters: Staging the City." In *Land/Scape/Theater*, edited by Elinor Fuchs and Una Chaudhuri. Ann Arbor, MI: University of Michigan Press, 2002.

Geertz, Clifford. "Afterword." In *Senses of Place*, edited by Steven Feld and Keith H. Basso, 13–52. Santa Fe, NM: School of American Research Press, 1996.

———. *Available Light*. Princeton: Princeton University Press, 2000.

Glassie, Henry. *Passing the Time in Ballymenone*. Philadelphia, PA: University of Pennsylvania Press, 1982.

Grimes, Ronald L. "Ritual Theory and the Environment." In *Nature Performed: Environment, Culture and Performance*, edited by Bronislaw Szerszynski, Wallace Heim and Claire Waterton, 31–45. Oxford: Blackwell Publishing Ltd., 2003.

Grotowski, Jerzy. *Towards a Poor Theatre*, edited by Eugenio Barba. New York, NY: Routledge, 2002.

Hahn, Tomie. *Sensational Knowledge: Embodying Culture through Japanese Dance*. Middletown, CT: Wesleyan University Press, 2007.

Henderson, John A. *The First Avant-Garde, 1887–1894: Sources of the Modern French Theatre*. London: GG Harrap, 1971.

Hill, Leslie. "On Location: Introduction." In *Performance and Place*, edited by Leslie Hill and Helen Paris. New York, NY: Palgrave Macmillan, 2006.

Hobsbawm, Eric and Terence Ranger. *The Invention of Tradition*. New York, NY: Cambridge University Press, 1983.

Hodge, Alison, ed. *Twentieth Century Actor Training*. Abington, PA: Routledge, 2006.

Hughes-Freeland, Felicia, ed. *Ritual, Performance, Media*. New York, NY and London: Routledge, 1998.

Hunter, Victoria. "Embodying the Site: The Here and Now in Site-Specific Dance Performance." *New Theatre Quarterly* 21.4, 2005: 367–81.

Johnson, E. Patrick. "Introduction: 'Opening and Interpreting Lives." In *Cultural Struggles: Performance, Ethnography, Praxis*, edited by Dwight Conquergood and E. Patrick Johnson, 1–14. Ann Arbor, MI: The University of Michigan Press, 2013.

Kapchan, Deborah A. "Performance." *The Journal of American Folklore* 108.430, Autumn 1995: 479–508.

Kaplan, Donald M. "Theatre Architecture: A Derivation of the Primal Cavity." *The Drama Review* 12.3, Spring 1968: 105–16.

Knowles, Richard. *Reading the Material Theatre*. Cambridge: Cambridge University Press, 2004.

Knopf, Robert, ed. *Theatre of the Avant-Garde, 1890–1950*. New Haven, CT: Yale University Press, 2015.

Kuper, Hilda. "The Language of Sites in the Politics of Space." In *The Anthropology of Space and Place: Locating Culture*, edited by Setha M. Low and Denise Lawrence-Zúñiga, 247–63. Oxford: Blackwell Publishing Ltd., 2003.

Landis, Judson R. *Sociology: Concepts and Characteristics*, 8th edition. Belmont, CA: Wadsworth, Inc., 1992.

Landis, Kevin. "Dreaming in Place." *American Theatre* 26.6, July/August 2009: 28–79.

———. "Culinary Pataphysics: Food, Theatre and the Historical Avant-Garde." *Gastronomica: The Journal of Food and Culture* 14.2, Summer 2014, 46–55.

Lawlor, Barbara. "Celebrating Grandpa Bredo - corpse on ice." *The Mountain-Ear*, 1 March 2001: 5.

Leacroft, Richard and Helen Leacroft. *Theatre and Playhouse: An Illustrated Survey of Theatre Buildings from Ancient Greece to the Present Day*. New York, NY: Methuen, 1984.

Ley, Graham. *Ancient Greek Theater*. Chicago, IL and London: The University of Chicago Press, 1991.

Lewis, George E. "Improvised Music After 1950: Afrological and Eurological Perspectives." *Black Music Research Journal* 16.1, Spring, 1996: 91–122.

Low, Setha M. and Denise Lawrence-Zúñiga. "Locating Culture." In *The Anthropology of Space and Place: Locating Culture*, edited by Setha M. Low and Denise Lawrence-Zúñiga, 1–47. Oxford: Blackwell Publishing Ltd., 2003.

MacAulay, Suzanne P. *Stitching Rites: Colcha Embroidery Along the Northern Rio Grande*. Tucson, AZ: The University of Arizona Press, 2000.

———. "Communities and the Poetic Imaginary." *Journal of Literature and Art Studies* 6.2, February 2016: 105–20.

Madison, D. Soyini. *Critical Ethnography*, 2nd edition. Los Angeles, CA: SAGE Publications Inc., 2012.

Marchand, Trevor J. "Place-making in the Holy of Holies: The Church of the Holy Sepulcher, Jerusalem." In *Ritual, Performance and the Senses*, edited by Michael Bull and Jon P. Mitchell, 63–83. London: Bloomsbury Academic, 2015.

Marvin, Garry. "A Passionate Pursuit: Foxhunting as Performance." In *Nature Performed: Environment, Culture and Performance*, edited by Bronislaw Szerszynski, Wallace Heim and Claire Waterton, 46–60. Oxford: Blackwell Publishing Ltd., 2003.

———. "The Art of Fierceness: The Performance of the Spanish Fighting Bull." In *Performing Animality: Animals in Performance Practices*, edited by Lourdes Orozco and Jennifer Parker-Starbuck, 39–56. Basingstoke: Palgrave Macmillan, 2015.

McAuley, Gay. *Space in Performance: Making Meaning in the Theatre*. Ann Arbor, MI: The University of Michigan Press, 1999.

Medina, Juan Estevan. Interview with Suzanne MacAulay, Fort Garland Morada, Fort Garland, Colorado, 23 September, 1993.

Moore, Alexander. "Walt Disney World: Bounded Ritual Space and the Playful Pilgrimage Center." *Anthropological Quarterly* 53.4, October 1980: 207–18.

Mirecka, Rena. Interview with Kevin Landis, Sardinia, Italy, 19 June, 2008.

Newhall, Mary Anne Santos. *Mary Wigman*. London: Routledge, 2009.

Noyes, Dorothy. "Group." *The Journal of American Folklore* 108.430, Autumn 1995: 449–78.

Orozco, Lourdes and Jennifer Parker-Starbuck. *Performing Animality: Animals in Performance Practices*. Basingstoke: Palgrave Macmillan, 2015.

Parker-Starbuck, Jennifer and Roberta Mock. "Researching the Body in/as Performance." In *Research Methods in Theatre and Performance*, edited by Baz Kershaw and Helen Nicholson, 210–35. Edinburgh: Edinburgh University Press, 2011.

Pearson, Mike. *"In Comes I" Performance, Memory and Landscape*. Exeter: University of Exeter Press, 2006.

Ridout, Nicholas. *Stage Fright, Animals and Other Theatrical Problems*. Cambridge: Cambridge University Press, 2006.

Rodman, Margaret C. "Empowering Place: Multilocality and Multivocality." In *The Anthropology of Space and Place: Locating Culture*, edited by Setha M. Low and Denise Lawrence-Zúñiga, 204–23. Oxford: Blackwell Publishing Ltd., 2003.

Royce, Anya Peterson. *Anthropology of the Performing Arts*. New York, NY: Altamira Press, 2004.

Ruprecht, Lucia. "Gesture, Interruption, Vibration: Rethinking Early Twentieth-Century Gestural Theory and Practice in Walter Benjamin, Rudolf von Laban, and Mary Wigman." *Dance Research Journal* 47.2, August 2015: 23–41.

Schechner, Richard. *Performance Studies: An Introduction*, 2nd edition. London: Routledge, 2006.

Schechner, Richard and Lisa Wolford, eds. *The Grotowski Sourcebook*. London and New York, NY: Routledge, 1997, 286.

Schechner, Richard and Willa Appel. "Introduction." In *By Means of Performance: Intercultural Studies of Theatre and Ritual*, edited by Richard Schechner and Willa Appel. Cambridge: Cambridge University Press, 1990.

Senelick, Laurence. "Consuming Passions: Eating and the Stage at the Fin de Siècle." *Gastronomica: The Journal of Food and Culture* 5.2, Spring 2005: 43–9.

Singer, Milton. *Traditional India: Structure and Change*. Philadelphia, PA: The American Folklore Society, 1959.

Sklar, Deidre. "Reprise: On Dance Ethnography." *Dance Research Journal* 32.1, Summer 2000: 70–7.

———. "Unearthing Kinesthesia: Groping Among Cross-Cultural Models of the Senses in Performance." In *The Senses in Performance*, edited by Sally Banes and André Lepecki, 38–46. New York, NY and London: Routledge, 2007.

Smith, Matthew Wilson. "Beyreuth, Disneyland, and the Return to Nature." In *Land/Scape/Theater*, edited by Elinor Fuchs and Una Chaudhuri. Ann Arbor, MI: University of Michigan Press, 2002.

Stockho, Pamalla. *One Too Many Frozen Dead Guys*. Westminster, CO: Hawthorn Cottage Press, 2005.

Stoeltje, Beverly J. "Riding, Roping, and Reunion." In *Time out of Time: Essays on the Festival*, edited by Alessandro Falassi, 137–51. Albuquerque, NM: University of New Mexico Press, 1987.

Stoller, Paul. *The Taste of Ethnographic Things: The Senses in Anthropology*. Philadelphia, PA: University of Pennsylvania Press, 1989.

Stowell, Laurel. "Garden's Occupation Remembered as Iwi Celebrate." *Wanganui Chronicle* (Friday, 21 February 2014).

Sutton, David E. *Remembrances of Repasts*. Oxford and New York, NY: Berg, 2001.

Suzuki, Tadashi. *Culture is the Body: The Theatre Writings of Tadashi Suzuki*, trans. Kameron H. Steele. New York, NY: Theatre Communications Group, 2015.

Szerszynski, Bronislaw, Wallace Heim and Claire Waterton, eds. *Nature Performed: Environment, Culture and Performance*. Oxford: Blackwell Publishing Ltd., 2003.

Tauroa, Hiwi and Pat. *Te Marae: A Guide to Customs and Protocol*. Reprint. Auckland: Reed Publishing (NZ), Ltd., 1993.

Thomas, Nicholas. "The Inversion of Tradition." *American Ethnologist* 19.2, May 1992: 213–32.

Tilley, Christopher. "Introduction: Identity, Landscape and Heritage." *Journal of Material Culture* 11, 2006: 7–31.

Toelken, Barre. *The Dynamics of Folklore*. Logan, UT: Utah State University Press, 1996.

Tuan, Yi-Fu. *Space and Place: The Perspective of Experience*. Minneapolis, MN: University of Minnesota Press, 1977.

Tuleja, Tad, ed. *Usable Pasts: Traditions and Group Expressions in North America*. Logan, UT: Utah State University Press, 1997.

Turner, Victor. *The Ritual Process: Structure and Anti-Structure*. New Brunswick and London: Routledge, 1997.

———. *Dramas, Fields, and Metaphors*. Ithaca, NY and London: Cornell University Press, 1974.

———. *On the Edge of the Bush: Anthropology as Experience*. Tucson, AZ: The University of Arizona Press, 1985.

Valentine, Kristin and Gordon Matsumoto. "Cultural Analysis Spheres: An Integrated Ethnographic Methodology." *Field Methods* 13.1, 2001: 68–87.

———. "Yaqui Easter Ceremonies and the Ethics of Intense Spectatorship." *Text and Performance Quarterly* 22.4, 2002: 280–96.

Walker, Peter. "Maori War." *Granta* 58, 4 July 1997.

Wanganui Chronicle "Filipinos mark Easter with crucifixions." Wanganui, New Zealand, April 1999: 1).

Webber, Sabra J. *Folklore Unbound: A Concise Introduction.* Long Grove, IL: Waveland Press, 2015.

Williams, Sean. *The Ethnomusicologists Cookbook.* New York, NY: Routledge, 2006.

Index

Abrahams, Roger, xviii, 184
acting workshop, exploring
    Grotowski's work, 158–9, 161
admission, free, 208
aesthetics, 15–18, 195–6
agency, 45–6, 183
Akan storytelling, 18–28
aleatoric music, 157
Anansesem, 20, 22–27
anarchy, and Frozen Dead
    Guy Days, 187–8
animals
    bullfighting, 196
    deer mating rituals, 182–3
    hyena baiting, 4–5, 10, 15, 17–18,
        190
    interspecies performance, 191–2
    Longhorn Cattle Drive, 191–6
    nonhuman frolics, 190–1
    performances created for, 196–7
    spontaneous, 192–5
architecture of performance, 73, 77–8
    ambulatory experience, 80–4
    location affecting reception, 80
    queering, 88–9
aroma, in somatic performance, 154
Artaud, Antonin, 160–1
atmospheric space, 83
audience
    acceptance of space, 73
    and somatic performance, 160
    types, 51–3
audience participation
    Anansesem storytelling, 24–5

How to Build a Forest, 209–12
    Punch Drunk, 162
audience/performer element, 6–9
authenticity, and cultural
    mirage, 18

Basso, Keith, 182
Bauman, Richard, xviii, 50
Bauge, Trygve, 184–9
Baynes-Rock, Marcus, 17–18
Bayreuth, 74
beauty. *See* aesthetics
Belasco, David, 154
Bell, John, 153
Ben-Amos, Dan, xviii
Bestor, Kurt, 124
Betsky, Aaron, 91, 99
Bidgood, James, 94
Bluebeard, 88–100
    at Christopher's End, 94–6
    at the Performing Garage, 97–9
    structure and intent, 92–4
    touring, 98–9
    two productions architected, 89
body, corporeal context of
    performance, xxii. *See also*
    somatic performance
Bonnemaison, Jöel, 75
Boucheres, Les, 154
Brantley, Ben, 193
Bread and Puppet Theatre, 153
Brook, Peter, 6–7, 70–1, 193
builders, interaction in *How to Build
    a Forest*, 211

239

Made in the USA
Middletown, DE
16 September 2019